D0556079

Named in remembrance of

the onetime *Antioch Review* editor

and longtime Bay Area resident,

the Lawrence Grauman, Jr. Fund

supports books that address

a wide range of human rights,

free speech, and social justice issues.

The publisher and the University of California Press Foundation
gratefully acknowledge the generous support
of the Lawrence Grauman, Jr. Fund.

The publisher and the University of California Press Foundation
also gratefully acknowledge the generous support
of the Barbara S. Isgur Endowment Fund in Public Affairs.

Dispossessed

CALIFORNIA SERIES IN PUBLIC ANTHROPOLOGY

The California Series in Public Anthropology emphasizes the anthropologist's role as an engaged intellectual. It continues anthropology's commitment to being an ethnographic witness, to describing, in human terms, how life is lived beyond the borders of many readers' experiences. But it also adds a commitment, through ethnography, to reframing the terms of public debate—transforming received, accepted understandings of social issues with new insights, new framings.

Series Editor: Robert Borofsky (Hawaii Pacific University)

Contributing Editors: Philippe Bourgois (UCLA), Paul Farmer (Partners In Health), Alex Hinton (Rutgers University), Carolyn Nordstrom (University of Notre Dame), and Nancy Scheper-Hughes (UC Berkeley)

University of California Press Editor: Naomi Schneider

Dispossessed

How Predatory Bureaucracy Foreclosed
on the American Middle Class

Noelle Stout

UNIVERSITY OF CALIFORNIA PRESS

University of California Press, one of the most
distinguished university presses in the United States,
enriches lives around the world by advancing scholarship
in the humanities, social sciences, and natural sciences. Its
activities are supported by the UC Press Foundation and
by philanthropic contributions from individuals and
institutions. For more information, visit www.ucpress.edu.

University of California Press
Oakland, California

Library of Congress Cataloging-in-Publication Data

Names: Stout, Noelle M., 1976– author.
Title: Dispossessed : how predatory bureaucracy
    foreclosed on the American middle class / Noelle
    Stout.
Description: Oakland, California : University of
    California Press, [2019] | Series: California series in
    public anthropology ; 44 | Includes bibliographical
    references and index. |
Identifiers: LCCN 2018055942 (print) | LCCN 2018060131
    (ebook) | ISBN 9780520965423 (ebook) |
    ISBN 9780520291775 (cloth : alk. paper) |
    ISBN 9780520291782 (pbk : alk. paper)
Subjects: LCSH: Predatory lending—California—
    Sacramento. | Reverse discrimination in mortgage
    loans—California—Sacramento. | Collection
    laws—Moral and ethical aspects—California—
    Sacramento.
Classification: LCC HG2040.5.U62 (ebook) |
    LCC HG2040.5.U62 S76 2019 (print) |
    DDC 332.1/7530979454—dc23
LC record available at https://lccn.loc.gov/2018055942

Manufactured in the United States of America

27   26   25   24   23   22   21   20   19
10   9   8   7   6   5   4   3   2   1

For my mom, Lori,
and my boys, Bohdy and Damian

You can't go back home … to the old forms and systems of things which once seemed everlasting but which are changing all the time.

—Thomas Wolfe

Contents

Illustrations

DOCUMENTS

DRAWINGS

Once Sold, Twice Taken

A Life Undone

Brooke handed me a paper towel so I could wipe the sweat from my forehead. The temperature had broken a hundred degrees, and the thick air in her garage smelled like baked asphalt and dusty wood. Perspiration dotted the back of her neck, where strands of blonde hair escaped from a thick, messy bun. A white plastic table fan, propped on a pile of movers' blankets, hummed as it pushed hot air from one side of the garage to the other, skimming over towers of moving boxes. She took a seat next to me, our knees almost touching as we cowered in a small island of space near her open garage door—a futile attempt to capture a late afternoon July breeze. Neither of us complained about the heat, silently shifting our weight on the boxes where we sat surveying the garage.

Brooke Young, a thirty-eight-year-old whose light eyes and tall physique betrayed her distant Scandinavian roots, was going through foreclosure in her lower-middle-class suburban neighborhood in Northern California. "Dealing with packing the garage," she had told me six months earlier, "is the first thing I think about when I think that we might really lose our house." A self-described pack rat, Brooke hated moving. And moving because of her foreclosure made it an atypical move. Unable to hold back tears, she had said, "When we bought the house I thought we'd be there forever. It's where my son took his first steps, celebrated his first birthday and Christmas. We planted a tree in the yard when he was born, marked his height on the wall in the kitchen." Tending to avoid big life changes, Brooke had lived in San Jose her entire life. She had taught sixth grade at the same public middle school since finishing her teaching credential over a decade before.

We had been in the garage most of the day. The artifacts of Brooke's family life closed in around us. On one side were white garbage bags stuffed with clothes atop cardboard boxes bursting with stuffed animals and other toys. Disassembled Ikea furniture leaned against one wall next to towers of paperback books. In the back of the garage sat floor lamps missing shades and bulbs, sports equipment, and bicycles. Knick-knacks and keepsakes, including a Ziploc baggie of half-melted birthday candles from her son's birthdays, old thank-you cards from her former students, and shells from beach trips, had broken free from their original containers and were littered across box tops. Brown paper grocery bags from Trader Joe's barely contained Brooke's school papers, with work sheets popping out like white flags. Given the circumstances, one greeting card seemed especially tone-deaf, with a smiling baby gorilla wearing a party hat under neon balloon letters proclaiming, "Life's a party!"

At the center of the garage, where a car would have been parked under more civilized circumstances, sat three heaping mounds: trash, donate, and pack. Towering over the piles was a broken grandfather clock Brooke had inherited from her grandmother, a family heirloom caught off guard in a whirlwind of downward mobility.

Our packing had stalled when Brooke reached a section of the garage filled with storage boxes of her son's outgrown baby clothes. Bending over an infant car seat, she pulled a wrinkled, yellow cotton onesie out of a box. Months earlier, when Brooke had told me about their impending foreclosure, she confessed that she and her husband, Jarred, desperately wanted a second child but were delaying their plans because of their money troubles. Nearing forty, she felt as if time was running out. Losing their home might also mean letting go of the family she had always envisioned. "Should we take all of this?" she asked, stuffing the onesie back in the box. "Keep it, pack it," I said, trying to sound nonchalant, as if her favorite David Sedaris paperback was at stake. Instead of talking about it, we sat on our boxes to take a break.

Three years older than I am, Brooke has been one of my best friends since high school. By the time we became friends, her father had already abandoned the family, and her mother, an office manager, had been raising Brooke and her brother on her own. Brooke's extended family was tight-knit and proud of their working-class roots. "We have kegs at weddings," she once quipped. An athlete, Brooke had played basketball and run track in school. With a generous spirit and a sharp sense of humor, she was well loved. After high school, Brooke had attended community college and then San Jose State University along with her brother, a high school football star. After graduating, she had met Jarred, an African American high school teacher originally from Tennessee, who had recently retired from playing professional basketball in Europe. They had married in a small beach ceremony on the California coast.

The couple bought a two-bedroom house in San Jose after their son was born in 2006. Struggling to keep up with a housing market that had exploded along with the growth of Silicon Valley, Brooke and Jarred had gone along with the suggestion of a college buddy of Jarred's who had become a real estate broker and convinced the couple to take out a jumbo subprime mortgage they could barely afford. When the teaser introductory rate expired after a few years and their payments jumped, the couple struggled to make high monthly payments. Brooke gave up her cell phone service, and they canceled their annual trip to Tennessee to visit Jarred's family. Brooke had hoped to stay home with her son for some months after his birth, but the school district offered no maternity leave, and with their mortgage payments, they couldn't afford to live on one salary. Brooke worked until the day she went into labor and returned to teaching twelve weeks after the baby's birth, leaving her newborn for nine hours a day with a family friend, pumping her milk in the bathroom during recess, and crying many days on the drive to school.

Then the housing bubble burst in 2008, and their house lost much of its value. Brooke and her husband found themselves owing more on their mortgage than the house was worth. There was almost no chance they would recover their equity. For months, Brooke refused to move, even though she told me that she felt she was throwing money away by paying on her mortgage. She and Jarred began blaming each other, arguing late into the night after putting their son to bed. When their savings were wiped out, Brooke conceded. In 2010, they negotiated a short sale with TrustWorth Financial.*

Brooke was just one of the approximately 13.7 million Americans who entered the foreclosure process between 2006 and 2013, and by some estimates, at least 9 million households lost their home to foreclosure in the years following the 2008 U.S. mortgage crash.[1] In hard-hit states like California, residents saw generations of hard-earned family savings wiped out, home values plunged, homelessness and urban blight erupted, and entire cities went bankrupt. Even if homeowners hadn't signed on for high-fee, risky subprime mortgages as Brooke and Jarred had, the crash of the U.S. housing market sent property values plummeting, leaving them with mortgage payments that far outpaced the value of their homes. At the same time, the ensuing financial crisis triggered a recession that stranded millions without work and left them unable to pay their mortgages. And Americans were not the only ones suffering—as credit evaporated, global markets entered a steep recession that shuttered factories from Singapore to Mexico, and people struggled with unemployment around the world.

By now the story of how the 2008 financial crisis—which collapsed housing prices, decimated stocks and retirement accounts, and shut down businesses—triggered downward mobility for many middle-class Americans like Brooke is familiar. A decade after the financial crisis of 2008, Americans who faced losses during the Great Recession have

---

* In the context of individual respondents, all banks, lenders, and mortgage modification companies that are still in business as of 2018 have been given fictitious names. (The rationale will be discussed in more detail later in this introduction.) Whenever a fictitious corporate name appears for the first time, that first usage will be marked with an asterisk.

reported an uneven recovery, with many never finding the stability and prosperity they enjoyed before 2008.[2] But absent from these increasingly familiar cultural narratives is *why* so many people were unable to bounce back from the devastating losses incurred during the mortgage crash and its aftermath.

Statistics describing mortgage defaults after 2008, while staggering, fail to capture the traumatic and lasting effects of the failed recovery efforts rolled out in 2009. Beginning in 2012, I spent two years in California's Sacramento Valley, one of the hardest-hit regions in the nation, studying these enduring aftershocks. Foreclosures tore apart families, as marriages withered in the face of financial ruin, and intergenerational bonds were stressed by financial decisions to walk away from homes. Depression and suicidal thoughts were common among homeowners confronting the loss of their home and life savings, and stress-related illnesses took hold. The high cost of living meant that families straddling the lower end of the middle class found themselves worse off than their parents, who often had less education but better benefits and more financial security. Just like millions of Americans who had grown up with the American Dream as a backdrop for their everyday ambitions and life choices, people in the Sacramento Valley now lived its reverse: higher education, hard work, and prudent financial decision-making no longer guaranteed that life would be better or more secure than it was for earlier generations.

For many homeowners, their ongoing Kafkaesque confrontations with mortgage lenders amplified their suffering. Struggling to secure federally mandated assistance from corporate lenders, Sacramento Valley residents were ensnarled in bureaucratic tragedies that ended in near-universal denials and evictions. These rejections from corporate lenders have proven to be more damaging to the social contracts implicit in American debt ties than the financial losses of foreclosure alone. I found that many of these California homeowners who had begun the process with feelings of shame and grief ultimately came to interpret their foreclosure experience as a form of social and economic abandonment. I discovered that low-level corporate lending employees living and working in the

Sacramento Valley often went through a parallel progression of disillusionment, beginning with a hopeful optimism that their corporate employers would rescue struggling homeowners, only to confront bureaucratic obstacles at every turn. I came to see how people struggling to stave off foreclosure could arrive at a place of moral outrage rather than acquiescence—a moral stance in which some homeowners confronting looming evictions would even refuse to pack their garages and leave.

The Sacramento Valley had seen a boom in real estate development before the crash and after 2007 consistently ranked in the top ten in foreclosure for U.S. metro areas. A mid-sized city, Sacramento's rate of mortgage defaults jumped 482 percent from 2008 to 2009, with one in every sixty-three households in foreclosure. The Sacramento Valley's cities and towns are surrounded by open agricultural lands—industrial farms, sprawling ranches, orchards planted in symmetrical rows—and crisscrossed by the Sacramento River and its tributaries. Approached from the quaint college town of Davis to the west, Sacramento's downtown juts from an expanse of endless green and yellow fields. Beginning in 2008, foreclosures stretched across these towns and cities dotting Highway 80 from the state capital of Sacramento. Surrounding suburbs in the Sacramento Valley fared even worse; for example, the municipality of Elk Grove went from being the fastest-growing city in the nation, a "development miracle" as investors labeled it, to a city marked by blight, with half-finished developments haunting the landscape and one of the highest rates of mortgage default in the country. As development projects came to a halt, residents working in fields like construction and real estate were stranded without jobs.

In that period, Sacramento's foreclosure crisis gained national prominence. Former homeowners and their families moved into a swelling tent city that found its way onto Oprah Winfrey's popular daytime talk show as a symbol of the tragic consequences of the 2008 financial crisis. After the segment, the encampment became, to the residents' chagrin, a tourist destination. One local elected official gave tours, and camera crews from CNN, the *Today* show, and even a Swedish newspaper joined the spectators. "We're a circus for sightseers," Michael Borchardt, an unemployed truck driver living in the camp, told the *New York Times*.[3]

Rather than fixate on these dramatic and often voyeuristic representations of Sacramento's foreclosure epidemic, I turn to the stories of homeowners struggling to stop bank seizures in Sacramento and its surrounding towns, people who insisted that the real tragedy lay in the nature of their exchanges with lenders as they appealed to save their homes.[4] For them, dispossession appeared in daily life not as one vivid (telegenic) moment such as an eviction but as continuous mundane, monotonous bureaucratic exchanges—a series of frustrating phone calls to the bank, lost paperwork, misinformation, missing faxes, cryptic warnings from debt collectors, and formulaic eviction notices. It was these protracted tragedies between corporate lenders and homeowners, sometimes lasting for years, that ruptured the social contracts implicit in American debt relations.

My task is to make these bureaucratic dramas as vivid and memorable as the more visible scenes, the evictions and tent cities that dominated the news coverage of the crisis, and to show their ongoing consequences. These bureaucratic ephemera changed the lives of Americans by restructuring their feelings toward the U.S. government and mainstream financial institutions, shifting dominant American moral economies in the process. Triggered by one of the largest bank seizures of residential homes in American history, this metamorphosis inspired unprecedented distrust and disaffection, with lasting consequences for the political future of families and neighborhoods in the Sacramento Valley, as well as the nation at large.

FAILED RECOVERY EFFORTS

The 2008 mortgage crash was triggered by an orchestrated effort by lenders to convince Americans, many of whom would not have previously qualified for mortgages, into taking on hundreds of thousands of dollars in risky mortgage debt so that debt could be commodified and sold on secondary markets to investors. Wall Street investment firms diced subprime, high-risk mortgages into bits, bundled them with other kinds of debt, mislabeled them as safe investments, and sold them for windfall profits as mortgage-backed securities. Regulatory bodies tasked with keeping Wall Street schemes in check failed to perform due diligence on the suspect mortgages that had become a mainstay of investment funds, leaving families, elderly retirees, school districts, and city governments vulnerable to insurmountable losses.

As the scheme began to unravel in 2007, U.S. housing markets soon took a nose dive, and unemployment soared. In 2008, as government leaders began to recognize the scope of the financial crisis, the George W. Bush administration pushed through the Emergency Economic Stabilization Act, which injected $700 billion of capital into failing Wall Street firms through the Troubled Asset Relief Program, or TARP.[5] The primary architect of TARP was the then U.S. secretary of the treasury, Henry Paulson, former CEO of Goldman Sachs, who was criticized at the time for operating with a conflict of interest: Goldman Sachs received $10 billion of TARP funds (which the firm would repay) and an additional $43.4 billion of bailout payouts.[6]

The plan, which relied on public funds to infuse Wall Street with capital and reestablish securities markets, remained intact, however, with the presidential inauguration of Barack Obama in 2009. That year, the Obama administration executed a number of homeowner assistance programs, the most popular being the Home Affordable Modification Program (HAMP), through which corporate lenders would receive financial incentives to modify mortgages. For mortgages that originated before 2009 and were attached to owner-occupied homes, these lenders or mortgage servicers were encouraged to lower interest rates or reduce the principal amounts on loans for homeowners whose houses were considered "underwater"—that is, valued at far less than the purchase price. In plain terms: if you had purchased a home during the housing bubble and now owed more on your mortgage than your house was worth and subsequently lost your job during the recession, you could appeal to your mortgage lender to lower your monthly payments.

Unlike the federal mortgage assistance programs during the Great Depression, in which the government took on the toxic mortgage debt of Americans, these programs created contracts between the U.S. Treasury and 140 Wall Street mortgage servicers to manage and adjudicate homeowners' cases. The government outsourced the task to the same corporate lenders who had fomented or at least profited from the growth in subprime lending. Abuses were rampant; corporate lenders including Bank of America, Wells Fargo, and Ocwen Financial Corporation erected byzantine bureaucracies that denied applicants who were eligible for mortgage assistance and moved ahead with foreclosures even as homeowners made modified payments. By 2016, HAMP had received over nine million requests for loan modifications, with a million more in the pipeline.[7] But between 2009 and 2015, 70 percent of these homeowner applicants were denied assistance. Only a minuscule fraction of the $317 billion TARP bailout program reached homeowners. As a result, millions of American homeowners who wanted to keep paying their mortgages were forced to default.

Meanwhile, the profit motives of the mortgage assistance programs remained out of public view, as television commercials, billboards, and mailers ubiquitous in the Sacramento Valley falsely suggested that if homeowners were proactive and persistent, calling their lenders and loan servicers, they could secure assistance and save their homes. Although the publicized intent of mortgage assistance policies was to help struggling homeowners avoid default, the legislation favored lenders' profit margins over the social good. It required lenders or loan servicers to calculate if they would save money by modifying qualifying mortgages and, if so and only then, to halt bank seizures. For every completed permanent modification that a lender or loan servicer granted to a homeowner, the government paid that servicer $1,000. Even if the lender canceled the modification after the first month, the lender kept the payment. In other words, the program was designed to benefit corporate lenders and investors in place of funneling taxpayers' dollars directly to homeowners.

Even more egregious, major lenders and loan servicers running the programs, including Bank of America, Wells Fargo, CitiMortgage, and JPMorgan Chase, manipulated HAMP incentive structures to defraud taxpayers of billions of dollars. Six of the seven largest HAMP servicers wrongly dropped homeowners from the program while continuing to collect government payments. According to the Office of the Special Inspector General for TARP (SIGTARP), a federal law enforcement agency monitoring the bailout, taxpayers paid $2.4 billion to mortgage servicers and investors for 575,000 homeowners dropped from HAMP before they received assistance.[8] Corporate lenders were charging the U.S. Treasury, and taxpayers by extension, for bailouts to homeowners who never received relief. Even as officials within the Treasury acknowledged that Bank of America, CitiMortgage, JPMorgan Chase, Ocwen, Wells Fargo, and Nationstar Mortgage—the largest servicers administering HAMP— needed "substantial improvement," the Treasury paid those servicers $448 million during the same periods for which SIGTARP found them guilty of mismanagement. Without a provision in the original legislation that allowed the Treasury to block payments to HAMP, misdeeds and mismanagement would go unpunished. The official solution to the crisis substituted a kleptocracy for an economic depression.

Individual cases when corporate lenders misplace a homeowner's paperwork or offer misinformation on a claim might seem innocuous annoyances typical of interactions with modern corporations. But when these bureaucratic failures reach epic proportions, in the millions, a pattern emerges: they become forms of *predatory bureaucracy*, a collection of private-sector bureaucratic techniques aimed to extract profits while masking these goals through a rhetoric of assistance.[9]

Corporate loan modification bureaucracies justified the bank seizures of millions of American homes, disguising a political problem as a technical and bureaucratic one. In a similar vein, anthropologist Vincanne

Adams uncovered "privately organized, publicly funded bureaucratic failures" in her research on post–Hurricane Katrina housing recovery programs. It was not only government bureaucracy that contributed to the colossal failure of relief funds to reach New Orleans residents, Adams notes, but also the "inefficiencies of profit" that caused insufferable delays.[10] Disaster relief has been, since the early 2000s, outsourced to private contractors who profit from public funds, a trend journalist Naomi Klein aptly identifies as "disaster capitalism."[11] The dominance of these corporate players, who often bid for U.S. government contracts for disasters occurring around the world, means that only a small percentage of the billions of dollars of aid, flowing either through domestic bailouts or international USAID, reaches the people in whose name funding was approved.[12] What makes the U.S. foreclosure epidemic unique among such catastrophes was that lending companies and loan servicing agencies profited from a "disaster" that they facilitated and then claimed that they were the entity best qualified to resolve it.

In conversation, I asked Timothy Geithner, the U.S. secretary of the treasury in the Obama administration, why the government could not administer mortgage assistance programs as it had during the Great Depression, when it took on the toxic mortgages of Americans. He admitted that a similar state-run program would have been ideal but insisted that the political will to fund such a massive undertaking didn't exist, even with a Democratic majority in Congress. "Even the little program we pushed through," he told me, referring to HAMP, "ignited the Tea Party movement and enraged Americans" who saw themselves as "paying for their neighbors' mortgages" when "their neighbor had remodeled and bought an Escalade."

Unlike his predecessor Henry Paulson, Geithner had not arrived at his post entrenched in a personal history of Wall Street executive management. Born a left-leaning Republican who challenged cultural conservatism, Geithner later identified as a right-leaning Democrat who became an expert on debt crises around the world.[13] Despite a subtle political agnosticism that inflected his views, his time at the New York

Federal Reserve (from 2003 to 2008), I would argue, led him to adopt a perspective that conflates the health of the United States economy with the wealth of Wall Street. In his memoir *Stress Test: Reflections on Financial Crises*, Geithner makes clear, for example, that he did not blame Wall Street for the economic devastation caused by the crash.[14] Instead, he argues that Wall Street executives, like everyone else, were innocents caught in the same misguided optimism that led them to speculate on housing. Geithner writes, "It began with a mania—the widespread belief that devastating financial crises were a thing of the past, that future recessions would be mild, that gravity-defying home prices would never crash to earth."[15] While Geithner's narrative accurately describes the backlash to HAMP, it downplays crucial ideological assumptions guiding the Treasury's approach to the crisis. If invisible and universal forces instead of the concrete practices of Wall Street executives triggered the crisis, officials must frame federal assistance as relief rather than restitution.

By using the label mortgage "assistance" or "relief," the programs insinuate that homeowners faced foreclosure as the result of a *natural* disaster—as if the capitalist boom and bust, itself the result of quasi-criminal activity by Wall Street investment firms, rating agencies, and mortgage brokers, had happened on its own. In the programs' own narratives, loan modifications were created to "assist" the survivors, as opposed to offering damages for faulty underwriting standards or to make fair adjustments to erroneous, predatory mortgage contracts. The discourse of modifications suggested that homeowners were receiving handouts rather than that lenders and loan servicers were taking taxpayer dollars to cover the fallout from their own highly profitable, highly risky business practices. Because mortgage assistance programs were misrepresented as offering relief (from an unpredictable disaster) in lieu of restitution (for human errors and fraud), the creation of publicly sponsored mortgage assistance programs sparked intense public debate about the morality of the individuals who received this so-called relief, whereas the larger question of whether this money was relief or restitution was, for the most part, obscured.

As mortgage markets collapsed and property values plummeted after 2008, TV shows like *60 Minutes* described homeowners who defaulted on their mortgages as moral hazards, while Fox News pundits declared them deadbeats and losers, likening them to those who handed Europe to the Nazis.[16] Talking heads claimed that mortgage assistance programs like HAMP misused taxpayer money to benefit homeowners living beyond their means. The most famous attack was leveled by CNBC correspondent Rick Santelli, who in February 2009 launched into a rant against the newly established mortgage modification programs on the floor of the Chicago stock exchange. Santelli compared the programs to Cuban socialism, and his tirade culminated when he invited viewers to throw tea into the harbor in protest, a moment credited as having birthed the libertarian Tea Party movement.

Local news reports in the Sacramento Valley presented a more sympathetic view of families facing eviction and default, as the scope of the crisis garnered compassion among some reporters and writers living there. Yet in an attempt to preserve the illusion of journalistic "fairness," news programs on English- and Spanish-language networks such as Univision also emphasized the perspectives of lending executives at the expense of more in-depth analyses.[17] Like national news stories, these discussions failed to address the bigger picture: how racial and economic inequalities endemic to American late-liberal capitalism spawned the housing crash in the first place.[18]

As I participated in the daily lives of homeowners trying to avoid foreclosure by applying for mortgage assistance, a radically different vision emerged. Most homeowners wanted to continue to pay their mortgages at a reduced rate that would still generate substantial profits for lenders. But achieving this outcome was next to impossible, despite the best efforts of lending employees trying to help homeowners reduce their mortgage payments to prevent evictions. Far from the socialist forms of redistribution Santelli suggested, loan modification plans were profit driven. The mortgage crisis, like myriad disasters natural and manufactured, became a gold rush for profiteers who absorbed multimillion-dollar government relief packages and failed to distribute funds, with little or no consequence.

MIDDLE-CLASS SWAN SONG

As my respondents and I sat together at their kitchen tables or waited in sterile customer service centers, endemic foreclosures became a poignant symbol of middle-class decline. Evictions drove a growing resentment among Northern Californian lower-middle- and middle-class residents, as the economic stability of earlier generations was increasingly out of reach.[19] Homeowners described confrontations with lenders in ways that illuminated how inequalities were becoming all the more entrenched in U.S. society, and long-standing histories of class and racial discrimination often festered beneath the surface of daily life. Collectively, these experiences, what I refer to as *post-middle-class-life projects,* show how post–World War II middle-class formations—a collection of aspirations, performative styles, forms of work and leisure, ideas about privacy and decorum, gendered and racialized assumptions, and uses of money and investments—were unraveling. Being or becoming middle class, as a subject position, was foreclosed, in part, by the predatory mortgage modifications bureaucracies of corporate banks.

The mounting unattainability of middle-class-life projects to the Northern Californians in this book must be read as the latest chapter in a longer story of Americans struggling to find security since the onset of neoliberal economic policies in the early 1980s, which shifted public funding toward major financial corporations and away from social safety nets. What political scientist Jacob Hacker identifies as the "great risk shift" has meant that individuals and families increasingly bear the burdens of health insurance, pension benefits, and job security that were previously understood as the responsibility of corporate employers and the government.[20] Debt is essential to this neoliberal vision of society, as anthropologists Hugh Gusterson and Catherine Besteman argue, serving as a primary apparatus for transferring wealth "via foreclosures and interest payments, from those who need money to those who already have more."[21]

As think tanks, academic networks, and foundations promoted neoliberal ideas in the 1980s, deregulation ensued. The epic rise of Wall Street finance commenced, leading to massive downsizing, outsourcing, and deindustrialization.[22] With the inception of downsizing during this era, sociologist Katherine Newman described a growing unease and intense shame about downward mobility among the middle class.[23] These fears about instability gained momentum in the 1990s, as anthropologist Rachel Heiman shows in her ethnography of middle-class suburbanites in New Jersey. Jobs were a tremendous source of anxiety, although wages increased, because, as Heiman describes, job security was ever more fleeting, resources for public education diminished, and retirement and college funds were more vulnerable to a volatile market.[24] In California's Silicon Valley, middle-class families more recently described similar circumstances to sociologist Marianne Cooper, as they struggled without guarantees of lifelong employment to fund their health benefits and retirement, typically taking on insurmountable debt to cope with daily expenses.[25]

Anthropologist Karen Ho's groundbreaking work digs deeper into the daily practices among Wall Street firms that contributed to this shift in the U.S. economy, emphasizing downsizing and the rise of shareholder value in the 1990s as engines driving these changes.[26] With shareholder value as the ultimate goal, Wall Street financiers were increasingly willing to risk the productivity and the health of corporations and their workers, triggering massive layoffs and downsizing for millions of Americans. Layoffs, Ho shows, grew ever more common for employees at all levels of Wall Street firms because downsizing propped up shareholder value. These frequent layoffs naturalized firings as a process that was good for companies and the economy, with little attention paid to the social costs to workers and their families.

In this setting, income inequality in the United States has exploded. As economist Thomas Piketty shows, the top decile's share of national income increased from around 30 percent in the 1970s to as high as 50 percent in the 2000s.[27] The richest 10 percent appropriated three-quarters of the growth in national income, with the top 1 percent alone absorbing nearly 60 percent of the total increase in U.S. national income in this period. For those Americans in the bottom 90 percent, the rate of income growth was less than 0.5 percent per year.[28] These inequalities, Piketty argues, make the United States more vulnerable to market instability, with the 2008 financial crisis a prime example. The stagnation of the purchasing power of the lower and middle classes in the United States, Piketty explains, forced households to take on more debt, a process that was bolstered by deregulation and a flood of cheap credit.[29]

Facing underwater mortgages would not have been so daunting for California homeowners if they had had the financial reserves to weather a downturn in housing prices. Housing markets fluctuate. Mortgaging, as a long-term commitment, is designed to insulate homeowners from some of the volatility. But the post-2008 landscape was different because home values dropped so drastically, often cutting property values in half, leaving homeowners feeling as if recovery was unlikely. Adding to this uncertainty was the fact that most families were already stretched financially by the rising costs of daily expenses. As homeowners saw their wages garnished and jobs lost because of the recession, struggled with rising costs of healthcare, or simply could not save for retirement, their ability to keep paying a mortgage on even a modest home became impossible.

Within two generations, the home, once imagined as a source of intergenerational wealth anchoring working-class families to an expanding American middle class, has come to replace the social benefits once provided by employers and the government. These dynamics played out in the ruptured inheritance cycle of my own blue-collar Northern Californian family. My paternal and maternal grandparents, without college educations and employed in working-class jobs, benefited from their employers' retirement and health plans and government home loan programs. They purchased homes, retired comfortably, and left their houses to their children. But my divorced parents, a farmer and a vocational nurse, found themselves without those same social safety nets and were unable to hold onto my grandparents' houses to pass them down through the family, as my grandparents had imagined. Instead, my parents sold the houses to put money toward more modest homes, using the remaining profits to fund basic expenses. When the money ran out, my father turned to a reverse mortgage on his own home, a loan for seniors that allows them to take out equity each month, adding interest to the growing loan balance. The reverse mortgage payments serve as retirement cash and allow him to pay for private health insurance, which constitutes over half his monthly expenses. As of 2018, my mother is in line for the same plan. The possibility of inheritance is wiped out, forcing younger generations to fend for themselves, building familial savings and security nets from nothing, putting them even farther away from accumulating wealth than the previous generation had been.

If neoliberal economic policies have left white lower-middle- and middle-class Americans more vulnerable to hard times than their parents, who themselves benefited from Keynesian economic redistribution to the middle class after World War II, communities of color confront even more dramatic declines. In the case of foreclosures, widespread bank seizures are only the latest chapter in an overarching historical trajectory of race and class discrimination within American housing, extending recent histories of redlining and exacerbating the effects of deindustrialization.[30] In the 2008 economic recession, foreclosures disproportionately affected African American and Latino borrowers, for instance, who were twice as likely to have suffered significant financial losses due to the crash. By 2011, according to the Center for Responsible Lending, one-quarter of all Latino and African American borrowers in the United States had lost their homes to foreclosure or were seriously delinquent, compared to just 12 percent of white borrowers.[31] Asian borrowers, especially those in urban areas, fared better than Latino and African American homeowners but still suffered more losses than whites. These racial inequities persist even among higher-income homeowners;

relatively wealthy African Americans were more likely to receive sub-prime loans than relatively poor whites.[32] In the Sacramento Valley, sub-prime lending, predatory bureaucracies, and the bank seizures they produced disproportionately punished poor communities of color while also dragging white lower-middle- and middle-class families into economic insecurity.

In the context of cheap mortgage credit and widespread mortgage default, postwar categories such as working class and middle class can often fail to capture the complex interplay of income, social and cultural capital, and life experience that places Sacramento Valley residents on a continuum of class privilege and precarity. As an alternative to positing class as a fixed category, determined by income and education, for example, I conceive of class subjectivities as heuristic devices that combine people's own views of their social position with markers of traditional status such as homeownership and employment. My use of class subjectivity also accounts for the interdependence of class with racial and ethnic histories, gendered and sexual identities, religious affiliation, and rural and urban identifiers. Because class subjectivities are formed relationally, I present stories of encounters between customer service representatives and clients.

These contests over legitimate homeownership offer an illuminating view into class formations in the United States; where one lives, as anthropologist Sherry Ortner points out, is often a proxy for class relations that are otherwise obscured.[33] Housing defines familial and social ties, determines educational opportunities for children, and serves as a locus for identity performance and consumption. My approach echoes the work of sociologist Julie Bettie on the boundary work that defined symbolic class distinctions among high school girls in California's Central Valley, neighboring Sacramento. Bettie shows how the micropolitics of a high school reflect broader economic shifts from factories to the service sector.[34] In a similar vein, my fine-grained study of the daily lives of homeowners and lending employees in the Sacramento Valley shows how class subjectivities shift and change in the face of a growing predominance of late-liberal finance—how they come into being in light of changing life circumstances, one moment disguised as personal failure and at another moment offering a platform to resist dispossession.

THE SOCIAL BONDS OF EXCHANGE

Rising inequalities and the sharp decline of postwar stability for American middle-class families help to explain why Sacramento Valley residents reacted with such ire when caught in faulty mortgage assistance programs after 2009. But these historical trends fail to account for why they might expect corporate lenders to help in the first place. It was a surprising discovery in my research that homeowners relied on terms like *obligation, duty,* and *help* to describe a lender's role, while many lending employees similarly articulated an ideal relationship between borrower and lender that their employers were failing to fulfill. By referring to terms of mutuality, these homeowners and lending employees challenged a fundamental tenet of market economies—in the context of a profit-driven mortgage industry, why would people expect anything but bald self-interest to prevail among mortgage lenders?

Drawing on long-standing anthropological theories of exchange, throughout this book I argue that mortgaging generates a social tie between borrower and lender. Homeowners and those processing their appeals described an imagined bond of mutuality that united borrower and lender in a relationship of *financial reciprocity,* an implicit social contract of mutuality. It is no coincidence that mortgaging, a financial contract governing the domestic sphere, would coconstitute market and reciprocal exchanges. Anthropologists have long recognized exchange as a unifying cultural practice that links economics to ostensibly noneconomic spheres such as kinship and political systems. In the late nineteenth century, anthropologists argued that so-called primitive societies were ruled by reciprocal ties based on human relationships, and capitalist ones were governed by the rules of the market.[35] These ethnographic studies paralleled social theorists, influenced by Karl Marx and

Friedrich Engels, who argued that industrial capitalism in Europe and the United States dissolved the social bonds and obligations that served as the glue of Western society. Industrial capitalism, theorists argued, with its key principles of wage labor, private property, and the nuclear family, replaced the sociality of the peasantry with power-laden transactional relations. French sociologist Marcel Mauss in *The Gift* amended this depiction to argue that pockets of reciprocal relations could exist within a broader context of commodification.[36] Gift giving would persist, opening the door for communistic relations between people, even in the hard, cold world of transactional exchange.

These Maussian nuances were later taken up by anthropologists pursuing ethnographic investigations of the interplay between commodified exchange and noncommodified forms of reciprocity. In the 1980s anthropologists such as Marilyn Strathern and Christopher Gregory, for example, posited the division between "gift economies" and "market economies" as anachronistic, instead focusing on how multiple types of exchange commingled within each society's economic system.[37] Anthropologists explored how people drew imagined boundaries between "the social" and "the economic" as a power-laden exercise that naturalized inequalities. More recently, feminist anthropologists have reinvigorated these inquiries to argue that selfhood, kinship and family, and community are, as Laura Bear, Karen Ho, Anna Tsing, and Sylvia Yanagisako write, "always 'inside' and mutually constitutive of capitalist social relations and vice versa."[38] In other words, the sociality of markets shapes people's expectations and allows them to erect boundaries around classed, racialized, and gendered forms of belonging.[39]

The prevalence of notions of financial reciprocity in the context of the U.S. mortgage crash shows how commodified forms of market exchange *generate* implicit reciprocal social contracts and vice versa. Because mortgage agreements involved the home, a site of moral personhood and citizenship within postwar ideologies, homeowners and many corporate service representatives came to view mortgage debt as an ongoing social relationship in which lenders had an implicit obligation to offer relief.

Yet, more than illustrating the sociality of mortgage markets, people's views of foreclosure highlight how reciprocal expectations were deeply classed and raced from the outset: entitlements to reciprocity were only available to residents in lower-middle- and middle-class neighborhoods who embodied an embrace of American upward mobility. By exposing middle-class residents to evictions, penalties for economic hardship in the form of fees and fines, and endless bureaucratic runaround—all commonplace in the daily lives of poorer residents—the foreclosure crisis eroded these lower-middle- and middle-class forms of respectability and personhood. Homeowners in solidly lower-middle-class milieus, many of whom had been protected by racial privilege or professional roles, witnessed a growing social and financial exclusion. To challenge these experiences of marginalization, Sacramento Valley residents emphasized the social relations of exchange and reframed mortgaging and foreclosure in moral terms, highlighting the moral underpinnings of economic action. Indeed, theories of moral economy originated in historical analysis of the reciprocal rights and obligations between landlords and peasants, ties that exceeded a market relationship.[40] How a society determines who owes debts to whom is a deeply moral question that gains a veneer of rationality as it is cycled through monetary calculation and bureaucratic mechanisms.[41]

STUDYING EVERYDAY DISPOSSESSION

It was October 2014, another sunny fall day in the middle-class Sacramento suburb where I had been living. The weather was so mild, the sunlight so pristine, and the lawns so trim that I felt as if I were driving through a location shot for a television show. Unlike the picturesque TV suburbs, the Pocket was also one of the most racially diverse neighborhoods in the country. The streets were empty, save for a retired neighbor, Judy Dong, wearing her morning uniform of walking shoes and an oversized white sun hat, and a gardener pushing a leaf blower whose roar dominated the otherwise quiet street.

A delta breeze flowed over the levee of the Sacramento River, bringing fresh air in through my car window. As I drove that morning to the freeway entrance to make my way to a low-income neighborhood where I was attending a baptism, the car radio spun through stations dominated by classic rock, stopping where the signal was strongest, on Pink Floyd's "Another Brick in the Wall (Part 2)." As the song ended, a woman's voice cut in: "Are you losing your home? Answer just a few simple questions to find out if you are eligible for a free assistance program. Go to keepyourhomeCalifornia.org today."

It had been six years since subprime mortgages had begun to default in Sacramento, but just that morning the *Sacramento Bee* had featured the third segment of a story about a woman in Citrus Heights, a small suburban city in Sacramento County, who, with her four daughters, was facing foreclosure. The family's story made the paper because the mother's lawyer was using the newly passed Homeowner Bill of Rights to try to challenge the eviction, which would leave her and her daughters homeless. The story ignited an outpouring of support—readers offered to provide rent and free storage and to adopt the family's two dogs and three cats.

While the national news was no longer reporting on the foreclosure epidemic, in the Sacramento Valley the lasting effects of the crash were omnipresent. For Sale signs lined residential streets, and billboards for mortgage assistance lined the highways. Passing acquaintances shared their struggles with mortgage defaults: parents I met at the playground, my hairdresser, my dental hygienist, the barista at my coffee shop. Even the doula who attended my son's birth while I was living in Sacramento was a former real estate agent who had lost her home and had, after the crash, reinvented herself as a birthing assistant.

As residents struggled to recover from the hard-learned lessons of 2008, real estate remained a constant if ambivalent backdrop. For example, days before the Fourth of July an endless row of American flags mysteriously appeared on all the front lawns in my neighborhood. Wrapped around the wooden stick of each flag was a sticker with a headshot advertising the services of a friendly-looking real estate agent

A home in the Pocket neighborhood of Sacramento, where the author lived during fieldwork, with a small American flag advertising real estate services on the lawn. Photo by the author.

with a coiffed blond bob. I immediately recognized her face from a handful of weathered mailers that had piled up outside the front door of a foreclosed-upon home down the street from my own house; the tattered front door of the home was plastered with city violation notices citing the overgrown foliage. As we neared Independence Day, the advertising flags seemed to imply that nothing could be more American than real estate. The region's real estate machine, desperate in 2014 for a comeback, kept churning, despite evidence of its glaring failures and dystopian effects.

It was in this environment that I spent twenty-six months conducting ethnographic research among homeowners facing foreclosure and the lending employees processing their appeals in the Sacramento Valley.[42] Between 2012 and 2016, I focused my efforts in three neighborhoods that have suffered from inordinately high rates of foreclosure since 2007: a low-income black and Latino neighborhood with a concentration of high-risk lending; a predominantly white upper-income residential area suffering from overbuilding and inflated home prices; and the racially integrated middle-income suburb where I was living.[43] I followed twelve families closely as they struggled with mortgage default, integrating myself into their daily lives, from baptisms to birthday parties. I also conducted participant observation and in-depth interviews with thirty-two additional homeowners, observing their interactions with lenders, including phone calls, paperwork submission, loan counseling sessions, financial literacy training, and foreclosure prevention workshops.[44] I sat with them as they ventured online to seek assistance and navigate modification applications. More than once, when evictions were inevitable, I helped pack and carry moving boxes.

On the lending side, I conducted twenty-five interviews with employees or former employees of major mortgage lenders and loan servicers in Sacramento, including Bank of America, Wells Fargo, Litton Loan Servicing, and now-defunct Countrywide Financial.[45] I also spoke with a handful of high-level executives and industry lobbyists and visited various lenders' customer service centers in and around Sacramento. Most of the lending employees I interviewed were current or former entry- or midlevel corporate lending employees who, like homeowners, were seeing postcrash America through a more cynical lens. Often real estate agents or loan officers laid off after the crash, many of these men and women had been retrained to work in the newly developed modification bureaucracies of major lenders such as Bank of America, Wells Fargo, and Ocwen Financial Corporation. As "loan modification specialists," employees were ostensibly tasked with amending loan agreements to prevent foreclosures. But they spent most of their time shuffling paperwork, ferrying documents from one department to another, placing homeowners on hold, and ultimately doling out denials to people seeking assistance.

I also spent time with intermediaries assigned to assist homeowners applying for loan modifications, including staff members at housing counseling agencies funded by the U.S. Department of Housing and Urban Development (HUD) and grassroots community organizations. I observed not only public servants in action but also activists' meetings, community events, and loan counseling sessions and conducted open-ended interviews with fifteen housing activists, many active in a small chapter of Occupy Homes.

Drawn to the Sacramento Valley by high rates of foreclosure, I also chose to conduct research there because I have deep family roots in the region. My paternal great-grandparents had left Oklahoma after the Dust Bowl, traveling to Northern California in a scene straight out of Steinbeck's *The Grapes of Wrath*. My great-grandfather Frank Nation, a Cherokee-German farmer, and his wife, Maggie, of English descent, had badly weathered the Great Depression only to watch the Arkansas River flood in 1945 devour their small farm. Looking for work in California, they left behind a shoddy wooden shack, where you could see the sunrise through every wood-slat wall in the house, and brought their six children—Everett, Frank, Jean, LaVeta, "Poochie," and Doris Ruth, my grandmother—cross country, landing in Paradise, just north of the Sacramento Valley, where Frank secured work as a foreman in an apple orchard, a job that included a three-room house for his family. My grandmother Doris Ruth, or Maw-maw, would grow up to work as a Safeway checker north of Sacramento in Chico, a good job with benefits, as she described it. She married a house painter who started his own business.

By the time I was born, my grandparents had saved enough to build a three-bedroom ranch-style home with a sunken formal living room, a dining room with a window seat, and an acre of garden where Maw-maw grew okra, string beans, cucumbers for pickling, tomatoes, and melons every summer. Their home stood at the end of a quiet cul-de-sac with their beloved two-door white Cadillac Seville with red leather interior parked in the driveway, a weighty ship anchoring them to a new middle-class life. Maw-maw retired early, channeling her energy into cleaning every inch of the house, taking breaks to smoke Benson & Hedges Gold cigarettes and drink homemade iced tea on the back porch. She made a weekly visit to the beauty shop, where she gossiped with other Okie transplants while getting her bleach, perm, and blow-dry. Maw-maw was a staunch Democrat, and she openly criticized family members who "got two paychecks ahead and became goddamn Republicans." When I was a young child, after my parents divorced, my mother and I moved two hours south to San Jose, but I would spend summers with Maw-maw, my father, and his sister, playing in the garden and running around the creeks of the oppressively hot rural towns north of Sacramento.

When I entered middle school, my mother and I benefited from a California public housing program that subsidized low-income units in buildings with full-price apartments—a program aimed to temper the detrimental effects of concentrated poverty. My mother, working a low-paying job and dedicating her nights to community college classes, spent hours on the phone fighting to get us on the housing list. Eventually, we were accepted. After I became the first in my family to graduate from a four-year university, where I was first exposed to American elite institutions (Stanford and later Harvard University for my doctorate), the role of the public housing program loomed large in my tale of upward mobility. This background made me sympathetic to homeowners who themselves were now spending hours on the phone struggling to secure government assistance to hold onto their homes. In the early days of the 2008 meltdown, I was optimistic, perhaps naively, about the potential for public programs to ameliorate the housing crisis, because I had positive experiences growing up in government-subsidized housing in Northern California.

After nearly two decades on the East Coast, first Boston and then New York City, returning to the working- and lower-middle-class neighborhoods of Northern California in 2012 inspired an acute sense of relief. I could abandon the airs of my newly acquired professional class— loosen my language, overshare without regret, unabashedly call out the injustices of daily life, and laugh too loud. Joan Didion, iconic American author and Sacramento native, sums it up best in "California Notes": "I am at home in the West. The hills of the coastal ranges look 'right' to me, the particular flat expanse of the Central Valley comforts my eye. The place names have the ring of real places to me.... I am easy here in a way that I am not easy in other places."[46]

Like anyone with working-class roots in the region, I had family members struggling with foreclosure and underwater mortgages in the Sacramento Valley after 2007. In some ways, this positioned me as an insider, and it was easy to find people going through foreclosure. Strangers seemed more inclined to open up to me after hearing about my family's struggles. Often, I could relate to the psychological and emotional toll of their losses, the hard decisions and nagging disappointments that accompanied financial hardship. The intimate aftereffects were also familiar: feeling disheveled, judged, ashamed, and somehow chronically out of place.

But, like California's midsize capital city, I had changed. I was returning as a researcher to study the lives of my close friends and relatives and their neighbors, a stance that could put an awkward distance between us. How would Brooke feel about having a private, intimate moment between old friends turned into the opening anecdote for a book? Similarly, after listening to a close relative as she cried late into the night about her failing marriage and the shock of her impending eviction, I found myself taking notes, thinking it might serve as a powerful conclusion, but wondering if it remained off-limits. (I left her story out of this book.) What was too personal, too much of our family's dirty laundry?

Put simply, I was also an outsider. By the time I began my project, I had spent just as many years in elite educational institutions as I had in government housing. I was, most likely, ascending to a shrinking upper-middle class, not going the other way. My remoteness from my respondents was exacerbated in the most deprived neighborhoods, where my white-skin privilege and status as a citizen structured my daily life in a way that rendered people's infinite forms of struggle illegible. I had grown up working class, spending a brief stint on welfare, but my family's poverty was never criminalized; we might have been stigmatized, but we never worried that the men in our family would be wrongly killed by the police. Teachers gave me the benefit of the doubt, transferring me from the remedial track, where I had been placed in kindergarten, to an advanced academic path by second grade. My grandparents weren't redlined out of homeownership in their neighborhoods, denied mortgage loans, or forced into jobs reserved for second-class citizens because of their ethnicity.

My status as an outsider was, at times, painfully apparent. One afternoon, I met with Jesus Hernandez, UC Davis sociologist and veteran real estate agent. A tall white Latino with a shock of black hair, broad shoulders, and wide eyes, Hernandez had the frazzled look of an academic, but his button-down shirt tucked into pleated slacks betrayed his twenty years working in Sacramento's real estate industry. He is a leading expert on racial discrimination in Sacramento's housing markets, and his work argues, convincingly, that racism is fundamental to the history of American mortgage lending. After I joined him at the bar of a Davis restaurant to talk about my project, Hernandez wanted to know where I had been in Sacramento. He seemed dismayed about my ignorance about the history of local real estate markets. "So, how did you get interested in this?" he asked.

"You mean, who the hell are you?" I said.

Hernandez laughed. "Well, yeah. Exactly."

I told him I had family in the area who had been through foreclosure. I wanted to understand people's encounters with lenders after the crash.

Hernandez wasn't impressed. "What can you give these people that they need?" he asked.

It was a question that I had considered myself. "Money? A stipend for their time?" I said, realizing immediately that my knee-jerk response missed the point.

"Not enough," he said. "They need jobs and houses; can you give them that?"

"No, I don't know. I think some people want to tell their stories. They're mad and they want to set the record straight," I said, finding my footing.

Hernandez had stopped listening. He was scrolling through a Power-Point presentation on his laptop. "This is it!" he said, quickly turning his computer around. It was an image of a doughnut with the names of Sacramento's neighborhoods circling the edge. We would talk housing, but I never won the impression that this would ever be my turf.

In our frequent conversations about family foreclosures, my mother often voiced similar concerns, but from a different vantage point: "You better not tell them that you *know* these people," she'd say. For her, my proximity to the stories I was telling could serve as a liability, threatening to reveal my background and puncturing the professional veneer that I had encased myself in through years of education, both formal and informal, which had let me pass among upper-middle-class colleagues. My mother's sentiment echoed what Lila Abu-Lughod was getting at in her notion of "halfie anthropology," authored by a "halfie" anthropologist who navigates an uneasy split between "speaking for" and "speaking from."[47] Halfies face many dilemmas, Abu-Lughod points out, positioned as they are between two or more communities; "because when they present the Other they are presenting themselves." Being both insider and outsider raised unique challenges; I was painstakingly aware of how family and friends imagined their lives playing out before an audience that could be unforgiving.

Indeed, homeowners defaulting on their mortgages faced intense public scrutiny after 2008, as media pundits on cable news shows derided them as deadbeats. In presenting their stories, I could counter this harsh public criticism by focusing on homeowners who were victims of predatory subprime lenders, an issue I explore in chapter 2. But this approach would be myopic. It is more important to understand how working families made bad financial decisions, some taking on traditional, fixed-rate mortgages they could not afford or signing contracts they could not understand, and others failing to save for retirement or using equity lines to remodel their homes. These homeowners made honest mistakes as they struggled to keep up with rising costs of living and stagnating salaries. Once they faced foreclosure, these homeowners found themselves trapped in the impenetrable bureaucracies of big banks, a reckoning that upended people's assumptions about the solvency of middle-class life projects.

In other words, even as my sympathies were with Brooke and other homeowners facing foreclosure, the direction of my research was not determined by those empathies alone. When I began this project, I never imagined the extent to which homeowners had been taken advantage of by corporate lenders. Initially, I was interested in personal shame and foreclosure—the scope of my inquiry was designed to stay within the confines of Brooke's unruly garage. Instead, homeowners led me in another direction, forcing me into a world of privatized government assistance, mismanaged corporate bureaucracy, and failed mortgage modification programs, an administrative universe that absconds with our time and energy but rarely sees the light of public exposure.

TELLING THE STORY

By the time TrustWorth Financial took Brooke's home in the summer of 2012, Oprah's viewers had long forgotten Sacramento's homeless, and the dramatic news coverage of the American mortgage crash had petered out. But this meant that the real story of how corporate lenders continued patterns of abusive behavior after 2008, obstructing the recovery of the American middle class, remains untold—and this is the truth that mattered most to those suffering through foreclosures.

Homeowners' experiences had already begun to suffer erasure, largely absent from the explosion of financial crisis literature—nearly a hundred books—published after 2008. Instead, these publications focused on the Wall Street corruption that had induced the Great Recession. Journalist George Packer laments in his *New Yorker* review of the crash literature, "It's as if no one could be induced to read a story about the crisis without a disgraced celebrity plutocrat as the protagonist."[48] In *The Big Short,* Michael Lewis's compelling book that was made into an Oscar-nominated Hollywood film, investors uncover the subprime debacle before the collapse and make a killing betting against the U.S. housing market. But in the film, the only speaking role for a homeowner is a thirty-second cameo of a Florida stripper who owns four condos and who gives actor Steve Carell's character a lap dance. Not the most sympathetic or even representative portrait of homeowners suffering through the crash.

Essential works tried to counteract this deafening silence, among them books such as Packer's own *The Unwinding: An Inner History of the New America,* Dale Maharidge and Michael Williamson's *Someplace Like America: Tales from the New Great Depression,* and Barbara Garson's *Down the Up Escalator: How the 99 Percent Live in the Great Recession.*[49] Taken together they offer a powerful and disturbing view of the realities of downward mobility for hardworking Americans living on the precarious edge of the lower middle class. Adding to these stories, I tell the hidden tale of how the collusion of federal programs and big banks robbed lower-middle- and middle-class homeowners of their chance to recover fully after the crash—a critical piece of this larger puzzle that remains, to my knowledge, missing from most popular and scholarly accounts. Nearly a decade after the 2008 crash, those Americans most affected by it are using new metrics to decide what they owe society and what is owed to them, a story that remains invisible in narratives of the U.S. financial crisis.

To elevate the voices of ordinary Americans struggling to recover after 2008, I had to promise them confidentiality. To make good on that promise, I was forced to anonymize the names of the major lenders and loan servicers that mismanaged homeowners' applications and denied them mortgage assistance. Were the big banks I describe in this book to take legal action, I would be forced to reveal my respondents' identities to prove that my characterizations are based in fact. So erasing the names of lenders has become the only way to guarantee my subjects' privacy. In a similar vein, many lending employees I interviewed signed nondisclosure agreements that would put them at risk should their identities be discovered. Although it was painful to disguise rather than to expose the actions of specific corporate banks, my ultimate aim in

Dispossessed is to illuminate a larger picture of predatory finance and corporate-state collusion rather than to fuel a movement to bring down a specific bank.

Dispossessed thereby taps into an archive of daily experiences to analyze the unidentified, enduring consequences of the botched recovery efforts following the 2008 mortgage crash and the ensuing foreclosure epidemic. As I describe throughout this book, these failed bureaucratic programs are the thread that joins the stories of Sacramento homeowners—from residents in low-income areas plagued with drugs and crime to those in shiny new suburban developments—with the stories of the lending employees charged with helping them. In the following chapters, you will meet David Sanchez, a Latino veteran in his sixties who lost a protracted battle with Leviathan Bank to save his home after losing his wife to cancer and who decided to squat in his house until he was evicted. You will also come to know Jason Silva, a loan modification officer at Sacramento's Leviathan Bank call center tasked with handling cases like David's who became disillusioned with his inability to deliver mortgage assistance to deserving homeowners. Both described how Leviathan, like most corporate lending institutions, destroyed a relationship of mutual obligation that David and Jason imagined existed between debtor and creditor. Extending far beyond the 2008 crash, David's and Jason's experiences changed their worldviews, changes that took their lives in unexpected new directions.

In chapter 1, I provide some critical background by describing the history and setting of the Sacramento Valley, exploring older models of mortgaging and the systems of financial reciprocity produced within them. I consider where the imagined ideal relationship between a borrower and a lender originated for residents, many of whom identified with the rural roots of this midsized capital and the surrounding cities. I show how these local cultural histories, although laden with earlier eras of dispossession and legacies of colonial and racial violence, encouraged homeowners and real estate professionals to infuse financial transactions with nostalgic ideals of economic fairness and loyalty.

I then turn, in chapter 2, to the stories of homeowners in Oak Park, the first neighborhood to suffer widespread bank seizures as early as 2007, before local news media had declared an official crisis. In Oak Park, a tight-knit, low-income, predominantly black and Latino neighborhood within Sacramento, some of the city's most vulnerable residents were heavily targeted with risky mortgage products. The distance between these borrowers and trustworthy financial information exposed them to unreliable financial offers from relatives, acquaintances, and so-called experts hawking dangerous financial products. As a result, most homeowners faced with foreclosures lost their homes before government assistance and loan modifications became available after 2009. Despite their victimization and exclusion at the hands of financial institutions, most residents were less likely to feel entitled to restitution from lenders or loan services, instead mobilizing community resources and organizations to contest their evictions.

After detailing the foreclosure stories of Oak Park residents, in chapter 3 I venture into the households of families on the brink of eviction in lower-middle-class and middle-class neighborhoods to which the mortgage crisis had spread by 2008. Exploring the prevalence of discourses of financial reciprocity in greater depth, I show how mortgage contracts imbued these homeowners struggling to maintain postwar middle-class identities with a social status and type of moral personhood that, many suggested to me, entitled them to assistance from lenders. But by the time I arrived in 2012, homeowners were still languishing in protracted entanglements with lenders and loan servicers. Among these post-middle-class mortgagors, the prospect of foreclosure initially evoked feelings of shame, but when faced with tortuous lending bureaucracies that made errors and miscalculations, doled out misinformation, and lost paperwork, many described how indignity morphed into indignation and then into forms of debt refusal and default.

Having raised queries about the baffling process of corporate loan modifications for residents in middle- and lower-middle-class neighborhoods, in chapter 4 I turn to lending employees for answers. Drawing on interviews with current and former entry- and midlevel loan modification specialists processing homeowners' appeals, I show how predatory bureaucracies embodied a post-Weberian administrative form, maintaining the hierarchies of 1960s and 1970s corporate bureaucracies but using inefficiencies in the service of capital. Focusing on their critiques of outdated technologies and reliance on temporary staff, I show how lending employees often became disillusioned with mortgage modifications and came to share homeowners' expectations for assistance and mutuality between lenders and borrowers.

In chapter 5, I turn to acts of debt refusal, showing how homeowners' outrage at lenders' abandonment of the imagined moral contracts of debt obligations inspired resistance. While a sustained revolution in debt relations eluded most homeowners facing evictions due to the 2008 crash, their responses to mass dispossession were neither simple nor straightforward. Homeowners were now engaging in novel forms of debt refusal, from political organizing to online protest to refusing to leave their homes, halting mortgage payments until banks evicted them as a moral alternative to repayment. Whereas foreclosure had once been a financial scarlet letter, marking those who defaulted with shame and years of bad credit, in the postcrash era homeowners' feelings of shame were complicated by the abuses of corporate lenders and emergent economic realities that put middle-class propriety out of reach.

As we approach 2020, the significant social transformations of personhood and indebtedness brought about by the crash continue to shape daily life for millions of Americans. In the book's conclusion, I ask, What if mortgage modifications had been, as Rick Santelli falsely claimed, an overt attempt to redistribute wealth? What would Brooke Young's life look like if she hadn't had to leave her house, putting her plans for a family on hold? How might David Sanchez have sailed into his retirement after a lifetime of hard work in manufacturing and military service, rather than spending his nights online searching for someone to help him stay in his home and his days anxiously waiting for Leviathan Bank to evict him? If public entities had implemented mortgage assistance for the social good, rather than for the benefit of the corporate sector, they could have reallocated some of the concentrated wealth back to the middle class. Corporate banks would still have turned significant long-term profits from the interest on home loans, but lower-middle- and middle-class homeowners would have regained some stability. Although failed assistance programs hijacked a clear opportunity to reverse the decline of the American middle classes, ideologies of financial reciprocity emerged from these episodes of administrative obstruction. Corporate lenders handed down denials for mortgage relief, and millions of homeowners packed up their boxes and left their homes, but these actions should not be interpreted as an easy acquiescence to dominant debt ties. There is much more to the story.

CHAPTER ONE

Dream It, Own It

*Genealogies of Speculation and
Dispossession in the Valley*

It was a bright spring afternoon, and a deer ran across David Sanchez's gravel road as I pulled through the gate. Empty horse corrals lined his driveway, where his faded red Ford pickup was parked. Inside, his house was dim and musty, each room cluttered with exotic knickknacks, handmade stone sculptures, and painting supplies. A xylophone, the size of a love seat, dominated the living room. Balding on top, with his curly gray hair pulled into a ponytail, David, a sixty-eight-old veteran, had a charming smile, an easy laugh, and a soft, ironic tone of voice that kept even the most disheartening conversations upbeat.

As David fed his three cats, wiry strays from the surrounding hills, on the kitchen counter, he explained how "a street-smart Chicano from East L.A. ended up in Sacramento." David told me he had had a good job in Los Angeles as a factory manager, but his first wife had succumbed to drug and alcohol addiction shortly after their daughter was born. His older brother had secured a stable manufacturing job in the Sacramento Valley, and on his advice David, then in his early twenties, moved there so that his young daughter could have a fresh start. In Sacramento, he worked in manufacturing, but after the factories shut down, David reinvented himself as a video tech for a community college, where he landed a job in the 1990s.

Working at the college, David met Karen, a gentle and hardworking white school counselor fifteen years his junior. Karen, originally from Santa Barbara, had traveled north to attend Sacramento State. After graduating, she had taken a position counseling students and coordinating adult night courses; they met when David was hired as a video technician and used his position to develop an arts curriculum for the adult program. After some back-and-forth, the couple settled into a relationship. They traveled, rode horses (Karen was an avid equestrian), and spent time with friends. In their social circle, David said, the couple developed a reputation for lighting up a room whenever they walked in together.

After five years, in 2001, they married. David described his outdoor wedding to "the love of my life" as he led me to a parade of photographs hanging in his hallway. In my favorite photo, Karen smiled straight into the camera, her mouth caught wide in mid-laugh, while David stood with his gaze fixed adoringly on his bride and his hands awkwardly angling toward her trim waist. The sun setting over the foothills cast shadows over their guests standing in the background.

Soon after, Karen was diagnosed with an aggressive ovarian cancer. They were living in what David called their "safety home," a two-bedroom house they bought after the wedding. It was nothing like the house they had imagined living in. "My wife had survived the first operation and chemo," David explained, "and she was looking dazed." On a mission to return some of the vitality cancer had stolen, David found their dream home four blocks away, a four-bedroom California ranch-style house nestled in the woods back from a country road. "It was a fixer-upper; it needed some TLC. And it had room for Karen's horses." David secured a loan through Countrywide Financial, and they borrowed $15,000 from a friend for the down payment. The couple signed a contract in 2004.

When the payments ballooned, their new mortgage stretched the couple financially. Karen had stopped working when she started chemotherapy, and they were barely scraping by on David's income. When they bought the house, they agreed, David joked, that they wouldn't eat for ten years, but if they qualified for the mortgage, they qualified. The market had been going up for years; property was a sound investment. Besides, Karen had fallen in love with the place, declaring it her dream home, and David was desperate "to give her something to live for."

For David and Karen, a home purchase was much more than a commodity or a sound investment; it represented a second chance at a life that seemed suddenly all too fragile. David described the purchase as emotionally driven, one that would give them a place where they could be together "with room to breathe." Like David and Karen, most homeowners I came to know in the Sacramento Valley described their motivation for homeownership as a combination of emotion and finances: a graduation into adulthood, a place to grow a family, a stable ground to live out the golden years. An empty structure, a dwelling, became the scaffolding that would support tremendous psychic weight and was infused with a magical power to give a child solid footing or to save a life. These visions of homeownership, enabled by a financial exchange but not determined by it, would later encourage people to rethink the moral valence of debt repayment as foreclosures overtook the Sacramento Valley.

POSTWAR AMERICAN DREAMS

Lenders and loan servicers consistently perpetuated the idea that homeownership could cure the tragedies of modern life. Advertising campaigns selling mortgages promised familial bliss, personal belonging, and financial stability. In the Sacramento Valley, this sentiment imbued the marketing tag lines of mortgage lenders: "Dream it, own it." "Impossible." "Move up." "You're too smart to rent." Kinship references abounded; in these advertisements, babies, young children, and women either holding newborns or about to give birth were familiar tropes. Another advertising angle emphasized a link between homeownership and unlimited possibility. One Wells Fargo television spot from 2013 intercut scenes of the Wright brothers, Rosa Parks, a NASA control room erupting into cheers as a rover lands on Mars, and a newborn baby as a way to link, in the space of sixty seconds, mortgage lending with a broader dream of American possibility.

If the American Dream was grounded in the ideology that hard work guarantees opportunities for the good life, possession of a house was the post–World War II embodiment of that ideal. This imagined role of the home as a respite from the cold, hard calculations of the public sphere was already rooted in nineteenth-century notions of public and private divides under industrial capitalism, but it took on a new sheen as the suburbs expanded after World War II. After the war, the federal government fueled the growth of the suburbs by using tax policies to encourage developers to build large-scale suburban neighborhoods on farmland.[1] To help Americans to buy these homes, the government insured mortgages and built highways connecting commuters with the city centers where they worked. The new houses in these sprawling suburbs needed to be filled, in turn promoting a consumer culture of goods and appliances, the domestic manufacturing of which helped the United States transition out of a wartime economy. Rosie the Riveter had built bombs during the war, but once peace was declared, she and her sisters handed their manufacturing jobs back to their husbands and brothers coming home from Europe and the Pacific. Soon American factories were churning out washing machines instead of bombs, appliances that made housework more efficient for now-homebound Rosie and kept the men in her life employed.

The postwar suburban housing boom was part of a larger project of economic redistribution that sought to secure blue-collar livelihoods and ease workers' entry into the American middle class. In the Sacramento Valley, New Deal policies supported not only mortgaging but also massive employment and educational ventures. Federal programs funded projects including infrastructure developments that hired local labor to produce city murals and sculptures, expand city parks and the Sacramento airport, build public schools, and install sidewalks and water tanks. These policies paved the way for significant public works after World War II. Sacramento State University was founded in 1947 to meet the increased demand for higher education from veterans taking advantage of the GI Bill. For generations, public-sector jobs in the Sacramento Valley would offer residents secure employment with moderate but certain possibilities for advancement and with decent health and retirement benefits.

This growth of the American suburbs and mortgaging coincided with the expansion of a consumer credit market that would transform the social meaning of debt. Before the 1920s, Americans had considered it shameful to owe money. As historian Louis Hyman describes, U.S. lenders were prohibited from charging profitable interest rates, reselling debts, or borrowing against debts before 1917.[2] Some Americans did secure loans, but the stigma of debt meant that they borrowed primarily in a subterranean world of loan sharks and pawnbrokers.[3] However, the expansion of consumer credit, along with federal mortgaging, allowed long-term borrowing and debt repayment to become central to middle-class notions of stability. In the 1920s, consumer credit entered mainstream middle-class American social life, as business and government collaborated to enable Americans to purchase the goods of the developing manufacturing economy. Those who carried so-called good debt were considered good citizens.[4] Mortgaging and other forms of consumer credit, as Hyman points out, became an entitlement rather than a privilege for middle-class Americans, tightly woven into the spending habits of homeowners who took out mortgages, financed cars, and bought clothes with charge cards. "To be denied credit went beyond an economic inconvenience," he explains; "credit access cut to the core of what it meant to be an affluent responsible adult in postwar America."[5] This pervasive sense of entitlement among middle-class homeowners would fuel expectations of financial reciprocity and mutuality from mortgage lenders decades later in the aftermath of the mortgage crash.

Conversely, residents in Sacramento Valley's lower-income neighborhoods were less likely to anticipate help from lenders as the housing bubble imploded in 2008. The absence of feelings of entitlement to assistance and attention reflects residents' long-standing exclusion from mortgage lending and credit markets. Consumer credit and home loans became available beginning in the 1930s, democratizing credit and mortgage lending, but both were riddled with racial covenants. "It was not a boon for everyone," UC Davis sociologist and veteran Sacramento real estate agent Jesus Hernandez told me. An expert on the racist practices of American mortgaging, Hernandez showed me a slide of a local appraisal manual he had unearthed from a Sacramento archive from the 1930s that listed races in hierarchical order of the supposed risk that neighborhoods posed to mortgage lenders; housing officials had relegated "South Italians," "Negroes," and "Mexicans" to the bottom of the list. At a property in Sacramento, an appraiser's notes justified low property values because "goats, rabbits, and black babies" had been found on the property. "Fannie Mae," Hernandez said bluntly of the Federal National Mortgage Association, "would only do loans with white people." Military bases attracted African American and Latino service members and their families to the Sacramento Valley, forging among them a fragile middle class, but rampant redlining and de facto segregation kept them from enjoying access to many neighborhoods in the region.

The same types of discrimination existed in other forms of credit lending. Hyman shows how middle-class consumers, particularly white men, had easy access to consumer credit, but low-income people of color and women of all classes and races were denied loans. Divorced and married white women, for example, could not take out a loan without the signature of a husband or father. The organization of postwar suburban houses similarly helped to solidify the advantages of white middle-class masculinity. Cultural campaigns to relegate women's work to the domestic sphere proliferated. Whereas women had broken gender segregation during the war, working in factory jobs previously forbidden to them, these posts were now reserved for men returning from war, which put women of color and working-class white women who had always worked and had relied on these higher-paying factory jobs to support their families during the war at a particular disadvantage. The architecture, material culture, and spatial arrangements of postwar suburbanization generated and exacerbated inequalities of class, race, and gender.[6]

Federally sponsored educational and employment opportunities likewise failed to benefit Sacramento Valley residents equally. Most prominently, during World War II, Japanese American residents in Sacramento had been detained and imprisoned in internment camps, suffering innumerable injustices and losing substantial amounts of family wealth in the process. Racial inequalities also plagued the farming industry, as large-scale farms took advantage of a largely Latino workforce. These inequities persisted into the 1960s, as Cesar Chavez led the most famous United Farm Workers civil rights march to Sacramento.

Without a doubt, the expansion of consumer credit consolidated white male privilege, but, ironically, the Keynesian philosophies driving these financial policies often celebrated credit markets as a tool of liberation. In the 1930s, policy makers often suggested that the best way to address social problems such as income inequality and discrimination was a massive expansion of consumer credit, making credit available to those previously excluded, such as nonwhite borrowers and white women.[7] In the 1960s, a second-wave feminist movement of credit activists emerged, in which women advocated for a fuller integration into capitalist economies as a way to secure equal rights, resulting in the passage of the Equal Credit Opportunity Act in 1974. Similarly, credit scoring was touted as a way to remove personal bias from the credit decisions made about consumers by outsourcing the human component of these decisions to a seemingly impartial mathematical system. That said, most often the rise of credit scoring merely concealed racism and classism behind a façade of formalized objectivity.

Postwar American consumer credit markets, especially mortgaging, endemic with forms of discrimination, were deeply flawed but still aimed to grease the wheels of manufacturing, supporting blue-collar and middle-class families with wages and benefits that allowed them to purchase manufactured goods. But 1980s neoliberal economic policies began dismantling those industries and sending factories abroad, replacing them with service industries in retail and finance. These industries relied on temporary workforces and flexible labor and offered few if any benefits to workers.[8] Moreover, this new deregulated economic order intensified the role of credit and debt for blue-collar and middle-class families. In what social theorist Andrew Ross describes as a "creditocracy," financiers would wrap debt around every possible asset and income stream, requiring basic goods like food and clothing to be debt-financed and making indebtedness the precondition for acquiring life's necessities.[9] Yet, disingenuously, financiers celebrated this amplification of indebtedness as an act of inclusion into previously discriminatory markets, especially subprime mortgage lending.

The restructuring of the American economy away from manufacturing and toward financial industries manifested in a transition from postwar to speculative mortgaging in California. Whereas the first post–World War II wave of suburban expansion had been driven by government policies that also created blue-collar jobs like the factory floor work David Sanchez and his brother had performed in their youth, the second wave of mortgage lending and suburban expansion in the early 2000s was tied to the same neoliberal policies that had shut down factories and forced workers into part-time or precarious work in the service industries, with no benefits. When David, for example, took his job as a video technician at the community college in middle age, he had to rely on his veteran's benefits for healthcare and his expectation of Social Security benefits for retirement, forms of redistribution grandfathered in from the postwar era. Despite historical obstacles to fair housing, many of my respondents from diverse racial and class backgrounds viewed the Sacramento Valley as a vestige of lower-middle- and middle-class affordability where families from almost any ethnic or class background could afford to purchase a home and find stable employment in the public sector. Historical developments had encouraged the growth of an American middle class through economic subsidies and ideologies of entitlement, making homeownership a centerpiece of this ideal and offering a moral high ground to those striving to achieve the implicit promise of postwar stability.

THE RISE OF REAL ESTATE SPECULATION

For David and Karen, postwar cultural ideologies motivated them to believe that homeownership could cure their emotional suffering, but the ethos of the mortgage industry had long been divorced from any sort of postwar romanticism about the American Dream. David and Karen's home purchase occurred during a boom in mortgage lending profoundly unlike that which prevailed during the postwar era of homeownership. By the late 1990s, the Sacramento Valley was experiencing a real estate explosion as mortgage brokers, land development corporations, and construction companies came to dominate the economic landscape, replacing more traditional livelihoods like industrial farming and manufacturing. As Wall Street investment firms took an interest in California mortgage markets, Sacramento mortgaging quickly transformed from a conservative investment into a sales-based market in which loan products were pushed onto consumers regardless of their needs or qualifications. Ameriquest Mortgage and Countrywide, two of the largest subprime lenders in the United States, launched national advertising campaigns with tag lines such as "Don't Judge Too Quickly. We Won't" and "Countrywide Can" and with promises not to "judge" the borrowers other lenders had turned down (often for good reason, in that people's financial solvency would crumble under the burden of repayment). Developments expanded onto farmland as sprawling down-on-their-luck horse and cattle ranches were transformed into nondescript suburbs in places like Elk Grove, which between 2004 and 2005 held the title as the fastest-growing large city in the United States, boasting subdivisions with ambitious names like Heritage Lakeside and Bruceville Meadows, and matching strip malls boasting retail grocery stores, fast-food drive-throughs, and nail salons.

In this context, Jason Silva, a bright and energetic eighteen-year-old, had arrived from a rural Northern California town to attend Sacramento State, from which he graduated in 2008 with a degree in economics. His mother was Punjabi Mexican American, and his father Portuguese American.[10] In college, Jason's friends were involved in real estate, and one classmate working in loan origination offered him $100 per document to convert W-2 forms and pay stubs into PDF files (his friend made $1,200 per loan). This was Jason's introduction to the mortgage industry. While still a student, Jason moved into a house in a rambling, newly built community near an exclusive golf course on the outskirts of Sacramento. Jason described his roommates as a "nucleus of guys," with most working in mortgage lending. He tended to describe his house in fraternity-like terms, whereby the parties and lavish living conditions were paid for by his roommates, three of whom worked for Ameriquest and who had graduated some years earlier and were "making a killing selling shady subprime loans" in real estate. The mortgage industry provided Jason's roommates with more than an education in mortgage lending; in the lead-up to the crash, they learned questionable and fraudulent practices that soon became de rigueur. Jason watched as his friends at Ameriquest "learned to be scumbags," adopting practices of lying and scheming to turn quick profits. They were "making so much cash," he told me, "spending it, wasting it."

Jason declined the higher-earning opportunities his friends pursued, instead taking a more measured and what he saw as a more ethical approach to real estate, originating loans for Leviathan Bank*. Despite the trouble in the mortgage industry, Jason, just out of college, still managed to earn nearly $180,000 in yearly salary, with five weeks off. He justified his decision to forgo million-dollar paychecks by describing his summers during high school working in his grandfather's grocery store. "You would go to that same grocery store because you had a connection," he told me. "My grandpa knew people who were actually stealing from him. What he would do, instead of calling them out, he would punch it up on the register when they actually bought stuff and charge them extra. Things like that you wouldn't see anymore." Jason believed business practices should respect people's pride and focus on the bigger picture—maintaining long-term loyalties rather than focusing on short-term profits.

Many older mortgage industry professionals in the Sacramento Valley interpreted the introduction of high finance into conservative local mortgage markets as a colonization of long-standing business practices. Sandra Washington, an African American mortgage broker in her forties, recalled how the marketing departments of Wall Street investment banks "descended" on her small firm, to the point where, each week, as many as ten representatives passed through her office with so-called innovative high-risk products. Sandra, whose husband commuted hours to work in the high-tech industry, sat on the boards of a handful of non-profit agencies; she was particularly active with Boys & Girls Clubs of America. She saw her role as building community ties by providing access to loans. But Washington was uneasy about changes she saw in the industry. She witnessed an influx of unqualified brokers who were prone to making questionable decisions and falling for the sales pitches of Wall Street firms. For her, the flood of cheap credit, subprime loan products, and loosened underwriting standards represented a financial foreign invasion, not a moment of liberation, for the communities where she had lived and worked for decades.[11]

Her concerns were well founded. As Wall Street executives were upending safeguards to protect consumers, Sacramento Valley brokers set about erasing boundaries that once had maintained ethical business practices. Beginning in the 1990s local brokers would start mortgage companies within their brokerage firms. "So, people selling you the loans," Jesus Hernandez told me, "were the people selling you the houses. It was a racket." Hernandez described how brokers no longer earned commissions solely on sales but began collecting commissions (called "desk fees") from the agents they hired. The more agents a broker hired, the more she earned. They prized quantity over quality.

"The commissions became a Ponzi scheme," Hernandez said. "You hire some agents, take some off of the top and pass it along to the agency, they do the same, and so on and so on."

HOMEOWNERS AS PAYMENT STREAMS

Just as consumer credit had been touted as a democratizing force beginning in the 1930s, similar rhetoric emerged during the 2000s real estate boom, as Wall Street mortgage lenders offered subprime mortgages as a way to "expand" credit markets to previously excluded Sacramento Valley residents, with devastating consequences. Lenders and brokers targeted neighborhoods in which most residents were people of color, a process I look at in greater detail in the next chapter. In my conversations with Jonathan Rudy, a former top-level executive at a major Wall Street financial firm notorious for its role in driving the subprime mortgage crash, he insisted that his organization had opened housing markets to residents who could not have previously afforded to purchase homes. "Just a week before the crash," he told me, "I was receiving an award from a community organization for housing justice for all the work we had done in poor neighborhoods. Overnight, we became the villains in the media, and our CEO was scared to leave his house." When pressed, Jonathan acknowledged that his firm, under his direction, may have "loosened underwriting standards" too much, encouraging loans that were destined to default, but he maintained that the firm failed to see the dangers at the time, which eventually bankrupted the company and ravaged the U.S. mortgage industry.

If anyone in the Sacramento Valley had a privileged vantage point from which to understand the risky practices inherent in subprime lending and the subsequent foreclosure epidemic, it was Sam Farber. Born and bred in Sacramento, Sam had spent a decade working on Wall Street on the technical side of mortgage securities markets. An animated, heavyset white straight shooter in his early fifties, Sam was partial to Hawaiian shirts and loafers on casual Fridays. He began his career in commercial real estate in Sacramento in the 1980s, moved into residential mortgaging, and then crafted a successful career on "the technological side," creating risk-assessment computer programs that determined if a buyer qualified for a mortgage for corporate lenders who outsourced much of this work under multimillion-dollar contracts. Although Sam's career took him to Wall Street, where he designed the subprime products firms then sold to local brokers, he always maintained a house in the Sacramento Valley just miles from where he had grown up.

Beginning in the early 2000s, Sam embarked on a lucrative career designing security-backed mortgages, which fueled the mortgage boom. More than once he detailed living the high life during the boom, posing the rhetorical question, "Do you realize what a *month-long* luxury vacation in Maui costs?" The real moneymaking clients for Wall Street mortgage lenders, he told me, were not the homeowners taking on mortgages but rather the investors who were securitizing the mortgages. He described the mindset in the industry as delusional thinking in part fueled by Wall Street's physical and psychic distance from the local realities of homeowners, especially those in the Sacramento Valley. "Most of the people I have worked with on Wall Street," he quipped, "lived in New York City and did not have a mortgage. Those guys were renters." The Wall Street mortgage industry had ordinary homeowners "trapped like rats." Homeowners, Sam pointed out, were unaware of this seismic shift in mortgaging. "You mentally separate yourself from the victims who are the borrowers," he told me. Instead, you focus on the beneficiaries, the people to whom you are selling the securitized mortgages. "When it's off your desk, that's when it's no longer your problem," he explained.

Despite his efforts to compartmentalize his work from the homeowners who would be affected, Sam occasionally challenged his Wall Street coworkers, who tended to shift blame to local mortgage brokers.

He remembered sitting at a conference on mortgage securitization at the New York Marriott Marquis hotel and listening to analysts and senior management blaming unscrupulous mortgage brokers for pushing subprime loans on unqualified borrowers. He recalled thinking,

> We sit here and we design these products, okay? We have no concern at all about [what] the impact is on the problem. We constructed these things so that if a borrower can't get out of it in two years, they're totally screwed. We offer five points in rebate to the broker to sell these products for us. Why is that substantially different compared to leaving a plate full of gold bricks on the sidewalk and then coming down tomorrow morning and fully expecting all the gold bricks to be sitting on the damn pallet?

Illustrating Sam's criticism, executives and upper-level managers developing risky mortgage products that overwhelmed the Sacramento Valley in the decades preceding the foreclosure epidemic rarely used the term "homeowner" in our conversations. Occasionally they mentioned "clients" or "customers" when discussing the problems of loan modification programs, but in describing their daily work before the crash, these professionals replaced "homeowners" with terms such as "commodities," "risk analysis," "securities," "products," and "income streams."

Brokers, in contrast, were involved in face-to-face exchanges with home buyers. Therefore, the misguided logic of executives went, they shouldered more responsibility for the tragic consequences.

When we met in 2013, Sam was atoning for his sins and reinventing himself after the industry collapsed. Now he was working as a housing advocate at a prominent nonprofit, helping to shape policies that delivered modifications and assistance to homeowners in foreclosure. He often talked about the stark differences between his luxurious precrash lifestyle and the modest existence he enjoyed once the layoffs had begun. Sam described the failures of lenders' mortgage modification programs after the crash as an extension of the questionable yet highly profitable mortgage strategies that had gripped the industry in the lead-up to the 2008 crisis.

Excerpts from "The Subprime Primer," a PowerPoint presentation that mortgage industry professionals circulated before the housing bubble imploded. Given to the author by Sam Farber.

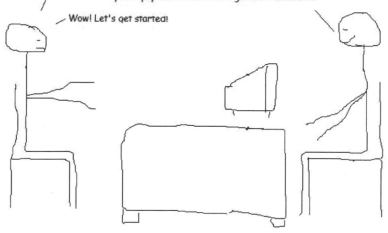

FROM PREDATORY LENDING TO
PREDACIOUS BUREAUCRACY

Judy Zaro, an elderly white Jewish retired civil servant, welcomed a mortgage broker into her living room in 2007, when brokers cold-called potential buyers and even knocked on doors. The broker, a former college basketball player with a buzz cut and a new suit, sat on Judy's plastic-covered sofa as he took in the ground floor of her three-bedroom town home in a quiet suburb of Sacramento. Photographs of her children and grandchildren crowded the mantel over the tiny fireplace. Her husband Bob had recently suffered a stroke. He sat in silence, perched next to a hospital bed they had added to the living room. After the three had spent an hour together, their small talk gave way to the broker's pitch.

"I can get you a great deal on an equity loan, no interest," he said. "With housing prices soaring like they are, the banks can't give the money away fast enough. Now is the time." He pointed to the staircase, then said, "You can use the cash to fit your home with a chairlift and remodel the bathrooms for you and your husband."

"Okay, we'll think about it," Judy said as she stood up to shake the broker's hand. She tried to sound self-assured, but Bob, a retired accountant, had always made the financial decisions. The presence of the broker in her living room overwhelmed her.

During dinner, Judy considered tapping into their fixed monthly income for the renovations they needed to stay in the condo and live independently. A cut in their budget meant they would miss their annual trips to visit their daughter and her family in the Midwest. They had worked hard to pay off their mortgage over thirty-seven years, so why not take advantage of their hard work by making their home equity work for them? Besides, the broker seemed trustworthy. It was 2007, and housing prices were on a continuous upswing. After a few days, she called the broker and told him they would sign the paperwork.

By 2009, the market had plummeted, and Judy and Bob no longer had the option to refinance when their monthly payments ballooned from $675 to $1,200. She realized that the broker had lied; he had reassured her that they would be out of the town home by the time the balloon payments began. Up late at night, she would replay those words in her head. What did he *mean* they would be out of the house by then? They had been in their home for over thirty years; they weren't going to flip the town house. They certainly did not plan on dying so soon. Judy lived on a modest pension from her career in school administration and later government service, and her husband relied solely on Social Security. The broker had signed them up for a loan payment that was a ticking time bomb, waiting to explode well beyond the limits of their modest fixed income.

Judy had been blindsided by the risks of a home equity loan contract she had signed in 2007. For good reason: until the late 1980s, home equity loans had been discouraged because they carried the risk of foreclosure. But home equity loans offered considerably higher returns for bankers than consumer loans did, so in the late 1990s, as suspect financial prac-

I don't want to lose my house.

888-995-HOPE

One of many ads for government-sponsored loan modification programs that appeared throughout the Sacramento Valley.

tices gained mainstream use, banks began promoting home equity loans through national advertising campaigns like Citibank's billion-dollar Live Richly campaign.[12]

Judy went to Vertex National Bank*, the lender that had bought her mortgage, hoping it would "make things right." But the service representative said there was nothing that could be done. "I talked to other people in my situation who were in the waiting room at [Vertex], and they told me the same thing: you can't get a short sale until you skip payments. That just didn't make sense; that's horrible."

Billboards for loan modification programs cluttered the Sacramento Valley skyline. Flyers advertising mortgage relief landed in mailboxes daily, and television commercials promising to save homes from foreclosure played on an endless loop during broadcasts. One typical commercial portrayed a middle-aged Latina grandmother, around Judy's age, who lived in a spacious middle-class home and who had fallen behind on her mortgage payments. She made a call, and within minutes she was frolicking in her sunny backyard with her grandchildren, her home now safe from bank seizure. Drawing on the same tropes that sold mortgages, these ads often harnessed powerful cultural narratives of saving one's family or preserving one's marriage by securing mortgage assistance.

Judy decided to apply for a government-sponsored loan modification but was overcome by the massive amount of paperwork required. With Bob unable to assist, Judy asked a neighbor to help her sort through the application and help her read the requirements. The piles of paperwork she needed to assemble for the application confused her. Learning to work her printer without Bob's help, she told me, took a day in itself. It seemed that every time she had everything in order, something, like her bank statements, were out of date and she had to begin again. Navigating her online account to find the correct documents was a challenge. Judy had never done her own taxes, much less compiled documents for a loan modification. After two attempts, the modification was approved, but it lowered their monthly payments by only $200, not enough to allow Judy to save their home.

During the modification process, Judy became ill with spinal stenosis, an illness she attributed to the stress of appealing to save her home. Fearful of upsetting Bob, Judy hid their dire situation from him. After nearly fifty years of marriage, Judy felt alone in her struggles. The stress of losing her home was exacerbated by the torturous modification process and her self-blame for taking on a risky loan when their home would have been paid for had they simply continued to pay their original mortgage. She stopped paying homeowners' dues on the town home and began turning to credit cards to keep them afloat.

After Bob and Judy lost their home in 2013, their daughter convinced them to move to a Jewish retirement community in a Minnesota suburb, where they would be closer to their daughter's family. Refusing to go outdoors during the winter, Judy described her new life in "Siberia" in dismal terms. Her daughter and son-in-law were paying for the cramped apartment Judy and Bob shared. "We had to get rid of all of our furniture," she said, "just giving things away we'd had for years, because we couldn't fit it in our new place." She desperately missed her home and friends in California. Plagued by a lingering depression, once a year Judy had a week of relief during which she hired a home health aide to care for her husband and flew to Sacramento to visit her close-knit group of female friends. "My girlfriend doesn't have a bar in the shower, so I don't bathe for a week, but I don't even mind," Judy told me. "I look forward to that trip all year." During her annual visit, Judy had considered going by the condo development to visit her former neighbors. But each time, the idea was daunting. "I'm too emotional to do it," she admitted. "I can't stand to look at everything we lost."

Had the broker not knocked on her door or had Vertex come through on its promises of substantial assistance, Judy would have been living out her retirement with her husband in her own community, as she had planned, spending time with her friends in the place she had lived and worked her entire adult life. Judy initially felt ashamed of her decision to take out an equity line and initially hid her impending default from her family and close friends; the idea of skipping payments, even to qualify for mortgage assistance, left her uneasy.

As lonely as she felt, she was not alone. At the start of the foreclosure epidemic in the Sacramento Valley, homeowners expressed fear that their friends, family, and coworkers would reject them or view them as incompetent or irresponsible for falling behind on mortgage payments. These impulses were in line with national surveys conducted in 2009, shortly after the crash began, that suggested that Americans believed they were morally responsible for repaying their mortgages even when they were underwater.[13] Seven of ten Americans surveyed who had defaulted on their mortgages still believed that it was unacceptable to stop payments on an underwater mortgage.[14]

Postwar ideologies of homeownership tying mortgaging to moral personhood were intensified by Sacramento's rural history, which emphasized small-town decency, heightening the stigma of nonpayment.[15] In a parallel case, during the Midwestern 1980s farm foreclosure crisis, anthropologist Kathryn Dudley observed the animosity community members expressed toward families undergoing bank seizures; instead of questioning how lenders had pushed cheap credit onto farmers, friends and neighbors concluded that anyone who had lost a farm had "done something to deserve it."[16] Government agencies and financial industries have intensified these tactics to cultivate borrowers' fear, shame, and guilt about foreclosures.[17] Traditional forms of public shaming, such as publishing delinquent mortgagors' names in newspapers and posting foreclosure notices on the fronts of houses, have disgraced homeowners and led them to pay even against their own financial best interests.

But in the Sacramento Valley these long-standing moral codes of debt repayment began to unravel after 2009 as foreclosures devastated neighborhoods across the region and homeowners became embroiled in nonsensical confrontations with corporate mortgage modification bureaucracies. Advertisements steered homeowners like Judy to loan modification hotlines and websites, but once homeowners initiated the process, they were immediately frustrated by an endless runaround. The promise of resolution suggested by the omnipresent television ads and billboards smacked of false advertising. Whether homeowners were forced to fall behind on payments to secure short sales or walked away from underwater loans of their own volition, these actions generated new attitudes and perspectives toward debt repayment among homeowners in the Sacramento Valley.

HISTORIES OF DISPOSSESSION

Everyday disputes over what qualified as wrongful bank seizures after the 2008 crash might, at first glance, seem markedly contemporary, reflecting the realities of suspect subprime lending and the failed promises of federal-corporate modification programs. But the changing meanings of landownership and speculative economic boom-and-bust cycles have been at the center of social and political struggles in the Sacramento Valley from the moment of Spanish conquest. Clashes over the legitimacy of landownership and dispossession defined the founding myth of the Sacramento Valley. Local interpretations of widespread seizures on the part of corporate lenders in the Sacramento Valley should be viewed through this lens of regional dispossessions—genealogies of financial speculation and protest in the shadow of a democratic ideal symbolized by the state capital.

Marxist geographer David Harvey argues that the unprecedented bank seizures during the recent foreclosure epidemic qualify as a form of what he terms "accumulation by dispossession," a modern variant of Marx's theory of primitive accumulation, which is a form of capitalist market expansion that relies on violence to remove people from their land, thereby making them into a landless proletariat, and then reselling their land as a means to accumulate capital.[18] Harvey emphasizes that primitive accumulation is not limited to a specific historic era—say, colonialism— as some orthodox Marxists insist, but instead involves the modern state in both backing and promoting these processes. In particular, Harvey emphasizes how neoliberalism, with its extreme concentration of wealth at the very top, relies on state-private entanglements and foments ongoing crises to move property to what he describes as the financial barons of American society.[19] Sociologist Saskia Sassen also points out how the mass expulsions triggered by the subprime crisis exemplify this modern-day incarnation of Marxist primitive accumulation.[20]

Understanding contemporary foreclosures as a form of accumulation by dispossession usefully links the unprecedented bank seizures after 2008 to violent forms of forced removal that defined the foundational history of the Sacramento Valley. The original Native American inhabitants, most prominently the Miwok and Maidu nations, confronted the genocidal encroachments of the Spanish and the missionizing movement of the Catholic church beginning in the eighteenth century. After they resisted the subsequent encroachment of the Mexican army in the 1800s, one of the most persistent threats to indigenous ways of life was John Sutter, a German-born Swiss pioneer who abandoned his wife, five children, and debts in Switzerland to travel to Mexican California in 1839. There he received the largest land title available for private ranchos, around 48,000 acres, encompassing all of modern-day Sacramento.

This bureaucratic technique of land titling gave an aura of rationality to a system of violent theft, an attempt to consolidate Mexico's hold over California against its original Native inhabitants, as well as against Russian, United States, and British colonial agents vying for ownership.

Violence initiated by Sutter but perpetuated in collusion with a growing state apparatus cemented the mass dispossessions under settler-colonial rule. Relying on the slave and coerced labor of Miwok and Maidu men, women, and children, Sutter created a settlement on Native Nisenan land, known to the people living there as the Cullumah Valley. Sutter enslaved Native Americans, incarcerating them in holding pens and locked rooms at night, punishing runaways by whipping or even executing them, and launching violent attacks on nearby Native villages, where people who refused to work for Sutter, including the elderly and children, were slaughtered. Sutter pitted clans against each other, maintaining his occupation of their lands even after 1846, when the United States took California away from Mexico during the Mexican-American War.

These brutal mass dispossessions were resisted by Natives but also contested by a growing population of poorer migrants to Northern California. After gold was discovered in Sutter's Mill in 1848, a speculative economy erupted. But prospectors fueling the Gold Rush frenzy faced a landscape that was closed to supposedly free homesteading—the act of claiming indigenous land that was imagined as "uninhabited"—as eight hundred families, including Sutter's, had already claimed fourteen million acres of California stolen from Native tribes. Newcomers were forced to lease land from Sutter and, often unable to afford rents, took to squatting on land surrounding the settlement. Squatters held public meetings, questioning Sutter's land titles and demanding the right to free homesteading. They formed a militia that, in 1850, clashed with police forces aiming to defend Sutter's titles, culminating in the famous "squatters' riots," a violent melee that is commemorated in downtown Sacramento with a plaque at the corner of J and Fourth Streets.[21] In addition to the plaque, this colonial history remains present in the rhythms of daily

A plaque commemorating the squatters' riots in downtown Sacramento. Photo by the author.

life in Sacramento through school tours of Sutter's Fort and Old Town, a popular historic district that offers residents and a steady stream of tourists a replica of Sacramento's Gold Rush life with horse-drawn carriages, museums, and performers strolling the street in costumes.

If eras of speculation and dispossession drive California's early history, banking offers a through line for these origin stories. The Wells Fargo History Museum in Sacramento's Old Town district belies this deep-rooted connection, embodying the bank's mythic status in conquest narratives that celebrate the so-called founding of the West. Aiming to capitalize on the potential wealth of the Gold Rush, Wells Fargo established itself in California in 1852 as a major player in transportation, communication, and shipping, especially transporting gold in its iconic stagecoaches across the continent. Founders Henry Wells and William Fargo instantiated the bank's presence in the daily lives of

Stagecoach replica parked over a map of California in the Wells Fargo History Museum in Old Town Sacramento. Photo by the author.

Californians who, according to a museum placard, "visited busy Wells Fargo offices to transfer money, send mail, receive packages, and pick up the latest newspapers." Administrative paraphernalia fill the museum's display cases—ledgers, handstamps, receipt books, precise scales for weighing gold, robbery reports. These incipient bureaucratic techniques of record keeping and accounting rationalized an unruly reality of conquest and seizure. Profits were nearly inconceivable at the time: $38 million in funds went through the Sacramento office in 1864 alone. (For comparison, a laborer's wage was around ninety cents a day.)

Those who ambushed stagecoaches and railcars, holding them up at gunpoint and running off with gold, cash, and documents, maintain an equally prominent place in the Wells Fargo museum. Although the museum's aim seems to be to feature the heroics of Wells Fargo's private security agents, who kept meticulous records of robbers and caught many of them, these tales also reveal an unintended narrative. Bureaucratic practices, like acts of policing, offered an aura of legitimacy to forms of profiteering that had not yet been naturalized to others living in the region. In other words, Wells Fargo was in the business of constructing criminality to cover for its own misconduct. Banking and, more specifically, documents like land titles formalized these seizures and relied on acts of overt violence to enforce them. Creating a private security force, offering rewards for infamous stagecoach and later railway robbers, the agents participated in shoring up an otherwise open question of legitimacy—the gold had been found on land stolen from Native Americans and then the Mexican government and finally Sutter, who abandoned his fort and the mill where gold was first discovered for a family farm on the Feather River. Seizure and theft were the defining values of Western expansion, not the exception to the rule of law.

Echoes of Wells Fargo's Wild West days reverberated for Northern California residents in the most recent era of speculation in three key ways. First, Wells Fargo, and banking more generally, had been romanticized as part of the social fabric and cultural history of the Sacramento Valley. This vision generated expectations of mutuality and reciprocity among present-day residents, fostering a pervasive sense that lenders shared a bond of mutuality with residents after the collapse of the market in 2008. Second, a nascent bureaucratic apparatus in the form of mortgage modification applications, documents, and agents, similar to those embryonic documents and procedures created in the 1800s, functioned to hold at bay pressing political questions about true and rightful proprietorship. Finally, these efforts to consolidate control in the aftermath of a speculative economy would often fail, as homeowners, not unlike the rustlers of the Wild West, would be framed as contemporary criminals, squatting in their homes and refusing to recognize the legitimacy of lenders in the context of unprecedented bank seizures.

The resistance of residents after the 2008 crash, absent the bloodshed of earlier riots against dispossession, often manifested as individual debt refusal or smaller organized collective protests on the courthouse steps where foreclosed-upon properties were being resold—tactics I explore in greater depth in chapter 5. If public protests were modest compared with those of previous eras, the private shifts in consciousness, less obvious to outside observers, were dramatic. The abuses of corporate lenders after the crash generated more than denials; they shaped subject positions from which homeowners and lending employees could question and refuse forms of administrative violence. Homeowners and lending employees alike explained that they had once labeled people who failed to repay their debts as deadbeats but that their views of the moral valence of mortgage default changed after they were caught in the modification process.

Blue-collar Americans' claims to hard-won forms of economic decency, which had dominated the period of high economic growth in the 1960s and 1970s, heard their death rattle by the time David and Karen Sanchez moved into their dream home in 2004. As manufacturing and small agricultural production were replaced by financial and service industries, which captured the lion's share of growth, executives had sent David's job abroad, pushed cheap credit on him and Karen (who were by all accounts unqualified borrowers), and eroded or eliminated employer-sponsored social safety nets, including healthcare and retirement, for which previous generations had fought hard. Failed mortgage modification programs, farcical performances of assistance plans, extended these late-liberal logics, seizing on postwar redistributive vernaculars of relief to obscure profit incentives. Wall Street firms pushed an economic transformation in which debts rather than labor became prime commodities for firms whose short-term, profit-driven mindset held shareholder value above job security for workers and above even the health of the firms.[22] It was against this backdrop of rural sensibilities and the existence of a thriving, secure lower-middle class in the Sacramento Valley that the Wall Street financialization of mortgage markets and the failure of lenders to provide relief would reshape the meanings of debt and dispossession.

Landscapes

At the center of this story there is a terrible secret, a kernel of
cyanide, and the secret is that the story doesn't matter, doesn't make
any difference, doesn't figure.... In the South they are convinced that
they have bloodied their place with history. In the West we do not
believe that anything we do can bloody the land, or change it, or
touch it.

   —Joan Didion, "California Notes"

Abandoned foreclosed home in low-income Oak Park, where predatory
lending was rampant, 2014. Photo by the author.

(*Top*) Vacant home abandoned after foreclosure in low-income Oak Park, 2013. Sign on door reads "SUBSTANDARD BUILDING DO NOT ENTER." Photo by the author.

(*Bottom*) Vacant home after foreclosure in Sacramento's middle-class Pocket neighborhood, 2012. City violation notices hang on the front door. Photo by the author.

(*Top*) Halted suburban development project blocks from Louise Walker's home in North Sacramento, 2012. Photo by the author.

(*Bottom*) Abandoned commercial development in North Sacramento, 2012. Photo by the author.

CHAPTER TWO

Put Out

Bank Seizure at the Poverty Line

Miguel Santos, a soft-spoken Mexican American carpenter in his early thirties, led me to Home Cash Market a few blocks away from the two-bedroom rental he shared with his wife, his four children, and his ailing mother-in-law in Sacramento's Oak Park neighborhood. It was a typical Tuesday in August, already creeping past ninety degrees and barely ten a.m. At the market he traded four crumpled dollar bills for a Diet Pepsi and three lottery tickets. Signs stapled to wooden telephone poles flanking the convenience store read, "We Buy Any House! All Cash 916-A-FLY-BUY" and "Sell Your House for Cash ... Fast! 855–99-Sell-Now."

As we passed an abandoned house, Miguel pointed out the foreclosures along the street. People who had lived in the neighborhood for decades had left. He explained that by 2008 the homes were all selling for between $15,000 and $20,000. "This house here," Miguel said, pointing to a run-down home with an overgrown yard, "sold at auction for under $10,000." You could walk down any street, he told me, and half the houses would be for sale or boarded up. "My brother had a house down this very block that he lost to foreclosure," he said, "But their situation—they're both illegal, so it made it hard to fight the bank. They could probably deport them." Within the tight boundaries of Oak Park, two miles wide and ten avenues long, residents witnessed nearly 6,200 foreclosures between 2008 and 2012.[1]

We passed a front yard marked by a waist-high chain link fence, where an unattended toddler wearing nothing but a diaper cried in her playpen. I remembered reading that nearly 40 percent of children in Oak Park lived below the poverty line. Catching the look on my face, Miguel shoved the lottery tickets into his jeans pockets. He told me that his third daughter was born eight weeks early and could fit into one of his hands. After he and his wife brought her home from the NICU, a home health nurse came to make a routine visit but was too scared to leave her car. "The lady called me from her car. I had to go and get her and walk her to our house," Miguel said, smiling. "The lady, a black lady, goes, 'I don't know how you do it. What about your family?' Everybody always asks me that."

Back at Miguel's house, we passed a makeshift clothesline sagging under the weight of children's clothes, with wrinkled Hello Kitty underwear hanging next to Ninja Turtle tank tops. His six-year-old son, hearing us approaching, peeked out of a small hole Miguel had cut near the bottom of the blinds. Miguel unlocked the two deadbolts and let us inside. His four children, ranging in age from fourteen months to nine years, sprawled before a large television watching *SpongeBob SquarePants*. His older boy, lanky with a buzz cut, home on summer break, sat on the sofa hunched over a worksheet, absentmindedly swatting at his sister's foot with his pencil when she occasionally kicked him.

Miguel and I sat down at his kitchen table to talk about his foreclosure. As we spoke, his youngest daughter climbed into his lap and wrapped her arms around his neck. Without pausing, he stroked her ponytails into place and told his story. In 2006 he and his wife had signed a subprime mortgage contract for $310,000 with no money down and no income verification. They had found the Oak Park two-bedroom through his cousin, who had left a job stocking shelves at Home Depot to work for a mortgage broker. I asked if he read the contract, and Miguel said it was in English, which he barely read, and he trusted his cousin. "It would have been an insult for me to ask too many questions," he said.

Then, in 2007, Miguel lost his job as a carpenter. He tried to find work as a day laborer, but the housing market was beginning to collapse and no one was hiring. His wife, who had been cleaning office buildings at night, picked up cleaning jobs during the day, stretching her working hours to twelve, sometimes fourteen consecutive hours. Miguel adjusted to life as a stay-at-home dad. "I had to learn to cook," he told me, pausing to unscrew a bottle of grape soda for his four-year-old daughter, who had wrangled it from the refrigerator. While she was waiting, she gently nibbled on her baby sister's earlobe. Miguel described how, at first, staying home with his children challenged his beliefs about what a man's role should be, but he came to accept it.

While he and his wife were struggling with Miguel's unemployment, their mortgage payments ballooned. Neither Miguel nor his cousin had fully understood how much the mortgage payments would spike. His neighbors were all losing their houses. When they were no longer able to make their payments, Miguel gave his last $1,000 to a scam artist who had come to Miguel's house and promised to negotiate with the bank on his behalf. But they were evicted from their home within the year. Miguel told me, "La única vez que el banco tiene una cara es cuando vienen a llevarse su casa. ¿Quien es el rostro de [Leviathan Bank]? Nunca dicen la verdad, nunca te ayuda." (The only time the bank shows up is to take your house. Who is the face of [Leviathan Bank]? They never tell the truth, never help you.) While Miguel and his wife didn't lose money on the down payment, Miguel had invested nearly all of their savings into fixing and improving their home.

Poverty, by necessity, fostered sociality and reciprocity between neighbors and kin in Oak Park, similar to the expansive social networks developed by African American residents of a low-income Midwestern neighborhood that anthropologist Carol Stack describes in the 1970s and 1980s. Friends and relatives relied on one another for food, clothing, shelter, and childcare. "In times of need," Stack writes of the poor black families she studied, "the only predictable resources that can be drawn upon are their own children and parents, and the fund of kin and friends obligated to them."[2] Toxic loans circulated in these tight-knit networks, combining blood and nonsanguine relatives; in Oak Park, subprime loans traveled to residents through people they had come to trust and depend upon in hard times. Their location within existing exchange systems made these mortgage loans all the more dangerous because borrowers were less likely to question their terms; doing so would introduce the shadow of distrust into otherwise loyal family ties.

Leaving Miguel's house, I passed a group of men standing on a nearby corner, a spot Miguel said had been overtaken by drug dealers. It made me think of a line in a song by neighborhood rapper Mozzy, who grew up with his grandmother, a former Black Panther, on Fourth Street a few blocks over from Miguel's rental: "Ain't no picket fences nice house and flowers / We live in the trenches you'll get devoured." Mozzy was rapping about the daily violence in his neighborhood, but it seemed that something even more vicious and covert was undermining residents' opportunities for a good life. During the boom years, low-income neighborhoods like Oak Park with mostly nonwhite residents were targeted with the riskiest, most predatory subprime loans. In these neighborhoods, families like Miguel's and his neighbors—Spanish-speaking farmworkers, disabled seniors, single mothers working at fast food chains, and unemployed factory workers—were convinced to take out loans they could not afford or, worse, to take out equity lines on homes they already owned.

As a result, the mortgage crisis hit these communities first, with bank seizures beginning as early as 2006, two years before the media declared an official crisis. "The global financial crisis," sociologist Jesus Hernandez explained, "started in the 'hood." When facing foreclosure, many residents had already defaulted by the time federal assistance programs became available in 2009. "By the time billboards for HAMP went up," a housing counselor in Oak Park told me, "the neediest home-owners in the most vulnerable neighborhoods were already gone with the wind." The foreclosure crisis shared a place in the local popular imagination with the crack epidemic of the 1980s and the ramped-up police and gang violence that followed—a calamity that could undermine familial survival and chip away at self-respect.

Some residents who were still confronting mortgage default in Oak Park after the rollout of mortgage assistance programs in 2009 had been conditioned by decades of financial exclusion to refrain from formally appealing to lenders for help. The handful of black and Latino families who had weathered the initial crash and did apply for modifications were less likely than homeowners in whiter neighborhoods to receive them.[3] In keeping with national trends, homeowners in Sacramento's low-income communities of color, where property values were lower, remained less likely than their white middle-class counterparts to obtain mortgage modifications.[4] According to national HAMP data released by the Treasury Department, Latinos and African Americans were more likely to receive denials of requests for loan modifications because of "incomplete modification requests" or because lenders lost documents. What's more, lenders rejected applications written in Spanish. Of particular interest is that the HAMP data reveals that lenders disproportionately canceled the trial modifications of African Americans in Sacramento, claiming that the loan modifications were "not accepted by the borrower."[5] But the idea that African Americans were more likely than other applicants to reject modifications after spending months, if not years, applying for them is suspect and implies that after the crash, predatory bureaucratic practices set up minority and low-income homeowners for failure, just as predatory lending had done during the housing boom.

Poverty in Oak Park stems from generations of economic exclusion, embodied by histories of residential segregation and intensified by deindustrialization over the last decades. The foreclosure crisis in Oak Park exacerbated the damage done by decades of redlining in Sacramento. Jesus Hernandez has shown how redlining kept nonwhite buyers out of the nearby West End neighborhood and pushed nonwhite residents over the border into Oak Park after the 1950s.[6] Nonwhite buyers, Hernandez recounts, were banned from obtaining mortgages in white neighbor-hoods by New Deal loan programs, which between the 1930s and the 1950s openly used racial categories to exclude minorities. As Oak Park became increasingly racially mixed, mainstream lending and financial institutions divested from it, and redlining restricted the use of feder-ally backed mortgages.[7] When lenders did extend credit to nonwhite borrowers, they systemically charged black and Latino applicants higher rates, even if their financial characteristics were identical to those of white borrowers.[8] In the 1950s and 1960s, the neighborhood faced crip-pling setbacks, as public transportation was cut and the construction of new highways stranded the community from the rest of the city. Unem-ployment soared as neighborhood businesses closed or moved. The Black Panthers organized community programs to help struggling resi-dents, including free breakfast, legal aid, and tutoring, but racial ten-sions with local police remained at an all-time high. In 1969, these sub-standard living conditions prompted residents to protest, which turned into riots and civil unrest when met with police opposition.[9]

These legacies of racial and class discrimination in housing markets gained new salience during the subprime mortgage boom and subse-quent crash in Oak Park.[10] Credit-starved residents had lived in a seg-regated financial universe in which traditional forms of lending were typically out of reach—payday lenders outpaced banks, money and debts circulated informally, collections and evictions were common-place. Here, residents' more desperate need for loans and lack of finan-cial literacy made them more vulnerable than homeowners in other neighborhoods to the predatory lending practices of subprime brokers. During the housing boom of the early 2000s, real estate speculators, often using government funds, took advantage of abandoned homes and low property values to buy and flip houses in the neighborhood. Bro-kers targeted residents with high-risk subprime mortgages, a process sociologist Gregory Squires describes as "reverse redlining": potential buyers who had been excluded from housing markets were flooded with offers to access mortgages they ordinarily could not afford without income verification or money down. Often these risky mortgage products traveled through kin networks, which I explore in the story of Carlos Lopez later in this chapter. The trends toward subprime lending in Oak Park reflect research showing that, as geographer and housing specialist Carolina Reid argues, regardless of their FICO scores, African Americans and Latinos were much more likely to receive a high-cost loan, even when controlling for local housing and mortgage market conditions and debt-to-income ratios.[11]

The predatory nature of lending and foreclosure in Oak Park exemplifies what I call predatory debt extraction—a process through which the most vulnerable Americans are no longer exploited for their surplus labor but now become key to capitalist accumulation through their debts, which are securitized and then sold and resold on global markets. Subprime mortgage lending is just one form of predatory debt extraction in which Wall Street industries target vulnerable populations. Other increasingly common forms of predatory debt extraction arise from payday lending, financial scams, and the exorbitant fees of debt collectors. These processes, all of which target vulnerable communities with unprecedented debt burdens, are often characterized by the absence of accountability and oversight, if not outright theft as formalized through semilegal practices. Being poor is not simply a matter of lacking opportunities to convert one's labor into a wage—or a living wage, for that matter—but rather of becoming indebted and, through the commodification of these debts, paying an ever-higher price for being poor.

Earlier epochs of primitive accumulation relied on brute force and face-to-face violence—formalized through administrative techniques such as land titles, bank ledgers, and robbery reports—to dispossess indigenous inhabitants and force them into working for settlers. Contemporary forms of accumulation by dispossession operate at a greater distance, using primarily bureaucratic governance—through suspect mortgage origination and obtuse foreclosure proceedings—to foster debt peonage among the most vulnerable citizens. These debts fuel the profits of financial industries and, when debtors cannot pay, embroil borrowers in bureaucratic systems that ultimately lead to a greater concentration of wealth through mass expulsions.

WHEN FRAUD COMES CALLING

The metal screen door stuck a little. After a few minutes Nancy Moore-Jones, a frail, hunched woman in her sixties with thin, pale skin, wispy gray hair, and thick-rimmed glasses, came to the door. Except for a sliver of sight in her left eye, Nancy was blind. She opened the door and invited me into a small living room with a bare linoleum floor. A tiny, wiry dog yipped at our heels. Nancy wore her cobalt pants high above her waist and decorated her thinning ponytail with rubber bands and silver trinkets, among them her deceased father's class ring and a small spoon she had twisted into a spiral. Nancy talked openly about her bipolar condition, her stories often meandering from traumatic events like her mother's suicide to mundane topics like the spelling of her doctor's name. "My dear wife, Joy, has saved my life many times," she often said. "Put that in your book, please."

Joy Moore-Jones, Nancy's wife, emerged from the back of the house, wearing a warm, open smile and a loose-fitting housedress. Joy, who had been blind her entire life, was also in her sixties, with smooth, soft-looking skin the color of rich mahogany and short cropped hair framed with spurts of gray. She had a grounded, supportive air about her. Even with the couple's challenges, they remained active in the community, volunteering to visit cancer survivors in the hospital and teaching Buddhist meditation. Before she met Nancy, Joy had spent years raising her foster son—rendered blind in his infancy by his stepfather's violent shaking—before the state returned him to his biological mother.

Joy and Nancy had lived in their home since 1985. Their landlord had suggested that they rent to own. Although they had no down payment, the landlord worked in real estate and did "some finagling" for the couple; they were able to buy the house in 1996. The home needed repairs, but Joy told me that it had been "a struggle to try to get a good loan that would make it so that [they] could still afford to pay." Then, in 2005, the phone rang. A representative from Independent National Mortgage Corporation, or IndyMac, offered a no-interest second mortgage on their home, assuring them that their payments would be lower than the $700 they were paying. They already lived on less than $1,600 a month in combined disability income and felt they could use the money to ret-rofit their bathroom to accommodate their disability. When they received the IndyMac mortgage contract in the mail, a friend read them the details and helped them to find a notary, and they signed and sent the paperwork. Joy explained that their friend was just as "bewildered" by the loan contract as they were. They read and reread the terms of the loan, but "the legalese," Joy said, "was just Greek to us."

It turned out that they had taken on an adjustable-rate mortgage with a teaser rate of $600 per month that would balloon to $1,300 within a few years, raising their mortgage payments to over 80 percent of their monthly income. The balloon payments deeply affected Joy. She told me:

> In 2006, right before the summer, we started getting statements from [Indy-Mac] that there was more owed. Our rent—our, um, mortgage payment was gonna go up. And we were pretty upset. They started really hassling us. And they were sending us threatening letters in the mail, ... they were calling us. It was just overwhelming. I was so upset that a lot of times I wasn't sleeping. [The doctors] really think now that that was what attrib-uted to my going into cardiac arrest all of a sudden. And [my heart] just got off-kilter and started beating so fast, I collapsed. I ended up going into the hospital for almost two weeks. And then we got the notice that there was foreclosure impending.

The stress-related physical illness that Joy experienced in response to their mounting debts, which left Nancy without help in the house, was widely reported among homeowners facing ballooning payments and evictions; they often described periods of acute illness as resulting from their mortgage ordeals.

Joy initially blamed herself for "consenting to the loan." A representative from the office of the California Real Estate Commissioner, however, visited their home to explain that they had been scammed. The IndyMac representative had falsified their income information to qualify them for the loan—deceptively claiming that Joy owned a daycare in a nearby county and supplying fraudulent details about their joint income. Often targeting seniors and minority borrowers like Joy and Nancy, IndyMac routinely exaggerated income data and conspired with mortgage brokers who misled borrowers about the terms and fees of their mortgages.[12] Indy-Mac then hid the level of risk inherent in its shoddy loans to resell them to investors at higher values.[13] A former IndyMac underwriter described how she would reject a loan, but then it would travel to upper management, where it would be approved.[14] A former IndyMac vice president similarly claimed that chief executive Michael Perry and other top managers emphasized loan volume and pushing through loans at all costs. IndyMac's fraudulent approach reaped massive short-term earnings for the company. Between 2003 and 2006, as IndyMac's loan origination jumped from $29 billion to $90 billion, the lender doubled its profits, which reached $343 million by 2006.[15] By 2008, however, IndyMac had collapsed.

Despite the fact that IndyMac had falsified its loan documents, the foreclosure nonetheless proceeded through the court system. Joy described how she and Nancy couldn't afford a lawyer but appeared in court three times, taking the bus two hours each way to the courthouse to appeal to the judge, who they mistakenly believed had the power to stop the foreclosure. Interpreting the legal proceedings as an opportunity to fight the foreclosure, Nancy confronted the lawyer pushing their eviction: "I stood face to face and looked him in the eye and told him, 'We are not leaving our home!'"

When the judge failed to stop their eviction, Joy and Nancy drew on their many years of involvement with a neighborhood activist organization to appeal to the public. (Both were longtime activists and had even been honored by the Southern Poverty Law Center.) Joy managed to get on the local news to tell their story. But ultimately their efforts failed.

When I spoke to a housing attorney about the judge's likelihood of intervening in Joy and Nancy's case, I learned that residential foreclosures in California were most often nonjudicial. By the time Nancy and Joy were summoned to court, they had already lost their home. It turns out that the hearings were part of a post-foreclosure eviction process in which the new owner was serving them notice. By the time they stood in front of the judge, the couple had already lost their home of more than twenty years without even knowing it.

The local Sacramento investor evicting them was in the courtroom and heard their story. After the hearing, he approached them, offered a hug, and told them they could stay in the house. He would charge them $800 a month in rent. Limitlessly optimistic in our conversations, Nancy and Joy described their new landlord as "a miracle," focusing on the fact that he had spared them the insurmountable challenges of moving and adjusting to a new home without the benefit of sight. (They didn't realize that the investor was present in the courtroom because he had initiated the eviction process once he owned the home.) After seeing the couple in the courtroom, he had a change of heart and decided not to pursue the eviction, instead renting it to Joy and Nancy at a price close to their original rent.

Nancy and Joy described this as a happy ending, but I had a hard time seeing it. Listening to people's foreclosure stories, I tended to match a homeowner's anger as a protective shell against adopting their grief. But for Joy and Nancy, gratitude had cast out righteous indignation. Their optimism cracked my defenses. Alone in my car, driving home after meeting Nancy and Joy the first time, I planted one hand on the wheel and used the other to wipe away a quiet, steady stream of tears the entire ride home.

Joy and Nancy had been victims of mortgage fraud and subsequently lost a home they had owned for more than a decade. Now they would pay rent on a house that had been theirs only a few short years before.

A decade of equity had been lost, as had been their ability to take out a reverse mortgage to help them secure full-time care in their old age. Like many Oak Park residents, however, they did not focus their outrage on the fraudulent practices of their lender, IndyMac. Whereas homeowners in middle-class neighborhoods, who had enjoyed historical access to financial institutions, approached foreclosure through official channels, duking it out with disorganized lending bureaucracies, Joy and Nancy sought assistance from a network of friends and individuals they encountered along the way—the friend who read the loan contract, fellow activists who helped them to get onto the local news, the judge overseeing their case, and the investor who ultimately bought their home. If the 2008 foreclosure crisis inspired homeowners in middle-income neighborhoods to think about mortgaging and foreclosure as a mutual obligation between creditor and debtor, Joy and Nancy did not feel entitled to the same kinds of mutuality. Instead of personalizing a financial relationship between borrower and lender, Joy and Nancy sought to use personal connections to cushion them from the harms of predatory finance.

When homeowners in middle-class neighborhoods confronted lending bureaucracies, discourses of financial reciprocity emerged. Experience with long-term mortgage contracts had entitled them to a form of moral personhood that reflected postwar ideas about middle-class belonging. These same expectations of reciprocity were not, however, available to the lowest-income borrowers; instead, the bonds these borrowers could access in poorer neighborhoods were personal, between themselves and their neighbors, community networks, and friends. Just as Carol Stack describes the prime importance of kin and non-kin support systems in poor black households, Kath Weston has shown a similar dynamic among working-class gays and lesbians in Northern California.[16] The creation of gay families, Weston shows, empowers those marginalized by society and their so-called blood kin to generate lasting support networks. Combining these cultural logics of care, Joy and Nancy for decades had recast friends as family as they relied on them for material and emotional support during difficult times. Mortgaging and foreclosure, for Joy and Nancy, traveled through a dense social landscape that reflected histories of community building and activism.

MORTGAGING SOCIAL NETWORKS

Toxic mortgages often circulated through these informal avenues of care and exchange, because abusive mortgage lending itself could become a family affair. Take Carlos Lopez, a twenty-two-year-old Mexican American high school graduate who had been working as a security guard when a mortgage broker looking to hire bilingual agents recruited him. Brokers paid agents per transaction rather than a set salary; the more mortgages they originated, the more money they would make. The position appealed to Carlos because it offered promise—working in an office, the immense financial promise of booming real estate markets, and a future career in real estate. For Carlos, his kinship and social networks were an obvious source of clients. He approached potential clients after church services, for example, and during gatherings of his large extended family.

Carlos knew that his cousin Joaquin and his wife, Dolores, had been saving to buy a home for some time and felt gratified that he could get them into a house by providing them with a mortgage. The couple was undocumented; Joaquin had come to California from Mexico in 2001 and worked as a day laborer in construction, and Dolores worked in the kitchen of a Mexican taqueria. The couple had three children and spoke no English, relying on their eldest children to translate for them in official circumstances. They had been saving their meager earnings since arriving in the United States in hopes of buying a home.

Carlos offered Joaquin and Dolores a subprime loan with an adjustable-rate mortgage whose teaser rate of $800 per month would balloon to $1,800 within a few years. Given rising property values, Carlos figured that Joaquin and Dolores could refinance into a fixed-rate mortgage and avoid the balloon payment. In the meantime, he would receive the commission, higher for subprime products, and his cousins could get into a house they couldn't otherwise afford. From his perspective, it was a win-win situation.

But the market crashed before Joaquin and Dolores could refinance. They lost their initial investment of $11,000, which had taken years to save. Carlos lost his job in real estate and returned to a part-time gig as a security officer at a mall. I didn't want to put him on the spot by asking if he blamed himself for what had happened to Joaquin and Dolores, instead keeping my questions vague about what happened to families after the crash. He remarked that he was able to give people a home they wouldn't have had otherwise, but then he paused and said he had learned a lot about "the way things work" before he lost his job.

If we compare European colonization to how Wall Street financial firms expanded mortgage markets to include low-income consumers, then the systems of financial governance that emerged were akin to forms of indirect colonial rule in which preexisting social structures became pathways for profit and debt extraction. It is significant that kinship systems in particular drove the spread of subprime lending to neighborhoods historically excluded from mainstream forms of credit lending, places where Wall Street investors and mortgage brokers had had little access but now were able to pursue unprecedented profits. Kin intimacies are often imagined as the antithesis of market transactions, but, as anthropologist Sylvia Yanagisako has shown, affective kin ties can play a central role in the reproduction of industrial capitalism, as demonstrated in her work on Italian family firms.[17] Here, the marshaling of sentiments of kinship also fuels the speculative economies of advanced neoliberalism.

The circulation of high-risk loans through community networks was common throughout California. As Carolina Reid shows in her in-depth study of mortgage lending, Northern California homeowners, particularly immigrant and African American borrowers in Stockton and Oakland, preferred brokers who were part of the local community. Reid's respondents believed that local brokers would understand their situations, refrain from judging them, and be more likely to produce positive results. "The shared identity that borrowers felt with their brokers," Reid reports, "coupled with the broker's perceived expertise about the mortgage process, led borrowers to trust their advice and not seek external validation of the information provided."[18] This tendency, however, often produced mortgage outcomes that were not in the best economic interests of homeowners. Moreover, brokers often had adverse incentives—collecting higher commissions for subprime loans, for example—and residents were unaware of these pricing structures, assuming that brokers were acting in the best interests of homeowners.

Cold calls and mailers targeted Oak Park residents with predatory and fraudulent loans but, more insidiously, close-knit networks of kin and friends trafficked in risky financial products. In both circumstances, the homeowners with whom I worked universally misunderstood the terms of the subprime loan contracts they signed. Without realizing that the rules of lending had changed, families in Oak Park trusted the brokers and banks to determine the correct amount of the loans, never questioning how they could qualify for hundreds of thousands of dollars in mortgage loans while subsisting on incomes below the poverty line. In contrast to homeowners in middle-class neighborhoods, homeowners in Oak Park lacked the opportunity to acquire the financial literacy needed to scrutinize the deluge of offers for toxic loans they received in the lead-up to the crash. Many, like Joy and Nancy Moore-Jones, similarly misunderstood the process of foreclosure and how they might contest it through formal, institutional means.

MANAGING FORECLOSURE WITH STREET SMARTS

Diego Ventana, fifty-seven years old when I first met him in 2012, short in stature with a gray beard and an easy smile, bought his house in Oak Park in 1980 and raised six children there. The family's living room was ornately decorated. Plastic covers protected polyester sofas flanked by dark wooden end tables, glass lamps, and vases, and doilies covered the tables. Devout Catholics, the family maintained a shrine to the Virgin, with candles and statues perched next to the television set. Photographs of their grown children and grandchildren lined the hallway to the bedrooms.

Diego had lived in Sacramento since childhood. In the 1960s, his family moved from Jalisco, Mexico, to Sacramento, where he started the fourth grade. He completed high school and spent a semester at city college. Starting after high school, he worked in a local factory that manufactured almond butter for General Mills. After almost thirty years, he lost his job after trying to organize a union and found part-time minimum-wage work as a janitor at his church. His wife Juana, a stout woman who was always in the kitchen during our visits, worked for fifteen years at a tomato cannery in a nearby town before the company moved out of state. They had two rental properties in Oak Park, bought in the mid-1990s, and the rental income was keeping the family afloat. The rentals, two houses across the street from each other, had belonged to an elderly woman who had lived in the neighborhood. She had no family, and when she died, the sellers, eager to off-load the properties, took $50,000 for both. Diego told me he found "a good loan officer" at Countrywide Financial that "cut corners" to help him get the loans. With the help of his wife and children, Diego remodeled one of his rental homes, adding an extra bedroom and bathroom.

Whereas it had been difficult to find a mortgage to buy the rental properties in the 1990s, when credit was mainly unavailable to working families in Oak Park, when Diego started looking for a second mortgage on his house in 2000, he received calls from more than twenty agents and brokers offering him deals. The family refinanced, taking on $213,000 of additional debt, using the money to pay off the rental properties and bring their mortgage to $1,400 a month. Just two months later, Diego lost his job at the almond plant. One of his rentals became vacant. He quickly spent his entire retirement savings, a little more than $15,000, to avoid foreclosure. Diego was contacted by a bogus company promising a loan modification. As instructed, he sent all of his paperwork, stopped paying his mortgage, and paid the company $1,000, the last of his retirement savings. Six months later he received a letter from the FBI explaining that he had been the victim of a loan modification scam.

In our conversations about his foreclosure experience, Diego talked less about the details of his mortgage loans—specific lenders and terms were foggy—and instead told stories about confrontations he had had in the neighborhood with dangerous elements. For example, he remembered a time when he confronted his next-door neighbor, a woman who sold crack from her house and whose customers were parking in Diego's driveway while copping drugs; they worked out a deal that kept the addicts and prostitutes away from his lawn. In an even more remarkable tale, a man was living across the street in a van, running electricity into the van from his mother's garage. Everyone knew the man was crazy; he had chased a neighbor down the street with a machete after a confrontation. Diego told me how he negotiated with the man, buying an air conditioner the man was selling as a way to appease him and to keep Diego's children safe. (The unit sat on the front porch for over a year before it was stolen for its aluminum parts.) Eventually, the police discovered that the man had murdered six women, burying five around the neighborhood. What did these stories, detailing how Diego had confronted a drug dealer and a serial killer to manage his family's safety, have to do with foreclosure?

Quite a bit. I realized that Diego saw foreclosure in much the same way: a threat of neighborhood violence. Instead of talking about the terms of the loans, his struggles with repayment, and lenders—the details of which were murky in his memory but which typically commanded center stage for borrowers in middle-class neighborhoods—Diego told me about the representative of the investor who had bought his house who came to his home to tell his family they were being evicted. In his narrative, which follows, Diego describes how his house was foreclosed on and how he negotiated with the investor to stay in his house as a rental. Notably, he skips the parts of his story in which he received notice of his impending eviction, glossing over the administrative details that constitute foreclosure narratives for other homeowners, and leaps quickly to the parts where he could make a deal with the new owner.

NOELLE: But how'd the new owner even buy the house?

DIEGO: At the public auction.

NOELLE: Oh. So this house went up?

DIEGO: Oh yeah. They sold it.

NOELLE: For short sale?

DIEGO: It was a ... yeah, it was ... it was out as a ... yeah, I would say short sale. So they bought it.

NOELLE: What year was that?

DIEGO: 2007. They bought it. They came over, they told me, you know. And then I got to get out. Right now.

NOELLE: I see. So it went through foreclosure and then it went up for auction.

DIEGO: Well, ... when it went for foreclosure ... this ... they sold it.

NOELLE: Right. Right away?

DIEGO: Yeah. So the ... yeah. So the guy that bought it, he was a private lender. He went to the auction, bought it. And then came back, told me it wasn't my house. I said, "Well, wh-what can we do?" So there was this Oriental lady that was handling all of his transactions.

NOELLE: Yeah.

DIEGO: After a week or so, she comes over and says, "Well, you can't be living here free." She says, "You've gotta pay rent and that," you know. Whatever. I said, "Well," I say, "what about selling the house to me?"

NOELLE: You're gonna buy back your own house?

DIEGO: Yeah. She goes, "Well, I don't know, you know. It's ... and I've gotta talk to the person ... but, you know, you've got to pay quite a bit of money." I go, "Well." So she goes, "Well, you know, he'll take so much." I go, "Come on." They paid $27,000 for this home.

Diego emphasized how the investor's representative arrived unannounced at his house and spoke to his wife and daughter even though he wasn't home, telling them, on his daughter's birthday, that they were being evicted. Addressing his wife and daughter on an important day for the family signaled for Diego a profound lack of respect. Using a representative seemed cowardly. "I don't know if it was his secretary or his wife," Diego told me.

The investor agreed to meet with Diego. In response, Diego arranged to repurchase his house for $55,000 using his rental properties as collateral. Diego brought his entire family with him to the meeting, a show of strength according to local logics but one that the investor could easily misinterpret as inappropriate for a business transaction. Three years after the foreclosure, Diego described how his credit was rendered clean and he could secure a loan to pay off the home. But the investor demanded an additional $15,000 beyond the $55,000 that Diego had already paid. "It's illegal," Diego told me, "because I have notes that he was paid off and everything." But the lawyer he consulted said he could resolve the situation for $5,000, more than Diego could afford. Diego decided to confront the investor. "I went over and I talked to him. We kind of settled things up, and he goes, 'Give me $3,500.' I go, 'I don't have $3,500.' Why should I give you $3,500 when you're all paid off? So, he's just a crook." In the end, Diego believed he lost his rental property over the disputed $3,500.

Unlike previous situations in the neighborhood in which Diego had confronted people threatening his family, when he faced the investor who had purchased his home, Diego didn't have the social or financial capital to resolve the situation. Diego had managed to negotiate with his new landlord once, but now the investor refused to release the lien on the rental. Diego admitted that he didn't read any of the paperwork that he had signed because they signed the papers at a title company. Diego trusted the title company, just as Joy and Nancy had trusted the notary who oversaw their loan application. "That's what they're there for," Diego said. "You trust them." These experiences reflect research that shows people tend not to read loan disclosures, instead trusting loan originators and the recommendations of friends.[19] Given how hazy the terms of the contract were for Diego, however, it was possible that the investor was legitimately charging Diego interest and fees that he hadn't understood at the time of the agreement. Either way, Diego needed professional assistance to regain his property, but a lawyer was too expensive and would take too long. Ultimately, however, Diego felt that it had been a good deal, because he originally had owed $250,000 with the second mortgage on his home. He lost his rental property, but his family had not been forced to move.

Here, the social capital of street culture fails to translate into authority and power in the world of finance and lending. In a similar vein, anthropologist Philippe Bourgois describes how Puerto Ricans in Spanish Harlem were forced into informal drug economies when they failed to navigate the official bureaucracies of the formal sector.[20] One resident, for example, lacked the literacy skills to navigate the city permit system to open a bar. Another failed to understand the cultural cues implicit in his office job, dressing in flashy, expensive street styles for work and answering phones when he was not supposed to have direct contact with clients. Bourgois shows how the transition from factory labor to a service economy left many poor Latino men lost in translation, as the macho, confrontational style of the factory floor that was compatible with street life was replaced by subservience, service with a smile, and female management.

Similarly, Diego had attempted to translate Oak Park real estate transactions into familiar vernaculars of loyalty, confrontation, and circumventing official avenues to make things work. In his foreclosure story, good guys tried to ward off and neutralize the misdeeds of bad guys. When describing real estate professionals operating in Oak Park, Diego used the terms "loan sharks," "scam artists," "lenders," and "investors" interchangeably. He believed, for example, that the Asian American woman representing the investor was "running her own scam" after she offered to broker Diego's contact with a lender. Bureaucratic terminology and the details of mortgaging contracts paled against the vivid confrontations with sellers, buyers, and brokers. These professionals became characters in a neighborhood drama in which Diego fought, as he always had, to keep his family from harm.

SEEING SCAMS

Residents' reliance on personal, face-to-face encounters to resolve their housing dilemmas often left them open to scam artists trolling the neighborhood offering bogus loan modification assistance. Families with limited English were especially vulnerable to loan modification scams that promised to negotiate with the lenders and financial institutions the residents imagined were a world away.

For example, Irma Machado, a seasonal farmworker, and her husband, a gardener, acquired a loan from Washington Mutual for $216,000 to buy a home in Oak Park with no down payment and no income verification. Their payments were around $2,000 for their small three-bedroom, two-bathroom home. When I asked if it was a fixed-rate loan, Irma said, "Well, they told me it was fixed, but I don't think it was a fixed rate. If it had been a fixed-rate loan, they wouldn't have taken our house, right?" (Pues así me han dicho que es fijo, pero no, yo pienso que no fue fijo. O sea, si hubiera sido fijo, no nos lo quitaron, ¿verdad?) Irma clarified that neither she nor her husband spoke English, saying, "I didn't understand what they explained, what they said, or what I signed." (No entendí nada de lo que explicaron, lo que dijeron, o lo que firmé.)

In 2006, Irma believed that she and her husband were refinancing to lower their payment, when in fact they were granted a second mortgage, an equity line of credit, that gave them cash but did not adjust the terms of their original loan. They used the money to make improvements to the house. Just a year later, as early signs of the coming recession began to surface in Sacramento, her husband's work started drying up. They fell behind on their mortgage. A representative from ProAssist Manager (a now-defunct company) telephoned and offered to come to their home to discuss how they could stop their impending foreclosure. In person, the representative, Lucy, explained that she could navigate the refinance process for Irma and her husband. They paid her their last $2,500. Irma believed they had been applying for a modification, but instead, Irma told me, they had been "dealing with this woman who was robbing us." They had given Lucy all the papers, and after weeks of back-and-forth, they had received an eviction notice. ProAssist Manager had never contacted the lender on Irma's behalf. She explained how they had trusted Lucy because she was Latina, but in hindsight she described her as a *pocha*, a Mexican American woman who speaks broken Spanish and has become a gringa. After the bank evicted Irma's family, it sold the house at auction for $40,000.

Irma asked me who sold the house when there was a foreclosure. When I told her the bank seized and sold the property, she was puzzled. When she and her husband were willing to continue paying a bigger mortgage, albeit at a reduced amount, why foreclose and sell the house for a fraction of the price? When I asked Irma if she felt the banks had a responsibility to help people, she said, "Yes, because there are so many abandoned houses, until they burn to the ground, and maybe that's what they want. I don't understand it. I say even though it would have been a small amount, we would have kept paying." (Sí, porque … hay tantas casas abandonadas que las están hasta quemando, y al lo mejor eso es lo que prefieren. Eso lo que no entiendo. Digo aunque sea poquito, pero dejarnos estar pagando.)

But more than losing the house, Irma was upset by how she and her husband had been victims of ProAssist Manager's scam. In thinking about the last bit of savings they gave to Lucy, Irma said, "[My husband] was going so far for work and arriving home so late, and he would say, 'All of those sacrifices I made, she just came and took it.'" (Él se iba a trabajar hasta bien lejos, llegaba bien tarde, y dice pues, "Todo mi sacrificio para que haya venido ella y se lo haya llevado.")

While Irma focused on the fraud they suffered through the mom-and-pop scam, she and her husband had also been caught in a larger fraud: the Washington Mutual scandal. A Senate panel found that Washington Mutual, or WaMu, had, much like IndyMac, structured its mortgage sales to encourage risky and often predatory lending practices. Loan officers received more money for originating high-risk loans, increasing their pay even more if they overcharged borrowers

through points or higher interest rates or applied stiff prepayment penalties.[21] Focusing on amassing short-term profits for shareholders,
WaMu executives dismantled internal controls designed to prevent the
bank from taking on too much risk and began promoting option adjustable-rate mortgages, or option ARMs, considered one of the most toxic
products that fueled the crash.[22] Although indictments were rare, fraud
at WaMu was rampant.[23] WaMu began to favor subprime loans with little or no documentation, meaning no income verification through pay
stubs or tax returns was required—the riskier, the more profitable. As a
consequence, WaMu's subprime loans failed at the highest rates in the
nation. Top executives made unprecedented bonuses selling suspect,
high-risk mortgages to financially vulnerable families like Irma's and
securitizing and selling those mortgages to investors and pension funds
that would unravel as borrowers began, in droves, the inevitable process of default. Between 2003 and 2008, WaMu CEO Kerry Killinger
made $103.2 million; the year he ran WaMu into the ground, he received
$25.1 million, including a $15.3 million severance payment.[24]

Irma did not know the details of WaMu's suspect lending practices
or how its CEO had profited from the suffering of her family. For Irma
and her family, the main betrayal centered on Lucy and the loan modification scam. The lender existed in a separate universe of financial
transactions that had long excluded Irma and her family from participation, and this sense of otherworldliness persisted even as mortgage
markets expanded to exploit undocumented families living under the
poverty line. Lucy's presence in Irma's home, as a Mexican American
immigrant who spoke Spanish and who shared cultural cues, mimicked
long-standing networks of support and assistance yet exploited this
familiarity to drain Irma's family of scarce resources. This breach of
trust, penetrating local systems of exchange and loyalty, defined the
tragedy of the crisis for Irma.

Irma's emphasis on the loan modification scam echoed the experiences of many of the more recent Mexican American immigrants I
came to know. Like Irma and Diego, they had given their last remain-

ing thousand dollars or more to a person who spoke Spanish and visited their homes, falsely promising to negotiate with lenders on the homeowners' behalf. These con artists were supposed to serve as a bridge between the local neighborhood and the distant universe of financial lending, which remained a mystery to many residents who had been systemically excluded from ecologies of credit. Unlike homeowners in middle-income neighborhoods, who felt entitled to lending institutions, these homeowners were segregated from financial domains in a way that bred misinformation. Ultimately, however, these person-to-person encounters with a secondary tier of real estate professionals and investors left residents open to misunderstandings and even abuse. The criminal practices of lenders, still distant, paled in contrast to visceral experiences of personal betrayal by individuals involved in the foreclosure tragedies in which residents were ensnarled.

FIGHTING FORECLOSURE

A soft-spoken man who wore sensible shoes and a cardigan over a button-down shirt tucked into his slacks, Ricardo Castro became animated when talking about how he and his wife Amalia landed in Oak Park by accident. Ricardo, trained as a computer programmer in Mexico, lacked the typing skills to succeed as a data analyst in the United States. He initially secured factory jobs through his cousins and later opened a janitorial business. Amalia worked her way up at Leviathan Bank from being a teller to originating loans. They were looking for an investment property to make some return on a small inheritance they had received when Amalia's father died. Originally from Mexico City, the couple and their two boys had been living in Vallejo, an affordable commuter suburb for the Silicon Valley. In 2000, the couple decided to look at potential rental properties in Sacramento, where they could get more house for their modest down payment. The real estate agent took them through Tahoe Park, an up-and-coming residential area with tree-lined streets, diverse families, and wide lots. They toured a small house priced at $80,000, a steal for such a desirable neighborhood. They bought the house and rented it out, but the tenants failed to pay the rent and tore up the place, so the Castros moved in. The first few nights in their house, the raucous noise of drug addicts on the corner fighting with sex workers led the Castros to the stark realization of how bad the neighborhood was. It wasn't Tahoe Park after all, but the easternmost tip of Oak Park.

Within weeks after Ricardo and Amalia moved into their home, a community organizer from ACORN, the Association for Community Organizations for Reform Now, later renamed the Alliance of Californians for Community Empowerment (ACCE), knocked on the door and explained that the group was trying to do something about crime in the neighborhood. Ricardo and Amalia signed on. Later, when residents began facing evictions in 2007, Ricardo would work with ACCE to mobilize against foreclosures, helping to run a free program that aided homeowners navigating the loan modification process. With an engineer's meticulous nature, Ricardo sat with homeowners to help them understand the mortgage agreements they had signed and to shepherd them through the complicated process of appealing impending foreclosures. In his free time, he also helped low-income families prepare their taxes.

Unlike other residents for whom the details of subprime mortgage lending and foreclosure remained inscrutable, Ricardo and Amalia proffered a nuanced analysis of subprime loans and foreclosures. As a loan originator for Leviathan Bank, Amalia pointed out the differences between more conservative lenders like Leviathan and TrustWorth Financial and suspect, high-risk lenders such as IndyMac and WaMu. During one conversation, Amalia explained how customers who could not qualify for mortgages had come to her at Leviathan Bank demanding loans. Clients would point out that their friends and family in similar financial straits had received loans from these risky lenders, some of them in six figures. Leviathan Bank lost a lot of business, Amalia said, because people would turn to the new breed of lender that disregarded a borrower's income and qualifications.

Yet even their firsthand knowledge of the intricacies of lending failed to protect Ricardo and Amalia from foreclosure. In 2003, they refinanced with Leviathan to add an extra room for their two boys. In 2005, they refinanced again, this time with Golden Gate Loan Servicing*, to lower their interest rate. By 2006, they owed $210,000 on a home that was worth $80,000. In December 2007, the foreclosure process started. Soon after they received the foreclosure notice, Ricardo was diagnosed with cancer. He could no longer work, and within a year, they had spent through their savings. In 2009, they applied for a loan modification, but the bank did not cooperate. Golden Gate Loan Servicing offered a deferment because of his cancer, which was not a modification but rather an agreement that the past-due payments would be paid off at the end of the loan. But then Golden Gate sold the mortgage debt to Edge Financial*, a new servicer that wouldn't accept the terms of deferment and demanded regular payments. For over a year Edge Financial consistently lost the Castros' paperwork while proceeding with the foreclosure. "People working at the servicer would ask for paperwork and then say they'd get back to you in two weeks if something was missing," Ricardo told me. "You never hear from them. You call in two weeks, and they say something is missing. Because the paperwork isn't complete, they move ahead with foreclosure." Because they lived in Oak Park, a low-income minority neighborhood with lower property values, the Castros were less likely to achieve a mortgage modification than their equally financially insolvent counterparts in predominantly white districts.

Twice the loan servicers tried to foreclose, but Ricardo organized ACCE members and reporters, orchestrating a protest on the steps of the courthouse in an attempt to disrupt the auctioning off of his home. "Why are they foreclosing," Ricardo asked into the cameras, "when we just want a modification?" Both times the protest delayed the foreclosure. The Castros eventually won a modification with Edge Financial, bringing their monthly payments to $1,800.

Activists like Ricardo helped to stall the foreclosures of his neighbors in Oak Park, either by helping residents with complex loan modification

Protest on the courthouse steps that saved Ricardo and Amalia Castro's
house from foreclosure. Photo by Anne Chadwick Williams.

applications or organizing protests on the courthouse steps.[25] Oak Park
residents' experiences of social and economic exclusion had fostered
participation in robust community networks. Neighbors worked through
community organizations to start a weekly farmers' market to address
food insecurity, hosted cookouts in public parks after gang shootings
had happened in them, worked through their churches to keep teens out
of gangs, and lobbied policy makers to reduce blight and crime in the
neighborhood.

Whereas homeowners in middle-income neighborhoods turned to
financial institutions for assistance when they faced mortgage default following unemployment or health crises, residents in Oak Park sought the
help of neighbors and community networks when facing evictions. For
middle-class homeowners, foreclosure was an individual, personal problem that had to be resolved through direct contact with lenders. Lower-
income homeowners in Oak Park were faster to recognize the common
aspects of the foreclosure crisis and approach the issue as a neighborhood

problem that demanded a community-wide approach. Homeowners had invested in community organizations that had addressed neighborhood troubles in the past, and the foreclosure crisis presented another challenge that collective organizing could overcome.

FROM FAMINE TO FLOOD

Oak Park homeowners' experiences of foreclosure often represented the worst in predatory lending—scams, fraud, and unscrupulous brokers taking advantage of buyers who spoke little or no English or had limited access to traditional forms of credit. The stories of homeowners in Oak Park support the earlier research of policy and planning scholar Dan Immergluck and his colleagues, which has shown that subprime lenders targeted areas of acute urban decline because there was less competition from other lenders. Likewise, the vulnerability of these residents shows how subprime borrowers knew less about the mortgage process, robbing them of the opportunity to make choices about their mortgages.[26] Intermediaries posed a more significant problem as well, as mortgage brokers have been shown to overcharge less financially sophisticated borrowers and to steer them into riskier loan products.[27]

These cases exemplify predatory debt extraction, a growing mode of economic exploitation that masquerades as financial inclusion by opening previously out-of-reach forms of consumption to the working poor, who then become trapped in growing cycles of indebtedness and default. Just as risky subprime loans were concentrated in U.S. neighborhoods with high concentrations of residents of color, after the crash, these homeowners were then less likely to achieve mortgage modifications.[28] Although a majority of residents in Oak Park in recent decades have been renters, those who do own their homes often struggled to buy them, working through informal networks to secure loans, making their losses during the foreclosure crisis all the more catastrophic because of the struggle it took to achieve homeownership in the first place.

Instead of imaging mutual ties with lenders, residents described endogenous reciprocal relations growing within families, churches, and the neighborhood. As foreclosures loomed in Oak Park, these dense social networks buffered individuals from the deleterious effects of default and dispossession. Facing foreclosures, residents relied on their interpersonal skills and local grassroots activist networks to stall evictions. If foreclosure narratives in middle-class neighborhoods focused on loan modification failures and the betrayals of lenders, stories of default in Oak Park—where money was scarce and evictions were commonplace—emphasized personal and collective perseverance against insurmountable odds. How people narrated their foreclosure experiences illuminates disparate universes of financial meaning. The narratives of homeowners in lower-middle- and middle-class neighborhoods, for whom the mortgage crash disrupted or upended upward financial trajectories, often centered on individual catastrophes, as I show in the next chapter, whereas for residents of Oak Park, one of the lowest-income neighborhoods in the nation, foreclosures represented yet another chapter in a long-standing history of neighborhood traumas.

An analysis of mortgage lending and foreclosure in Oak Park challenges dominant narratives that explain the mortgage debacle in terms of ignorant or morally inept borrowers who took out subprime loans and defaulted. On the one hand, media pundits often portray borrowers who took on subprime loans as greedy, naïve investors living beyond their means. Mortgagors, in these popular media discourses, succumbed to their desires for bigger houses and lacked the integrity to repay their debts. On the other hand, some scholars have suggested that subprime borrowers were just another breed of neoliberal subjects looking to maximize profits by taking out loans and defaulting strategically. Homeowners, framed this way, were investors swept up in the same frenzy that fueled Wall Street. But these narratives hinge on the financial agency and savvy of homeowners to identify lucrative opportunities and then to walk away from debts when markets slump. In actuality, many homeowners in Oak Park never *decided* to embrace high-risk loans or mortgage default. Quite the opposite: many were unknowingly saddled with risk and could not identify the moment they had lost their homes.

Although homeowners taking on mortgages in lower-middle- or middle-class neighborhoods had also been duped by brokers or had misunderstood the mechanisms of loans whose payments would spike in future years, these buyers typically had more opportunities to discover the terms of their mortgages before moving forward. In contrast, many residents in Oak Park who took on crushing mortgage debt were less likely to be aware of the conditions of the loans. Many spoke limited English, for example, or were elderly borrowers suffering from disabilities that made it nearly impossible to grasp the complicated and abstruse terminology of the contracts. With limited educational opportunities, many lacked access to informal networks of professionals who could give sound financial advice regarding the loans. Toxic loans traveled through family and friends, as brokers hired neighborhood residents with no industry experience to unwittingly push subprime products onto their loved ones, offering higher commissions for the riskiest loans. In the aftermath, scam artists like Lucy swept in to take advantage of homeowners whose vulnerabilities had been magnified by the mortgage crash. Unfortunately, their attempts to renegotiate their loans through individuals, instead of approaching institutions, often opened residents to scam artists who traveled door to door, misrepresenting themselves as loan modification agents and charging for their services; legally, loan modification assistance programs cannot charge a fee until after a successful modification is achieved. Dense social networks, comprising blood and nonblood kin, that had once delivered money, food, and childcare to keep neighborhood families afloat circulated dangerous mortgage products instead.

The steps of foreclosure and eviction were opaque, adding to the stress of uncertainty and leaving many feeling that anything could happen at any moment. Joy and Nancy did not realize that they had already lost their home and that they were going to court for their eviction hearing. It wasn't clear to Irma who seized her home in a case of foreclosure. The deal Diego made with a private investor left him vulnerable to what he believed was continuing extortion. Being cut off from conventional lines of credit resulted, for these residents, not only in financial exclusion but also in continued financial illiteracy. In this context of unintelligibility, scammers and fraudsters ran rampant. The opacity of the mortgaging and foreclosure process, riddled with obtuse legalese and a quasi-criminal lack of transparency, left the most vulnerable homeowners at risk for monumental losses.

In the stories of most Oak Park residents facing foreclosure, the criminal lending practices of banks and brokers faded into the background—financial institutions had never been trustworthy, since residents had experienced long-standing histories of housing discrimination. Joy and her elderly neighbors, other old-timers, had moved to Oak Park during an era in which nonwhites were excluded from other neighborhoods. Once Oak Park became a predominantly nonwhite area, lenders systematically denied standard mortgage loans to its residents. Those residents I came to know who managed to buy homes often did so through the creative assistance of real estate professionals they knew, usually their landlords. During the foreclosure epidemic, financial institutions seemed irrelevant, operating in a parallel universe that had little bearing on daily life. Instead of focusing on lenders who had falsified documents or provided them with fraudulent loans, residents focused their ire and feelings of betrayal on the con artists that circulated in the aftermath. The everyday imaginaries within the low-income financial landscape had never included financial institutions and lenders; IndyMac and WaMu, for instance, despite inflicting insufferable damages on families in the neighborhood, did not emerge as the primary villains in people's narratives of evictions.

Important trends distinguished the circulation of ideas regarding financial reciprocity among Oak Park residents from those of other homeowners in the Sacramento Valley. The sociality of mortgage markets did not mean that borrowers and lenders shared mutual interests and obligations. In fact, residents of Oak Park were more often victimized by predatory lending practices than their middle-income counterparts, but they expected less from the financial institutions that had taken advantage of them. The misdeeds of lenders and loan servicers, for example, held very little resonance for the residents of Oak Park, because, after all, mainstream financial institutions had rarely treated residents in ways that would suggest a bond of mutuality. Trends of racial and class discrimination had indelibly shaped people's expectations for the kinds of social bonds that markets would produce. Kinship and social ties still shaped the circulation of capital and debts, but in a distinct way from lower-middle- and middle-class neighborhoods.

What's more, fighting foreclosures proved difficult in practical terms. Many residents faced foreclosure at a time when government programs weren't yet up and running; residents victimized by fraudulent lending could not afford lawyers to contest illegal seizures; and appearing in court meant missing work or, for undocumented families, risking exposure. These realities show how racial and class identities and, even more, neighborhood segregation influence how members of different communities respond to foreclosure, as their experiences have been informed by disparate historical experiences of acquiring credit, relying on banking institutions, and owning property. Residential segregation by race has correlated with high-risk lending patterns and therefore has shaped the racial disparities of foreclosures.[29] As elsewhere, even white homeowners, like Nancy Moore-Jones, were subject to predatory lending and inordinate foreclosures if they lived in a low-income, predominantly black or Latino neighborhood.[30] Evictions, sociologist Matthew Desmond shows in his ethnography of Milwaukee's inner city, eviscerate poor black families' chances of catching up economically with white society in ways that have been underemphasized by scholars and policy makers.[31] If the inner-city Milwaukee landlords and renters Desmond describes are caught in a never-ending cycle that perpetuates abject poverty, homeowners in Oak Park and the predatory lenders swindling them were caught in a drama that pitched those families barely getting by into a maelstrom of evictions, destitution, and the extreme financial exclusion engendered by ruined credit. Families whose homeownership helped them to find a seeming grip on stability in a precarious neighborhood were uprooted by foreclosures in ways that further disenfranchised them.

The tragedy of these losses acquires even greater salience given that by 2015 Oak Park was undergoing gentrification. Media interest in the widespread losses of property and equity experienced by Oak Park residents was eclipsed by an influx of new renters: middle-income professionals who had been pushed out of their own rental markets following the crash. The countless residents of Oak Park who had defaulted and left the neighborhood before government-sponsored mortgage modification programs came into effect in 2009 would have seen significant gains on their initial investments, no matter how modest. Whereas 85 percent of zip codes in Sacramento County witnessed a drop in homeownership by 2014, Oak Park had the lowest rates in the county, at 58 percent.[32] If Joy and Nancy had been able to keep their home—if the IndyMac agent had not falsified their mortgage application—they would have been in a position to reap the rewards of rising property values, supporting themselves through old age. Those who stayed put after their foreclosures, like Diego, could not access loans to buy or refinance homes because foreclosure had ruined their credit. The economic benefits of rising property values are currently being reaped by outsiders, most often investors who bought properties at bargain prices after the crash and then rented them out to longtime residents like Joy and Nancy. These homeowners-turned-renters find themselves increasingly pushed out of the neighborhood as public safety increases, retailers move in, and rents rise accordingly.

The introduction of more financial insecurity to residents of Oak Park has affected not just homeowners caught in the subprime boom and bust but also the economic potential of their children and grandchildren. The disruption of intergenerational wealth through dispossession for those on the margins becomes even more egregious in the twenty-first-century United States when the possibility of earning one's way out of poverty is less likely than it was in the 1970s, as Thomas Piketty points out.[33] Since World War II, homeownership has become not only the gateway to middle-class stability but also a primary mechanism to pass on wealth to the next generation. Inheritance, as Piketty writes, becomes even more central to the accumulation of wealth in eras of slow economic growth. In Oak Park, not only did Miguel Santos lose his life savings, but through subprime lending, his four children have also missed a chance at financial stability.

If anyone deserved restitution, as opposed to mortgage relief after the 2008 crash, it was residents in Oak Park, where fraud and questionable mortgaging practices had defined the decade leading up to the 2008 debacle. Yet it was these homeowners, often unaware of the major financial scandals that had uprooted them, who felt the least entitled to reparations from lenders. Whereas homeowners in middle-class neighborhoods, as I will show in the next chapter, felt entitled to assistance from lenders, even if they had received standard loans and understood their terms, homeowners such as Joy and Nancy, victims of predatory mortgage fraud, did not feel authorized to make demands on IndyMac. In fact, Joy offhandedly mentioned that IndyMac owed them some money as restitution, but they had never received it. Instead of pursuing loan modifications, Oak Park homeowners fought their foreclosures by turning to local logics and community ties, drawing on their experiences fighting neighborhood threats and other forms of injustice they had encountered.

The stark contrasts between mortgaging and foreclosure among low-income families in Oak Park and among the middle-income homeowners that I explore in the next chapter show how interpretations of foreclosure are shaped by microecologies of neighborhoods, with their differences of race, class, and language. The stories of low-income, primarily black and Latino homeowners in Oak Park show how credit and debt are more than abstract financial instruments; instead, they are proxies for social exclusion and discrimination. At the same time, residents did not acquiesce to financial domination. Social reciprocity, while co-opted by the circulation of toxic mortgages through kin networks, could still work to residents' advantage as people counseled dispossessed neighbors to squat in their homes without paying or joined them on the courthouse steps to forestall evictions. More than their middle-class counterparts, these residents made their individual struggles collective by organizing and persevering against insurmountable odds.

CHAPTER THREE

Robbing Peter to Pay Paul

Relocating the Middle Class

What began in 2006 as a concentration of mortgage defaults in Oak Park, Sacramento's poorest neighborhood, had spread by 2008 to traditionally lower-middle-class and middle-class areas, plunging the Sacramento Valley into an economic recession. Government workers confronted furloughs, and the mortgage and construction industries collapsed; local businesses shuttered their doors and unemployment soared across the region; property values plummeted.

It was during this dismal season that David Sanchez, the Chicano veteran who had purchased a dream home with his wife, Karen, after she had survived cancer treatment, was laid off from his job as a video technician at a local public college in 2009. Just two months after David was laid off, they found out that Karen's cancer had progressed.

The costs of restarting Karen's cancer treatments left them unable to pay their mortgage. The couple approached Leviathan Bank for a federally sponsored HAMP mortgage modification. As required, they faxed their documents: an intake form requiring information about monthly expenses and debts, cash on hand, and credit card spending; a hardship letter; a tax authorization form; recent pay stubs that showed year-to-date earnings; a statement of Social Security and unemployment benefits; multiple bank statements; and federal tax returns.

But Leviathan lost their paperwork four times, each time telling them they would have to reapply. Once the application was finally recognized, the service representative explained that David and Karen had to be three months behind to qualify for a mortgage modification. "I had never been behind," David told me, "and that just really threw me for a loop. But at the time my wife was getting really sick, having a real difficult time, and we could see our funds were going to dwindle."

They halted payments and waited for a response from Leviathan Bank. Then Karen's health insurance through her job at the college fell through. One of Karen's doctors had checked the wrong box on a form, qualifying Karen to return to work although she was in the middle of intensive chemotherapy. Because of the mistake, Karen lost her health insurance, and the couple had to come up with an extra $800 a month to cover her cancer treatments. (They had to hire a lawyer to reinstate her coverage, but the process took months.)

While battling the health insurance company and the teachers' union over Karen's coverage, David also spent hours on the phone each week trying to get an answer from Leviathan about their modification. "Back and forth, back and forth at the bank—it got to the point you just don't want to talk on the phone," he told me. "You call up and try to talk to someone and you talk to some young lady that's still playing with Barbies, and [she says], 'Sir, we need a payment.' We need a payment? Okay. Call me when you get your braces off and you can talk instead of mumble."

David tried other avenues to secure mortgage assistance, including nonprofits that assisted homeowners in the modification process, to no avail. "You go to Save Your Home California and [they say], 'We're here to help you. We have to look at your finances and look at what you eat and what you drink and whether or not you smoke and if you pay for insurance. Do you have animals? Do you have private loans with other people? Are your pets vaccinated?' And you get a letter for a forum where they're going to answer some questions and give you some facts and it's always like four hundred miles away. I had called all of these programs; they were roadblocks. The programs were set up for people that were not behind."

After faxing reams of paperwork and spending months navigating Leviathan Bank's byzantine bureaucracy, David and Karen were enrolled in a trial modification plan, which promised to deliver a final decision regarding their modification after three months of reduced payments. They paid into the trial modification for nearly a year, submitting monthly financial statements along with their payments. But after that year, a Leviathan representative told David that the investor who actually held the mortgage would not accept the terms of the modification. Leviathan never had the final authority to approve their application in the first place.

Karen passed away three weeks later.

Two days after she died, David found a foreclosure notice from Leviathan in his mailbox.

Desperate and depressed, David tried going back to Leviathan to appeal his denial. One mortgage modification specialist said they could potentially lower his payments, but Karen would have to sign off on the agreement. "My wife is dead, and you guys still haven't recognized that," David said, his voice cracking. "That's the hardship, the entire reason I need the help."

That was the moment David gave up. "I crawled into my little cave," he told me, "and then basically I was alone and I didn't really care."

David's mortgage modification denial and subsequent foreclosure after a protracted struggle with Leviathan Bank compounded the devastating loss of his wife. Foreclosure notices burned like personal betrayals, exceeding the boundaries of a financial contract gone awry. Leviathan's failure to recognize Karen's death felt to David like an intimate disloyalty after years of blatant disregard. Because of the abuses by Leviathan, David had been forced to spend the last months of Karen's life on hold with service representatives and running to Kinko's to fax paperwork; the fight to save his home divided his attention at a time when Karen needed him most.

While devastating, David's foreclosure was, unfortunately, predictable. The odds were stacked against him. Decades of neoliberal restructuring had left David as a temporary employee at the college, the first category of staff to be laid off during an economic downturn. Even before the financial crisis, David would have been vulnerable after Karen's death because households headed by a widow or widower were twice as likely as households of married couples to struggle to pay their mortgages, even after controlling for income and net wealth.[1] As a Latino borrower, David was more likely to receive a subprime loan and less likely to receive a mortgage modification.[2] Perhaps worst of all, he was combating Leviathan, notorious for its mortgage modification abuses. Kafkaesque journeys through corporate administration show how the mortgage assistance application process continued legacies of deindustrialization, discrimination, and the stagnation of wages, cementing the dissolution of postwar American middle-class aspirations in the process.

Entanglements with mortgage modification bureaucracies defined the foreclosure experiences of many Sacramento Valley homeowners working to stop their impending evictions in lower-middle-class and middle-class neighborhoods. Customer service representatives at major lenders implementing HAMP stranded homeowners on hold and denied them mortgage assistance even when they qualified. Lenders moved forward with foreclosures while homeowners were stuck in modification applications. People described being ensnared in a dysfunctional system riddled with misinformation and mismanagement. Even worse was the common feeling that lenders were "lying," "cheating," and trying to force homeowners to "give up." Mortgage assistance programs were promoted as helping Americans maintain middle-class lifestyles and aspirations. Ads for mortgage assistance, for example, suggested that mortgage modifications would protect families and safeguard marriages, keeping worthy middle-class citizens in their picket-fenced homes. But the very act of submitting to the scrutiny and byzantine runarounds demanded by corporate lenders undermined applicants' already tenuous hold on middle-class status, disrupting forms of social capital that had defined them. Stonewalled by mainstream financial lenders, homeowners were hard-pressed to recognize that their own downward mobility had become the new normal.

The bureaucracies of corporate lenders therefore restructured an already decaying middle class and lower middle class, generating what I call a "post-middle-class" subject formation. Post-middle-classness is a psychic and material state of being in which the expectations for postwar middle-class life no longer function in the face of social and financial decline. Defined by more than income strata or a set of jobs and educational levels, post-middle-class subjects embody a double consciousness of sorts, in which their views and aspirations have been shaped by assumptions that hard work fosters financial security in a relatively fair marketplace even as they inhabit a liminal world in which their future opportunities are constricted beyond recognition. Often triggered by financial hardship, post-middle-class status exceeds the state of being broke, instead repositioning subjects in relation to financial institutions, government agencies, and one another in ways previously reserved for the working class or even the working poor. This postindustrial shift has had deep emotional repercussions for those most vulnerable to its losses, including men like David. Detailing the intimate traumas that followed the shuttering of the steel mills in southeast Chicago beginning in the 1980s, anthropologist Christine Walley traces in vivid detail the psychic dislocation of her father, a lifelong millworker. At times aimless, nonsensical, and fixated on seemingly arbitrary details of the closure of the mills, Walley's father shows his loss in palpable ways, his emotional suffering far exceeding the material effects of unemployment.[3] He, like David, confronts an ontological crisis in which manhood and meaning are radically redefined.

Consider how blue-collar life trajectories in the 1970s now describe the lives of Sacramento Valley middle-class residents in the aftermath of the financial crisis. Sociologist Joseph Howell differentiates between blue-collar "hard-living" families, prone to unpredictability and chaos because individuals relied on lower-paying, nonunion jobs, and "settled-living" families, who typically owned a modest home and enjoyed solid incomes and, often, health benefits.[4] Hard-living and settled-living families represented two ends of a continuum of working-class households before the onset of late-liberal economic policies in the 1980s. But by the time subprime mortgages flooded the market in the late 1990s, Sacramento Valley residents who inhabited traditionally lower-middle-class and middle-class neighborhoods were already living as their blue-collar counterparts had a generation earlier: struggling to secure modest homeownership and stable jobs with health benefits. Foreclosures and the insolent treatment Sacramento Valley homeowners received at the hands of corporate lenders pushed them into the down-and-out experiences of hard living, the dislocation and financial exclusion that had defined the lives of more vulnerable segments of working-class communities only a few decades before.

Ongoing confrontations with corporate modification specialists positioned lower-middle-income and middle-income homeowners as categorically suspect in a way that once had been reserved for poorer Americans. As David points out, to qualify for mortgage assistance, applicants had to submit to intensified levels of scrutiny over personal financial decision-making—opening up to strangers about topics previously off-limits within American middle-class decorum. (How much do you drink? How much do you spend on fast food? Are your pets vaccinated?) This process of providing detailed information about daily spending habits for months at a time exposed applicants' lives to surveillance and evaluation by the employees of corporate lending institutions.[5] Corporate lenders enmeshed homeowners in intensified modes of bureaucratic surveillance to keep their homes, the same forms of scrutiny that working-poor Americans had long been subjected to in order to secure basic needs such as public housing, food stamps, and welfare benefits, with the ever-looming threat that they would lose access to food, shelter, and even their children if they failed to comply with administrative rules. In other words, homeownership, the most powerful symbol of postwar middle-class security, no longer guaranteed the privileges of earlier generations.

RECIPROCAL TIES: WHY LENDERS SHOULD HELP US

I stood close behind Louise Walker, an African American retired medical assistant in her late sixties, as we rode up the steep escalators of Sacramento's expansive convention center to a foreclosure clinic.[6] It was 2014, my first experience at a public mortgage event, but Louise had been battling foreclosure for three years and had attended a number of these fairs. She had refused to accept the three previous denials for a loan modification handed down to her by TrustWorth Financial. During her most recent application process, she discovered that TrustWorth Financial had denied her appeal based on a bank miscalculation that overestimated her fixed Social Security income.

In 2002, at the height of the market, Louise and her husband, an African American retired UPS maintenance worker, had bought a new house in a booming northern Sacramento suburban development for $270,000. For almost a decade, they had cared for Louise's mother, who suffered from Alzheimer's disease, in Louise's childhood home in Marin County. After her mother died, Louise and her husband moved to Sacramento to be closer to her husband's family. They had signed a thirty-year fixed-rate mortgage contract, but the financial crisis had put them underwater, and they ran through their savings paying bills after retirement and could no longer afford their mortgage payments.

At the foreclosure clinic, at the top of the escalators, we were greeted by a smiling teenage volunteer with a clipboard who was perched in front of a balloon-filled display and who directed us into a large carpeted room. Employees from each lender wearing color-coded T-shirts sat at long folding tables. Fax machines and photocopiers lined one wall, and banner advertisements for government assistance programs hung around the room. Louise and I took seats in the carefully placed

The waiting area of a Sacramento loan modification fair. Photo by the author.

rows of chairs that constituted a waiting area. The mood was subdued, the room oddly quiet and organized despite the hundreds of people milling around. Most public spaces in Sacramento typically rang with loose, friendly chatter, but here no one made small talk. Homeowners, many dressed for professional jobs, sat silently and avoided eye contact, with arms crossed and their files on their laps as they watched a video. The homeowners seemed uncomfortable with the open, exposed space and the event's lack of privacy, finding themselves in the new position of requesting help in a public cattle call. In the video playing across a flat-screen television, black, white, and Latino professionals told their stories, detailing the stress and anxiety of facing foreclosure and the relief of receiving loan modifications. The narrator then explained the importance of having the correct documents, suggesting that these files would be the key to applicants' success. A checklist of documents appeared on the screen, and Louise and I glanced at the folder of paperwork stuffed into her purse.

A representative from TrustWorth Financial escorted us to a table where a white staffer in his early thirties with a sign on his laptop that read "Jared" proceeded to ask Louise for her intake information. We were sitting one chair away from another homeowner who detailed her struggles to a service representative. Louise glanced at the woman next to us and then began a recitation of the same information she had provided every time she called TrustWorth Financial. Fifteen minutes into the meeting, Jared told Louise that she had failed to include her latest bank statement when compiling her documents for the event. Without the bank statement, Jared could not do anything for her. "Aren't *you* my bank?" Louise asked, visibly upset. "You can look up my statement on your computer." Jared told us that he didn't have access to that information on his laptop. He gave Louise a card displaying a fax number where she could send her paperwork. She would have to start the process again. As we left the convention center, Louise shook her head and remarked, both to me and the young volunteer lingering by the escalator, how the ordeal had been an utter waste of her time.

The organized appearance of the foreclosure event implied that the loan modification process was simple, reasonable, and streamlined, as if lenders were doing everything they could to give personal attention to homeowners like Louise. It was, the video suggested, the homeowners' own disorganization, their failure to put their documents in order, for instance, that prevented modifications from moving forward. The upbeat volunteers, the color-coded outfits, and the use of service representatives' first names—all of it distracted from the frustrating realities of being forced to seek mortgage assistance in a massive convention center with no chance of privacy, a far cry from the institutional settings middle- and even lower-middle-class residents were used to navigating. But homeowners were forced to attend these events precisely because they had spent countless hours on the phone caught in Kafkaesque bureaucratic confrontations and were now desperate for face-to-face contact. Their hope to face a "real person," someone who could make decisions about their case, which had previously defined their middle-class experiences at mainstream social institutions, from education to finance, had brought them to this point, where they now faced volunteers and temporary workers with limited access to computer files.

Louise and many other homeowners waiting in the convention center had been spurred to attend the fair because they had seen an endless loop of television advertisements for loan modification programs. One of the most popular, "Frozen," featured homeowners who were frozen, literally paralyzed, standing still at work in a factory, at home in their kitchens, or while a marathon ran around them.[7] In the final scene, a smiling African American homeowner breaks the spell by picking up her phone, returning to life and gazing out her kitchen window as her son frolics in a manicured backyard with the family's golden retriever. Extolling the benefits of reaching out to one's lender, such advertisements uniformly encouraged homeowners to fight their paralysis and "get real answers and real help" by making a phone call. These commercials, like the organized appearance of the fair, misled applicants into believing that they *could* qualify if only they snapped out of their frozen state. Lenders wanted to help, the ads implied, but it was homeowners who kept getting in the way. Moreover, assistance could be achieved in the privacy of one's own home. But in reality, homeowners had to don the practices of the working poor, waiting in open, public venues for assistance, dealing with service agents unable to resolve their issues, and grappling with exposing their struggles to strangers, other applicants facing dire circumstances, sitting at arm's length.

The scene that unfolded at the convention center was markedly different from the one that played out in the mortgage assistance commercial. Even after Louise and I arrived back at her house, back in the privacy of her kitchen, things still looked nothing like the ad. Louise anxiously laid out piles of modification paperwork on her kitchen table in an attempt to find the bank statement she had misplaced. First she blamed herself for not having her papers, but then she said, "It wouldn't have mattered. They would have said no. I just have a fixed statement in my head that nobody is going to help me." When I asked Louise why lenders should help homeowners, she said:

> We help them. I mean buy a house, go through them. Pay on time and everything. And you start having a little problem, they should try to step in there and try to help you. They've got the money. I haven't heard not one person that they've helped. Not one. You meet a lot of people down there in those [events] and they feel the same too like I do.... I've done everything they said to do. All this paperwork they want me to fill out and still haven't gotten any help.... I got to just get the right papers.

The expectation for reciprocity animating Louise's demand for help from TrustWorth Financial reflects a long-standing notion of mutuality and respect between middle-class subjects and mainstream institutions, including health clinics, banks, and schools. For homeowners, reciprocal ties with lenders offered proof that middle-class clients and the institutions that served them were part of the same social networks. Faced with bureaucratic runaround, homeowners like Louise articulated an alternative ideal relationship with a mortgage lender: a relationship of financial reciprocity that tied borrowers and lenders over decades of payments and entitled her to help during hard times.

Lenders entering into mortgage contracts had previously treated homebuyers as equals. Before the Wall Street glut of subprime lending, homeownership offered a badge of proof that a borrower was a prudent financial subject (unlike transient and financially irresponsible renters), able to properly care for her property, build a stable community, and make sound long-term investments. As anthropologist Janet Roitman points out, the credit and debt relationship determines whether or not a subject is included in a community, defining hierarchies of exclusion and positioning people on a moral and economic spectrum.[8] Anthropologist David Graeber argues similarly that debt requires a relationship between two entities who "do not consider each other fundamentally different sorts of being, who are at least potential equals, who *are* equals in those ways that are really important, and who are not currently in a state of equality—but for whom there is some way to set matters straight."[9] If there is no way to repay a debt, Graeber concludes, we wouldn't be calling it "debt." For residents like Louise in lower-middle-class and middle-class neighborhoods, mortgaging in the postwar era had been seen as a lifelong tie that implied a relationship, not simply a faceless financial transaction. Homeowners expected to deal with a decision-maker at the bank, not a series of temporary, uninformed employees with no leverage to make real decisions. Becoming or aspiring to become middle class meant being able to find levers of influence within institutions, either through contacts in one's personal network or through a mutual recognition of one's place in a social order.

If only, as Louise said, she could get her papers in order, she could trigger the respect and assistance from TrustWorth Financial she had anticipated. But the right paperwork might not have been enough, as she suspected. In fact, SIGTARP, the federal enforcement agency monitoring the bailout, found that TrustWorth Financial along with other major lenders and loan servicers committed egregious offenses, among them failing to count homeowners' payments and then illegally dropping homeowners from the HAMP rolls while simultaneously collecting millions for these same homeowners. The diffuseness of administrative power within corporate bureaucracies now denied homeowners entitlements they had come to expect and, instead, bred a kind of forced helplessness, rendering homeowners as dislocated subjects unable to save their homes.

Expectations for mutuality with lenders was intensified because a home was not solely a commodity or a securitized payment stream but an object of profound sentimental and aspirational attachment and because homeowners applied to their lenders the standards and expectations of duty and forgiveness fostered in the domestic realm. The profound ways in which homes were invested with fantasies about kinship, stability, belonging, and citizenship meant that homeowners embroiled in loan modifications would expect reciprocity in the form of individualized attention and assistance as an "inalienable right."

Family ties, often posited as the counterpoint to markets, fueled the production and reproduction of housing markets. Sylvia Yanagisako discovers a similar confluence of kinship and industrial markets in her research on family firms in Italy, which are passed down from generation to generation. Kinship, with its affective ties, becomes the basis for the thriving of market economies rather than serving as a respite from relationships of market exchange.[10] The commercializing process of markets does not flatten social ties, as sociologist Viviana Zelizer has similarly shown in her study of the multiple social meanings of earmarking household money in the United States.[11] Zelizer's findings sharply counter Georg Simmel's claim that money liberates people from social obligations such as those of kinship. Obligations between people endure, if not proliferate, within markets.[12] Decades of postwar suburban expansion and government policies encouraging homeownership had fostered the sense that owning a home was both a right and a benchmark of middle-class citizenship that guaranteed mutuality with lenders. These social contracts implicit in mortgaging, however, were now anachronistic.

Louise's parents had moved to California from Louisiana seeking to escape the overt racism of the South and established themselves by buying a home in a blue-collar, middle-class black neighborhood in Marin County. They opened a number of grocery stores, where Louise had spent her youth working. Now in retirement Louise lived in a new suburban development, in a home that displayed the trappings of middle-class prosperity—window dressings, African artwork and sculptures, family antiques, framed original artwork. But she also lived on a minuscule fixed income and sat on the brink of eviction. Internalizing the broader economic shifts that had made her situation precarious and falling prey to the injuries of the modification rhetoric that put the onus on her to resolve widespread structural inequalities on her own, she now assumed responsibility for her predicament, saying she had been "stupid"—she should have been more careful with her modification paperwork, just as she should have saved more for retirement.

In many ways, the mere existence of loan modification programs fed American homeowners' enduring attachment to the possibility of living "the good life" despite the various ways the economy had been destabilized since the 1980s. For decades, declining wages and rising costs of living had put my respondents in a position where they had to pile up exorbitant debt to maintain middle-class lives that were just as or even more modest than their parents'. For many applicants, the mere *possibility* of procuring a loan modification was evidence that mortgage lenders had a duty to offer forbearance. In this sense, modification programs manufactured "cruel optimism," Lauren Berlant's term for an enduring attachment to something that prevents, rather than facilitates, one's flourishing.[13] The possibility of assistance indicated that an acute and contained moment of hardship in people's lives would pass when, in truth, structural changes rendered middle-class aspirations and expectations increasingly unachievable and anachronistic.

In other words, for many homeowners facing foreclosure, hardship had been ongoing for years. A decline in wages and rising healthcare costs had eroded their financial safety nets. Louise, for example, had been juggling bills for years, paying the mortgage some months and not others, and eventually falling delinquent. "I've been robbing Peter to pay Paul for years," she explained, "paying off the mortgage but skipping our utility payments because they don't like to stop picking up the garbage, but they will throw you out of your house." While the modification application required homeowners to narrate a specific event that caused them to fall behind, the exact point when many homeowners fell behind on their mortgages was often not the same moment that they started having financial trouble. These were not solidly middle-class families who faced a sudden crisis of unemployment, but post-middle-class Americans who had been living on the precipice of financial instability for decades. Louise had been holding onto settled living patterns of work, education, healthcare, and leisure readily available to her parents' generation by turning to widely available forms of consumer debt. Just as an explosion of suspect mortgage lending had put my respondents in a more vulnerable position, the rise of corporate bureaucracies in the aftermath of the crash put the onus on them to fight an uphill battle with little chance of success—maintaining a precarious hold on what had once seemed basic.

DUAL TRACKING: TRYING TO GET THROUGH

Rachel Leibrock, a bright and empathetic journalist, grew up in a working-class neighborhood in Texas with her single mother and two brothers.[14] She left home at thirteen and ended up in California, where she met her husband, Cory. The couple sacrificed higher-paying jobs to pursue careers in the arts, she in journalism and he in the music industry. Worried that they would be priced out of the rapidly escalating housing market, Rachel and Cory bought a two-bedroom home in 2005, at the height of the boom. Their first broker encouraged them to take an interest-only loan so they could purchase a home in the $500,000 range. He said the prices would only go up, and they could either flip the property for something bigger or stay and refinance their loan into one with a thirty-year fixed rate. The encounter left Rachel and Cory feeling uneasy; it was a lot to borrow, given their incomes, so they found another broker and started looking for homes in the $300,000 range, which would still be a stretch but which they considered the only way into the market. In 2005 they settled on a two-bedroom house for $330,000 in what Rachel described as a racially diverse, lower-middle-class neighborhood.

By 2006, Cory's company had gone bankrupt, and he had resorted to taking a lower-paying job. During a massive wave of newsroom cuts, Rachel had also been laid off from the *Sacramento Bee*. In the four years they owned their home, its value depreciated by nearly $150,000. Rachel contacted a loan officer at Coldwell Banker, their lender, who told her that they were not eligible for refinancing. He recommended contacting HUD. So, Rachel called the HAMP hotline.

She told me that the modification process took as much time as a part-time job. She and Cory managed to get into a trial modification program. If their application was approved, then they would begin a trial period in which they would make reduced payments through the HAMP program. After a period of a few months, they would be eligible to receive a permanent modification, which would include a reduced payment plan for a designated time, most likely keeping the principal amount intact, but extending payments ten years beyond the current life of the loan. The service representatives were optimistic that Rachel would get the modification.

Indeed, they were awarded a modification, but months into the process, Rachel opened a letter from Coldwell Banker stating that the mortgage on her property was in default. She had thirty days to pay the entire delinquent balance of the loan, an amount that disregarded their HAMP trial payments, or to face eviction. Coldwell Banker claimed to have no record of her HAMP payments. Rachel and Cory assumed it was a mistake, but when she called Coldwell, the service representative told Rachel that she "should have been making her regular mortgage payment in addition to the HAMP trial payment." Incensed, Rachel told the woman that if she could afford to pay her mortgage plus a modified payment, why would she need a modification in the first place?

Over the next two weeks, Rachel was caught in what she aptly described as a "three-ring circus of absurdity." She spoke to six different people and received six different answers. One person said the foreclosure threat was part of the process; another claimed that the money was in a "suspense account" but couldn't tell her what, exactly, a suspense account was. She explained that she was reluctant to make any more payments until they could show her where her money was going. In the course of one week, she received a letter from a department at Coldwell Banker claiming that she owed them $11,000, while another department sent a letter that put the figure at closer to $7,000. Meanwhile, a third department at Coldwell Banker inexplicably mailed her a check for $2,500.

A year after she had begun the modification process, Rachel learned that her permanent modification had been denied. In 2010, Rachel detailed her experience in a widely read feature article, "Default!," in the *Sacramento*

News & Review.[15] In vivid detail, she described how she and Cory had become victims of "dual tracking," an illegal practice in which homeowners pay into trial modification programs, such as HAMP, while lenders fail to count the payments and move ahead with wrongful foreclosures.

After her article was published, Rachel was contacted by a government caseworker who offered to shepherd her case through Coldwell's modification process so she and Cory could get a rate they could theoretically afford, albeit one that was still a financial strain. Before that moment, neither she nor her husband had ever missed a payment on a credit card or student loan. However, they decided to walk away from the mortgage. Rachel told me that they chose to pursue a short sale—in which the lender agrees to accept less than the amount owed on the house and the homeowner takes a hit to her credit score—because they had lost faith in their lender. The byzantine bureaucratic process felt like a form of humiliation. "At first, I was depressed," Rachel told me, "but it was like a divorce. We went through so much; by the time it was over, I could only see the things that were wrong with the house. It gets to the point that you can't remember what you loved about someone."

While Rachel's public voice and visibility gave her an opportunity for personalized attention that had been denied to homeowners in Oak Park, even for activists like David Castro, residents in Sacramento's lower-middle-class and middle-class neighborhoods faced innumerable roadblocks that positioned them as suspect in the eyes of mortgage lenders and debt collectors. Whereas residents with cultural capital, like Rachel and Cory, had taken for granted their knowledge of how to traverse mainstream institutions, mortgage modification bureaucracies were uncharted territory. Neither greater financial literacy nor formal education could illuminate the inner workings of labyrinthine mortgage modification systems. Rachel, for example, had described the dual-tracking fiasco as a miscommunication between a government agency, HAMP, and her lender, Coldwell Banker. Indeed, for months into my research, I, like Rachel and a handful of other middle-class homeowners I interviewed who had been dual-tracked into foreclosure,

imagined dual tracking as a communication problem between two separate entities—a government office set up to help homeowners and a
corporate lender who failed to recognize the payments. But during a
conversation with legal scholar Katherine Porter, who at the time was
also the California mortgage settlement monitor, she pointed out that
there was no such thing as a "HAMP hotline." There was no such thing
as a "HAMP office." The federal programs operated only through corporate lenders. Corporate banks had call centers administering HAMP
mortgage modifications.

The profound opacity of the system encouraged applicants to misplace blame and fostered political ambivalence about the outcomes of
failed modifications. The dual-tracking failure was much worse than
Rachel Leibrock or I had imagined. Rachel had been sending her HAMP
payments directly to Coldwell Banker without being aware of it. Coldwell Banker failed to count these modified mortgage payments it was
receiving, in effect pilfering Rachel's payments, and pushing through her
foreclosure. Rather than a case of miscommunication between two mammoth bureaucracies, one government and one private, the wrongful eviction was driven by a singular predatory bureaucracy mismanaging government funds and taking payments from Rachel without counting them
toward her mortgage. The lack of transparency about how mortgage
assistance programs worked allowed educated homeowners like Rachel
to blame frustrating bureaucratic snafus rather than to comprehend the
full extent of corporate lenders' malfeasance.

Dual tracking was widespread. In a 2012 survey of California housing counselors, 100 percent reported that they had witnessed how the
foreclosure process "often" or "sometimes" continued while a modification application was still under review, up from 95 percent of counselors in 2011. A majority indicated that these sales were in direct violation of government rules.[16] Succinctly describing dual tracking, one
housing counselor said, "One hand [at the lender] is telling you we need
this and that paper, while the other, the foreclosure department, has
the attorneys accelerating the legal process." Another respondent

described dual tracking as a "demoralizing process when people have the hope of a modification and then their home is suddenly up for sale or sold. In their desperation, clients become easy targets for scams or are pressured into a short sale or bankruptcy."[17] Corporate bureaucracies relegated homeowners to a lower social status through administrative techniques that promoted misrecognition and unresponsiveness, erasing the notion implicit in mortgage contracts that borrower and lender were potential equals. The unintelligibility of corporate bureaucracies likewise precluded homeowners, many of whom were expert researchers, from gaining the necessary social knowledge to negotiate successful outcomes and save their homes.

TAKING NAMES

I had met Darren Lewis, a white computer programmer in his early forties, through a mutual friend whose son attended preschool with mine. Darren and my friend had come to be close through many years of attending the Northern California Renaissance Faire, where attendees donned costumes and drank mead from Viking mugs. Darren had shoulder-length blond hair tucked behind his ears and was partial to an olive-hued fedora and simple, slightly wrinkled button-down shirts. He wore a gold wedding band and had a gardener's fingernails. His face looked serious, and he would take an extra beat when responding to questions, as if about to disagree, but then would flash a warm, reassuringly open smile.

Darren had grown up in Germany, the son of an engineer who worked as a military contractor. He had moved to Sacramento around his ninth birthday, and a few years later his parents divorced, with his mother moving over an hour away. His father eventually retired from the military to farm goats. As a teenager, Darren had dropped out of his high school in a wooded, upper-income suburb of Sacramento, as had the woman who became his wife, Michelle, now the owner of a small, in-home daycare center. The couple had three children, ages 22, 14, and 11.

The oldest daughter had recently graduated from UC Berkeley in political science. (Darren proudly explained that she had attended community college and realized she liked arguing on YouTube, so pursued the degree.)

In 2005 Darren and Michelle had found a house that they wanted to buy, and their real estate agent offered a loan through her lender. They had solicited a second opinion from another broker who told them that anyone who "loans to you is doing you a disservice." But Darren was making good money, a hundred dollars per hour, as a programmer contracting for a credit card firm, and the couple felt the house was close enough to the edge of what they could afford. "My career was going right then ... on a pretty sharp incline," Darren said. "So yeah, we knew it was a little bit of a stretch to get in there, but the trajectory of my career was pretty good."

Their Realtor devised a plan to offer two loans to cover the cost of the house, a little over $450,000. They invested around $10,000 for the down payment and would pay $2,422 monthly on the first, an adjustable-rate loan with Polestar Bank*, and $922 on the second, a fixed-rate loan with Lehman Brothers, until the payments ballooned in a few years. (Both loans ended up being serviced by Vertex National Bank.)

But by the time the mortgage payment adjusted in 2009, it increased by over $1,000 a month; meanwhile, their house was now worth only $240,000.

Darren's firm, largely based on offering easy access to consumer credit cards, collapsed after the crash. For Darren and Michelle, they could either "pay for the mortgage or buy food." Michelle closed her in-home daycare, adding to their financial burdens, because they could not predict if or when they would be evicted.

The representatives at Vertex National Bank told Darren that to qualify he had to be behind on his mortgage payments. But then he fell too far in arrears and was transferred to collections. Some weeks, Darren spent two or three hours on the phone trying to get accurate information on his application. During these marathon sessions, Darren took copious notes, documenting his interactions and holding onto the false hope that, by sheer force of evidence, he could compel his lender to be accountable.

At our first meeting, he handed me a photocopy of the four pages of typed notes he had written while being bounced to different departments at Vertex. Divided into two columns on each page, the abbreviated lines of the notes looked like a poem detailing his foreclosure story. It began with a simple list of items needed for his loan modification application, and then became more editorial as he transcribed a series of names, phone numbers, delinquent amounts, and conflicting information about the unit to which he should appeal. These included the names of service representatives that he spoke to at Vertex: Ms. White, Janise, Shelley, Colleen, Ronette, Coranda, Chelise, Kathy, Renada, Michael, Susan, Lewana, Reba, Mike, Chad, Gayle, Loretta, Bob, Ann, Eddie, Larry, Bruce, Victor, and finally Tekisha in the foreclosure department when there was no longer any hope. A typical sequence, playing out over several weeks, read:

> Called back 5/7 8am to tell her I faxed the papers and how many pages
>
> Ms white tells me that the account has now moved to a different department 800–834–9XXX—loss recovery.
>
> She tells me the [account] number I gave is the second mortgage even though it's the only number I've used since I began this process—it's the only one in my notes.
>
> Call new number.
>
> Says [the mortgage] is in restructuring still, has no idea what ms white was talking about. Hung up on me after 15 minutes on hold.
>
> Call again—says this is a general line....
>
> Janise says to call 877–838–1XXX I say no send me to a supervisor, she still sends me to 877–838–1XXX where I get hung up on.
>
> Call again—get most emphatically sent to 877–838–1XXX.

NO! NO! NO!

They don't have any of the info I've faxed?

Gonna start again?

Darren's notes illustrate the impossibility of getting access to the correct service representative and the frequency with which lenders and loan servicers lost files and forms.

At one point, a service representative confirmed that the couple had received a mortgage modification offer. Darren and Michelle saw cause for celebration. But when Darren received no contract in the mail, he followed up with the bank and spoke to a series of representatives who denied that a modification had been granted. "It was really strange, every person I spoke to said that that information doesn't exist. Nobody would have ever said that or could have made that assessment." Chasing a ghost of a promise, Darren started the process again.

After two years of trying to achieve a modification, they gave up. "We tried to do a short sale," Darren said, "and I don't know if we ever got an offer.... Eventually we just walked. Packed up our stuff and left. Didn't say boo. Yard got grown over and we went back later, somebody had already stolen the heater. It was vacant for a long time. We'd drive by and check it out. Part of me felt bad about it, but I was also vindictive. It was not by far the only vacant lot in the road."

Darren, like Rachel Leibrock, relied on strategies of persistence and institutional know-how in confronting Vertex National Bank's mortgage modification bureaucracy—asking to speak with managers, taking copious notes, following up on paperwork submissions—actions that would ordinarily lead to improved outcomes in legal battles or when dealing with health insurance snafus or erroneous credit card charges. Darren held up a stack of papers more than two inches thick to show me what he had faxed to Vertex. Other homeowners, unprompted by me, carted similar files to coffee shops for our interviews, dug through packed closets to find their records, and displayed their documents before me on their kitchen tables. It was as if the answers to mortgagors' stories might be unearthed from their plastic binders and repurposed school folders. Homeowners would then add to their stacks the useless automated form letters from lenders. Rachel Leibrock requested, when her story was featured in the *Sacramento News & Review*, that she be photographed sitting beside her pile of paperwork.

These skills, tracking conversations in detail and compiling correspondence, can translate into success when advocating for children's accommodations or dealing with doctors in health settings. But in the case of mortgage modifications, these middle-class dispositions often worked against applicants. "Homeowners might call their servicer and ask to speak to a manager," sociologist Lindsay Owens writes about her yearlong experience in a nonprofit mortgage modification help center, or "incessantly check up on the status of their application; appear at the local branch of their servicers to speak with someone in person; or contact influential authority figures," but these interventions, when implemented in the mortgage modification context, would often backfire.

TROUBLES WITH SECURITIZATION

Jorge Rivera, a forty-six-year-old white Ecuadorian American manager at a big-box retail store, described how his first loan servicer, Wellspring Loan Services*, agreed to a modification, but his loan was sold during the process, and the modification was canceled. His second servicer, Edge Financial, had different requirements, demanded that he begin the process again, and eventually denied his request. Jorge had a grueling schedule, working twelve-hour days with one day off every two weeks, and had spent hours on the phone to secure the initial modification, often locking himself in the restroom at his store to talk to customer service representatives. According to Jorge, the stress of the application process and the eventual loss of his home had irreparably damaged his health and marriage, which ended in divorce six months after the foreclosure. Now living alone and struggling to rebuild his credit, he described the break with his lender as the first in a series of broken relationships in his personal life, as if securitization represented a form of abandonment auguring others.

Securitization made it impossible for homeowners who were used to negotiating with financial institutions to find levers of influence within organizations, individuals who could help them to resolve their mortgage dilemmas.[18] Many homeowners suggested that mortgages held by secondary loan servicers rather than by banks were less likely to receive modifications and more likely to face foreclosure. Supporting this view, a study of mortgage modification outcomes conducted by the California Reinvestment Coalition found that the kind of assistance homeowners received often depended largely on who owned the loan. Banks, if they owned the loans, were more likely to reduce the loan principal, the most desirable outcome for homeowners, but these same banks were reluctant to do so for the loans they serviced on behalf of investors.[19] Before the crisis, my interlocutors thought little of the letters they received from lenders announcing that their mortgage debt had been sold, aside from noting where to send payments. Yet, in the context of the crisis, their specific lender or loan servicer gained critical importance as homeowners were forced into protracted negotiations over modifications, short sales, and foreclosures. In hindsight, many homeowners identified the initial sale of their mortgage as the first sign that lenders were abandoning their responsibilities to borrowers. Homeowners spoke critically about their lender "no longer being their lender." As one unemployed commercial real estate broker who faced foreclosure put it, "You can pick your lender, but you cannot choose who buys your loan."

The untraceable links between borrowers and lenders became painfully apparent as foreclosures became widespread. To seize a foreclosed home, a lender is required by law to record a paper trail that shows a chain of ownership transferred during each sale—evidence, for instance, that a mortgage originating with Countrywide was sold to Goldman Sachs and then to JP Morgan. However, in the aftermath of the crash, not only did banks foreclosing on homeowners fail to maintain reliable records of these complex trails of ownership, but they even went so far as to create cheap, hired "robo-signers" to fraudulently sign thousands of documents each month attesting to the banks' ownership of mortgages in an attempt to disguise their negligence.[20]

Struggles with Ocwen Financial Corporation, a large residential and commercial mortgage loan servicing company, were likewise common-place. The mortgage servicer receiving the lion's share of TARP funds, Ocwen continually abused the system, denying nearly 70 percent of homeowners' applications for mortgage modifications under HAMP, failing to apply homeowners' modified payments to their balances, and canceling the HAMP enrollment of more than 130,000 homeowners, meanwhile collecting more than $757 million from the Treasury for those expunged homeowners. In 2013, in an enforcement action by the Treasury, Ocwen was found guilty of "deception and shortcuts in mort-gage servicing" for the following misdeeds: "failing to properly process borrowers' applications and calculate their eligibility; [p]roviding false or misleading reasons for denying mortgage modifications; [f]ailing to honor previously agreed upon trial modifications with prior servicers; and [d]eceptively seeking to collect payments under the mortgage's original unmodified terms after the consumer had already begun a mortgage modification with the prior servicer."[21]

These entanglements between mortgage modifications and distant lenders during times of widespread adversity reflect dynamics that par-allel the U.S. farm foreclosure crisis of the 1980s, as Kathryn Dudley shows in her powerful book *Debt and Dispossession: Farm Loss in America's Heartland.* Farmers who borrowed from local banks expected, and often were granted, loan restructuring during times of hardship, whereas those who borrowed from more distant agricultural credit unions or the federal government were denied.[22] The dense social networks that allowed farmers to borrow from local banks also encouraged borrowers and lenders to view these debt ties as reciprocal obligations during times of economic crisis. Recognizing the relationship between lending and social ties, farmers who did not have the social capital to qualify for loans from local lenders turned to more distant sources of credit as a last resort.[23] When the crash hit, farmers who had borrowed from local, family-owned banks and whose debts remained in dense social networks were able to modify distressed mortgages. In a similar vein, during and after the housing crash, Sacramento homeowners expected mortgage contracts, brokered by local agents but immediately securitized, to create a lasting partnership of mutual interest to both parties.[24] The greater the distance between borrower and lender, Sacramento Valley residents observed, the more likely that a lender would deny assistance and seize the home.

PENNING HARDSHIP LETTERS

Although the concrete ties between borrower and lender were undermined by mortgage securitization, the hardship letters required by modification applications suggested the existence of communication between two parties—homeowners facing tenuous circumstances and lending employees able to help them. A required piece of the application in which homeowners narrate the adversities that prevent them from staying current on mortgage payments, the hardship letter would give applicants an opportunity to detail a so-called qualifying hardship—death, divorce, disability, or loss of income—to gain acceptance into a modification trial. For homeowners, the hardship letter reinforced the illusion of reciprocity by implying that lenders were invested in the personal lives of mortgagors. The notion of directly corresponding with a lender through a letter implied a relationship between people that could be equals, rather than a market transaction between unequal entities, spurring homeowners to become emotionally invested in the power of storytelling when appealing to their creditors.[25] The possibility that a well-penned letter could incite sympathy reinforced the idea that mortgage debt bonded borrowers with lenders.

But mortgage modification specialists who processed homeowners' paperwork told me that homeowners often "misinterpreted" the request for the letter as an invitation to "unload" too much personal information—evidence of the deep interpretative divide between contemporary financial mortgage markets and earlier imaginaries of middle-class status imbued within Main Street lending. At Leviathan Bank, for example, one representative considered the worst letters those that were handwritten, more than two pages long, and replete with every detail of everything happening in a homeowner's life, "from the cousin who got laid off to the cheating husband she had to divorce." In contrast, he described the appropriate letter as "less than a page, formally written, with one line of basic information about why the loan was delinquent." This notion that homeowners' letters were too personal—that the writers overshared, that they were unable to recognize the standards of decorum within the business world—enforces an ages-old hierarchy in which those with less economic, political, or social power are viewed as emotionally excessive. In a similar vein, another loan officer claimed that staff at his office never read hardship letters, insisting they were a mere technicality in a modification application. Another modification specialist, a midlevel staffer at Trust-Worth Financial, told me that employees did read the letters, but the letters did not have the same meaning that homeowners imagined. Instead, TrustWorth would not want the bad publicity that might come from certain cases. He told me, "If the hardship letter says, 'I bought four cars with my line of home equity credit,' no way, but if it's a senior citizen whose husband died and she'll be out on the street, they don't want that on the front page of the news."

Applicants were caught in a cruel hoax that suggested first that there was an enduring social relationship with their lenders, symbolized by the direct address of the hardship letter sent to lenders, and second that homeowners could win the lender's sympathy if only they decoded the correct form of address. This ruse supported an outdated vision of a financial world in which one's worthiness, defined by life choices and personal values, mattered. The hardship letter requirement placed the onus on homeowner-applicants to inspire the mercy of lenders, depoliticizing any rejections and encouraging homeowners to blame themselves for the denials they received.

Hardship letters doubled as disciplinary techniques of financial governance that brought corporate power to bear on the intricacies of individual acts. Loan counselors at one housing nonprofit I observed, for example, sent their clients to a law school clinic where students helped distressed homeowners write "appropriate" letters. When I asked homeowners about the first letters they had sent before working with the clinic, many described their letters with denigrating terms such as "garbage," "way off-base," or "with everything in it." Louise, for example, joked that she would be ashamed for me to see those early drafts, and, like many other homeowners, she had thrown away her original letter. Hence, even as these letters reinforced the idea of a social tie to lenders, they also encouraged homeowners to internalize the notion that their supposed shortcomings in communication or expression qualified as justifications for their failure to secure assistance. If applicants could mimic or embody a middle-class style of address, the logic went, they would garner respect and response.

In his analysis of the appeals that subjects wrote to the king of France during the seventeenth and eighteenth centuries, Foucault focuses on the petitioners' attempts to convince the sovereign power to take action in local disputes, a process that brought power to bear on the minutiae and squabbles of daily life.[26] Foucault shows how these forms of power became more diffuse with the establishment of modern techniques of governance, including the prison system, mental institutions, public education, and routine forms of self-discipline. Indeed, the complex forms of administrative authority circulating through mortgage modification bureaucracies suggest an evolution of financial governance in which power is exercised and subjects formed through the seemingly innocuous paper trails of business transactions. The so-called objective financial bureaucratic process meant to render these financial ties neutral had embedded them more deeply in the daily lives of homeowners, providing a smokescreen for questionable home seizures and unquestionable forms of loss.

BREAKING RECIPROCAL TIES

By expecting lenders to assume coresponsibility for mortgage debts after the 2008 crash, homeowners articulated an ideal of financial reciprocity between borrowers and lenders—a relationship that was at once moral, social, and financial. Forceful criticism of lenders' failures to provide mortgage modifications indicates the existence of expectations for mutuality in late-liberal mortgage markets. Homeowners felt *shocked* and *insulted* by the treatment they received at the hands of corporate lenders, a sentiment tied to reciprocal relations gone wrong in the ethnographic record.[27] Mortgaging, with its echoes of postwar good debt and long-term contracts, unlike healthcare debt or credit card balances, led homeowners to anticipate help and even sympathy from lenders during hard times.

Prevalent discourses of financial reciprocity in the heart of postcrash financial mortgage markets add nuance to long-standing anthropological theories regarding markets. Initially, nineteenth-century anthropologists mapped an opposition between societies engaged in market exchange and non-Western ones practicing forms of so-called gift exchange. According to this model, Western market exchange is impersonal, with both sides seeking maximum material benefits for themselves. The identities of buyers and sellers are irrelevant; either party can end the contract at any time.[28] In contrast, non-Western societies were imagined as entrenched in reciprocal trade, as the gift ties giver and receiver in a relationship of implicit future obligation. Who gives and who receives are of prime importance, and the exchange often involves forms of prestige, with no scorekeeping. Describing the social power of the gift, Marcel Mauss writes, "Souls are mixed with things; things with souls. Lives are mingled together, and this is how ... each emerges from their own sphere and mixes together."[29] As anthropologist Mary Douglass writes in her preface to Mauss's work, "A gift that does nothing to enhance solidarity is a contradiction."[30]

Influenced by postcolonial and feminist views, in the 1980s anthropologists such as Marilyn Strathern and Christopher Gregory posited the division between "gift economies" and "market economies" as anachronistic, instead focusing on how multiple types of exchange commingled within each society's economic system.[31] In her work on the Trobriand Islands, economic anthropologist Annette Weiner, for example, described the multiple forms of exchange that coexisted, citing her translator, who distinguished between market exchange and reciprocal kin ties this way: "If my father gives me [*mapula*] a coconut palm and several years later a strong wind comes and knocks down the palm, my father will give me another one. If I go to the trade store and buy a kerosene lamp and later the lamp breaks, do you think Mr. Holland [the store owner] will give me back my money?"[32]

After 2008, many U.S. homeowners metaphorically returned to the trade store to ask for their money back after their lamps had broken. But more than demonstrating the concurrence of market exchange and reciprocity within U.S. society, the case of postcrash foreclosures indicates that commodified forms of market exchange actually *generate* and *amplify* implicit reciprocal social contracts. Mortgage payments were recorded, which is a hallmark of distant market exchange. But rather than distancing the borrower and the lender, the long-term payments, projected over the course of thirty years, created mutuality. Mortgage payments were tracked (market exchange), but in that accounting, homeowners and lenders generated a kind of habitus over a lifetime of scheduled payments (reciprocity). When homeowners failed to make payments, lenders pushed through evictions (market exchange), but homeowners viewed this practice as a breach of trust and loyalty (reciprocity). Homeowners had misunderstood the offer of subprime loans as an initiation of a reciprocal relationship through a financial contract with a lender, when, in fact, lenders were giving without giving, offering mortgages but not holding them, transforming them into commodities that would be dispersed into the ether of the market.

Offering a view of commodities and gifts that illuminates these ties of financial mutuality, anthropologist Anna Tsing argues that "taking the gift out of the commodity is never easy."[33] Even after commodities are run through the machinery of private property, markets, and commodity fetishism, Tsing observes, the work of removing the reciprocal aura from market commodities must be reenacted again and again. Noncapitalist social relations are tapped and transformed to grease the wheels of late-liberal markets. Gifts and commodities, Tsing posits, "incorporate each other's characteristics, change into each other, or confuse different participants about their gift-versus-commodity identities."[34] Amid widespread financial ruin, mortgage debts spawn precisely this interplay between the reciprocal ethics associated with noncommodified exchange and the calculative impulse of mortgage markets.

The sense that lenders and borrowers owed one another, that they shared responsibility for distressed mortgages, persisted even as Wall Street investment firms commodified mortgage debt, making the links between borrowers and lenders indiscernible. But these realities did not render the social contracts implicit in mortgage debt ties obsolete. To the contrary, when lenders refused to grant mortgage modifications, homeowners viewed this refusal as a breach of trust and loyalty. More than a straightforward extension of sociality into the market, mortgage contracts functioned as boundary markers—symbolizing forms of inclusion and exclusion from social respectability and status and demarcating forms of gendered, racialized, and classed belonging. When homeownership is viewed as a marker of middle-class social inclusion rather than solely a financial contract, it becomes clearer how it would bestow entitlements to reciprocity.

It's no coincidence that we see these expectations for reciprocity emerging around mortgaging, which commodifies the domestic realm, imagined as the antithesis of the calculated world of the market. The complicated mix of affect and aspiration embedded in the home made the house itself an uneasy commodity from the start. It is singularized, as anthropologist Igor Kopytoff describes, spending most of its years off the market.[35] This respite from commodification lends the home a magical quality that allows a buyer to feel ownership and stewardship of it, even if, in purely economic terms, the bank actually owns the home. The narrative of mortgaging is shot through with fiction: home "ownership" is, in most cases, a misnomer. Lender and borrower enter into a tacit falsehood that a home owned by the bank and leased to the borrower for thirty years belongs to the homeowner rather than to the bank. The feeling of entitlement to one's home, regardless of how much of the mortgage balance had been paid, and histories that linked home-ownership to forms of racial and class privilege set the stage for home-owners to expect help and assistance from lenders and to question dis-possession when lenders failed to deliver.

When failed mortgage modifications are viewed through the lens of anthropological theories of reciprocity, the moral outrages produced by the Sacramento Valley foreclosure epidemic can be seen as more than straightforward reactions to bank seizures. More complexly, the indig-nation shared among homeowners and lending employees embroiled in botched mortgage modifications also resulted from corporate lenders' *refusal of the obligation to receive.* Reciprocal relationships entail not only an obligation to give but also an obligation to receive. As lenders denied mortgage modifications, they also denied homeowners the ability to continue paying on their mortgages—habitual acts that preserved the belief that a borrower and lender could be restored to equal status. Modified payments within a homeowner's means would have main-tained the implicit social contract of mortgaging, rectifying a depar-ture from postwar ideas of homeownership. Lenders' denials of home-owner applicants meant that the boom-and-bust cycle inspired by Wall Street investors was not an aberration that federal programs would remedy through redistribution and regulation, as the U.S. government had after the Great Depression. This refusal to accept ongoing pay-ments from homeowners therefore symbolized the death of an imag-ined social tie, a severed bond that homeowners, since World War II, had relied upon to define their moral standing and social status.

Across the nation, these frustrations and resentments at lenders and the government, according to legal scholar Brent White, distinguished homeowners who continued to pay on underwater loans after the 2008 crash and those who chose to abandon mortgage debts, even if they could afford to pay them.[36] Facing mortgage default and appealing to lenders and loan servicers for assistance, residents were forced to submit to ongoing forms of evaluation and scrutiny—both personal and financial that transformed them from potentially valued citizens to vulnerable subjects surveilled and managed by hybrid governmental-private entities. Ironically, at a moment when mortgages were capitalized to the greatest degree, chopped into bits to be resold on secondary markets, which would, in theory, sever ties between buyer and seller, homeowners came to expect assistance, sympathy even, from a human lender with whom they imagined a social bond. Wall Street deregulation and speculation had long replaced the conservative Main Street lending practices Sacramento Valley homeowners assumed were governing mortgaging.

HARD LIVING POST–MIDDLE CLASS

If dusty tent cities were the popular emblem of downward mobility during the Great Depression, then bureaucratic runaround and endless paperwork have become the symbols of the death rattle of postwar middle-class subjectivity during the Great Recession. The inequalities sowed by deindustrialization and stagnating incomes were amplified by widespread subprime lending and the rise of corporate mortgage modification bureaucracies after 2009. No longer limiting their evaluation to loan applicants' credit scores and incomes, corporate management tasked modification specialists with surveilling the daily spending habits, addictions, illnesses, divorces, and domestic decision-making of applicants who had identified as middle class through the extensive paperwork homeowners were required to submit. One collections agent at Leviathan Bank, for example, encouraged David Sanchez to get a roommate so he could better make his monthly payments. By 2012, these intrusions into the lives of struggling homeowners on behalf of corporate banks had become commonplace. The stories in this chapter thereby represent the increasing difficulty of daily life for a majority of homeowners in lower-middle-class and middle-class neighborhoods embroiled in mortgage modifications—people who were seeking government assistance but were enlisted into a battle with corporate bureaucracies, a battle whose outcome would define the solvency of their status within an American post–middle class.

Corporate bureaucracies used to be, for the most part, aligned with values that supported the formation of middle-class subjectivities, both as workers in corporations and as customers of these businesses. But within mortgage modification bureaucracies, homeowners who were accustomed to navigating bureaucratic systems with ease were subjected to long wait times on the phone, typically thirty minutes to an hour per call; they could not employ professionals to do the work for them (HAMP prohibited paid third-party assistance); and widespread securitization or reselling of loans had made finding levers of influence within big banks impossible.[37] These dynamics, combined with increased levels of scrutiny, meant that mortgage modification bureaucracies undermined the possibility of reproducing American middle-class subjectivities by crudely dispossessing residents of their homes and more subtly by treating them as expendable, which, of course, they now were under the logics of Wall Street financial debt economies.

Middle-class solutions, such as hiring expert attorneys or accountants to help navigate institutions, were unavailable to homeowners applying for modifications. HAMP, for example, prohibited charging fees for mortgage modification assistance.[38] Although homeownership had been a foundation of middle-class subjectivity in the postwar United States, sociologist Lindsay Owens in her research on mortgage modifications in the San Francisco Bay Area found that middle-class applicants lacked any advantages in securing mortgage modifications and fared even worse than their working-class counterparts, a finding confirmed by scholars looking solely at loan-level data.[39] Middle-class applicants, Owens shows, were accustomed to paying professionals, such as lawyers or financial advisors, and wanted to hire third parties to shepherd their applications through the modification process. David, for instance, wanted to hire someone to help with his modification, as he had in order to resolve Karen's health insurance mix-up. His impulse to outsource the work to a third party who could produce results was so profound that he paid two separate organizations over $1,000 each, even as he recognized that those businesses were most likely scams, because he felt he had to "do something" to save his home.

The design of HAMP modifications, routed through the corporate sector, reflected a divergence of corporate and middle-class interests that was only intensified through the bureaucratic mechanisms HAMP created. Alternatives existed. One bill proposed in 2009 before HAMP was established advocated having bankruptcy courts write down mortgages, which would have given homeowners from middle-class milieus with social capital and access to lawyers a better chance to navigate the system to hold onto their homes. The bill passed in the House, but was defeated in the Senate, because investors wanted to maintain control over mortgage amendments.[40] The interests of the mortgage holding companies, Owens argues, conflicted with the interests of both middle- and working-class homeowners.[41] The policy that passed—HAMP— prohibited the use of fee-earning professionals such as lawyers and financial advisors to guide modifications, leaving middle-class homeowners without typical recourse to resolve financial issues. Not only were middle-class homeowners unable to draw on their established social and professional networks to get modifications passed, but the help that was available often grated against middle-class identities. Owens details the discomfort many middle-class homeowners felt when they had to rely on nonprofit housing agencies, as David Sanchez's encounters with Save Your Home California demonstrated. This was a new type of crisis, where middle-class homeowners were forced into the position of accepting assistance from working-class housing counselors, the sort of assistance typically reserved for the working poor.

The foreclosure crisis and, most important, the mechanisms of corporate dispossession, formulated new subjectivities as residents with middle-class expectations and assumptions now faced a Wall Street reality in which lenders and loan servicers positioned applicants—who had once defined the boundary of social inclusion—as suspect, disposable, and disrespectable subjects. Homeownership, once a prudent financial decision that, much like a college degree, served as the foundation of middle-class stability, now demanded such overwhelming amounts of debt that it exposed families to downward mobility. Simply put, more debt, even of the sort once considered "good debt," meant greater vulnerability. Ironically, in the decades leading up to the 2008 mortgage crash, these families, most often straddling the lower rungs of the middle class, faced increasing debt burdens and diminishing incomes during a moment of economic growth in the United States, where gains were diverted to those at the very top of the income distribution.[42] Even before the 2008 crash, 90 percent of people declaring bankruptcy had traditional middle-class backgrounds with regard to education, occupation, and homeownership, as Elizabeth Warren and Deborah Thorne show.[43] Job instability, illness and injury, and family breakup were already leading middle-class families into "dramatic reversals of fortune" and financial collapse before the onslaught of bank seizures after 2008.[44]

A defining quality of post-middle-class reality is the increasing debt burdens of middle-class families beginning in the mid-1980s. As income growth slowed, Americans turned to consumer debt to obtain the basic necessities of daily life.[45] Between 2001 and 2004, the median American household's wealth declined, with the debt-to-equity ratio climbing from 37.4 percent in 1985 to 61 percent in 2004 and 2007.[46] Holding consumer debt became the unifying quality of middle-class Americans, more than owning a home, being married, obtaining a university degree, or attending church.[47] After the crash, things only deteriorated. By 2011, one study found that if faced with a financial emergency, half of middle-class families could not come up with $2,000 from savings, family or friends, or borrowing.[48] As anthropologist Brett Williams writes, this rise of consumer debt intensifies inequalities while simultaneously obscuring them, making debtors feel personally responsible for social problems.[49]

Homeowners in lower-middle-class and middle-class neighborhoods were not pressing for a debt jubilee like that of Biblical times that
would wipe out their mortgage debts. Their demands were much more
modest: they wanted to stay in their homes and *keep paying* on their
mortgages until they were paid off, reinstating homeowners' status as
equals within the logic of exchange. But, despite the promises of advertising campaigns, loan modification programs were not established to
restore pre-Wall-Street-takeover ideals of fairness to mortgage markets
or to rescue lower-middle-class and middle-class Americans' hopes for
the good life. These programs were established to incentivize lenders
and loan servicers to consider the possibility that forbearance would
reap higher profits than foreclosure and then, and only then, to stop
evictions. If foreclosures were halted, it was not because homeowners
were suddenly understood as real people whose hardships and histories
mattered to financial institutions, no matter how much the loan modification applications, with their attendant required hardship letters, suggested otherwise.

Homeowners' herculean efforts to amend their mortgages reflect the
lasting importance of homeownership and the profundity of a shared
belief that mortgage lenders are tied to American homeowners in an
ongoing bond of mutuality. Homeowners demonstrated great fortitude
as they wasted hours on the phone with lenders and kept applying for
modifications, trying to correct errors, seeking to set the record straight
in the face of the strategic incompetence of corporate bureaucracies.
Just as homeowners had embraced a blind faith in lending institutions
in the lead-up to the crash, these efforts suggest how few homeowners
realized that the outcomes of the modification applications had more to
do with the property values in an applicant's neighborhood and the
projected long-term profitability of the housing stock than with a
homeowner's worthiness. But the application process led homeowners
to believe they were denied aid because they gave the "wrong answers"
or failed to meet obscure standards. Hence, the loss of a home through
bank seizure and, more important, the treatment homeowners received

at the hands of lending bureaucracies while struggling to amend their mortgages depoliticized bank seizures while dramatically rupturing applicants' sense of self and the possibility of stability. As David Graeber shows, if a debtor cannot repay her debt, she cannot restore herself to equality; reigning logic suggests that it is her fault, that "there must be something wrong with her."[50] Lenders, by failing to acknowledge status and hardships, destroyed an imagined social contract that had governed mortgaging in the postwar era. This rupture in long-standing relations of financial reciprocity would inspire homeowners to consider forms of debt refusal and resistance unfathomable before the 2008 crash, tactics of resistance I explore in greater depth in chapter 5.

The nagging question that echoed across television news debates and kitchen table conversations after the crash was whether homeowners now facing foreclosure had lived beyond their means. If so, the logic goes, bank seizures offered the payback they deserved. (People don't want to pay for their neighbors' new Escalade, as Timothy Geithner quipped, describing the backlash to federal mortgage assistance.) Homeowners like David, Darren, and Rachel had strained themselves financially to buy their homes in the first place. These houses were not McMansions, as many critics claimed, but modest homes in lower-middle-class and middle-class neighborhoods where soaring prices due to the housing bubble stretched buyers to their limits. They couldn't predict the crash of the housing market, much less intuit the tanking of the global economy. Even more opaque were the slower but badgering changes to their own financial and social standing, eroding over decades before the crash. How were people to suddenly understand, much less accept, that they were going to be worse off than their parents? Or to assume that they should forgo homeownership and retirement because the scaffolding that had given shape to these plans had collapsed under the weight of Wall Street finance? Everything *looked* the same. People in the Sacramento Valley might have been using cheap credit and home equity rather than salaries and benefits to sustain their basic needs, but the realities of daily life did not betray those differences until it was too late.

Documents

Homeowners presented me with documents as evidence of their experience.

Louise Walker, a retired African American medical assistant, in her kitchen displaying her modification paperwork. Walker was denied a mortgage modification because TrustWorth Financial overestimated her fixed Social Security income, 2014. Photo by the author.

3/1/14

To whom it may concern:

Please accept this letter as evidence of the hardships my husband and I have faced that have caused us to fall behind on our mortgage. We are determined to stay in our house and implore you to work with us in crafting a rate we can afford.

Our difficulties began in 2006 when I retired from the Blood Center of the Pacific. My husband had become disabled in 1989 after working 20 years with UPS. An injury to his neck precluded him from working. Instead, he began caring for his father who was suffering from dementia. Since my retirement, we are both on a fixed income of approximately $2400 per month. At times, we have struggled to meet all of our payments. Sometimes we would not pay our utility bills in order to afford our $1,670 per month mortgage. Additionally, my mother-in-law and my father have also been diagnosed with dementia. Although insurance helps cover most of the medical costs, the emotional strain of caring for our parents has been intense. Regardless, we are determined to remain in the home we've lived this past decade and a half.

Please consider these circumstances when looking at modifying our loan. We want to pay, and satisfy our obligations, but need to ensure that we can keep our lights on. Thank you very much for your time and consideration.

Louise Walker's handwritten hardship letter to TrustWorth Financial, as required by the mortgage modification application. This is her final draft after receiving help from a law school clinic. Walker described her earlier versions as "garbage."

(*Top*) Darren Lewis holding a portion of his paperwork from his failed mortgage modification application, 2014. Photo by the author.

(*Bottom*) Irma Machado, a seasonal farmworker in Oak Park who was a victim of predatory lending. When asked if she kept the paperwork from her foreclosure, Irma showed this page from her address book—the name and number of a scam artist who falsely promised her a modification in exchange for $2,500, 2014. Photo by the author.

CHAPTER FOUR

Can't Work the System

The Troubled Sympathies of Corporate Bureaucrats

By 2011, Jason Silva, the thirty-one-year-old Punjabi Mexican–Portuguese American loan officer at Leviathan Bank, had been reassigned to a new modification division as sales slowed after the crash. Although his managers at Leviathan had grandfathered in his $180,000 salary for two years, placing his earnings well above those of new mortgage modification specialists, Jason admitted that he missed the environment of the fast-paced sales division where performance was tied to bonuses and commissions. He had become, he told me, a "paper pusher."

Jason worked at a behemoth Leviathan Bank building on the outskirts of Sacramento that had been converted from a large-scale mortgage sales compound into a massive call center that employed over one thousand workers processing mortgage modifications. Although mortgage modifications had existed before the mortgage crash, they had been infrequent, and few bank staffers were trained to handle them. Starting in 2009, as hundreds of thousands of homeowners faced mortgage default, modification programs came to dominate the mortgage divisions of major lenders. Because most lenders had little or no experience with lowering mortgage payments, having perhaps offered a handful each year on a case-by-case basis, none were prepared for the flood of applications for modifications or for the proliferation of legal guidelines that, starting in 2009, were created to manage them. At the peak of the crash, Leviathan Bank centers like the one where Jason worked fielded up to 50,000 calls a day from distressed homeowners.[1]

A technologically inclined fast thinker, Jason derided the antiquated computer system and inefficient interdepartmental communication tools he faced in the mortgage modification division, problems that led to disastrous results for homeowners. Each month, Jason received a new Excel spreadsheet listing a hundred homeowner applicants who would make up his cases for that month. These were not all new applicants for loan modifications; some had submitted their applications months before, but Leviathan Bank policy was to shuffle cases to a new loan modification officer each month, regardless of whether the file had been resolved. Plans to reduce a homeowner's mortgage payments were managed on sixteen different computer systems, one of them still running MS-DOS. When he contacted a customer, Jason explained that he would enter their information into a software program—ironically called Mortgage Rescue*—that would give a breakdown of their account status, linked to five other subdivisions of the software that would be used to establish trial plans. Miscommunications and errors were rampant. Jason elaborated:

> And that's where the processors, underwriters, all of these people had to go in there and use that [system] day-to-day to update notes and everything else. And that thing was a pain in the ass.... The problem was that your notes were supposed to carry over into other systems but, depending on what department you were in, some of those couldn't be viewed by everybody, so there was a lot of suppression going on within all of the different software systems. When a customer service representative would get his list of one hundred new clients, they would go into [Mortgage Rescue] and say, "Well, I don't see any notes in the system, no trial plan was started." It was all there, but it was just not accessible for you.

Many service representatives were new, Jason explained, without the experience or training to navigate the systems. "You could do your job," he said, "or you could just sit there and get lost."

A typical Bank of America mortgage modification call center in California, located in Simi Valley, outside Los Angeles. Photo by J. Emilio Flores for the *New York Times.*

The mandatory monthly reshuffling of cases around the office also caused confusion. Documents would be sent to an underwriter to pre-screen a mortgage adjustment, and by the time the underwriter responded with a request for more information, the account had been transferred off Jason's list. Even if a homeowner got lucky and reached a savvy employee familiar with the computer systems and able to locate the homeowner's records, there was a significant chance, for example, that the paperwork had passed a thirty-day window for documents before they were considered out-of-date and homeowners were required to update their application with their most recent pay stubs and bank statements. The default option was to require homeowners to start the process again, to resubmit their applications, as had been the case with David Sanchez and so many others.

More than a logistical inconvenience, the mismanagement of files and the erasure of notes on cases in the context of modification bureaucracies thwarted the ties between employees and their homeowner clients. Drawing on Foucault's notion of inscription, anthropologist Matthew Hull shows how the circulation of bureaucratic paperwork in urban Pakistan generates sociality, requiring broad participation both within bureaucracies and between state functionaries and citizens. The circulation of the documents themselves within the bureaucratic order, Hull maintains, links functionaries to people and things outside the bureaucratic domain.[2] As employees criticized the circuitous maze of paperwork channels, they also critiqued the constrained opportunities for mutual ties with borrower clients.

The computer technologies that lenders implemented after 2009 to track homeowners and their files were outdated and inadequate even at high-powered lenders such as Leviathan Bank and TrustWorth Financial, whose temporary service representative could not find Louise Walker's bank statement on the system installed on his laptop during the loan modification fair discussed in chapter 3. At the loan servicer Edge Financial, employees struggled to manage well over eight thousand different computer codes used to categorize issues within a borrower's file, with many confusing duplicates.[3] Daniel Matos, a white Latino midlevel modification specialist in his early thirties, admitted that when he told a homeowner that a file was incomplete, it reflected what he saw on the screen more than what was actually in a record. A Leviathan Bank modification specialist detailed the runaround for homeowners: "You [the homeowner] go into a line to find out that that person is not able to help. The rep thinks maybe the other person down here can help; you go to them and find out neither one of those two can help. Then you have to go all the way back to the beginning of the line and start over. This is every time you call." Customers would be transferred around and "nobody would have a clue what the hell was going on." The limited capabilities of software interfaces likewise led agents to misinterpret homeowners' circumstances. When denying a loan modification, for example, agents would be limited to selecting from a fixed drop-down menu of reasons for denial. Often, however, the reasons were incorrect, and many real-life

circumstances were not included in the menu, leading service representatives to misrecognize the hardships and daily realities of the homeowners they served, such as occurred when Leviathan Bank failed to recognize the death of David Sanchez's wife.

Individual cases when corporate lenders misplaced a homeowner's
paperwork might seem innocuous, if vexing, annoyances typical of the
workings of modern corporations seeking to maximize profits by relying on automated systems and temporary workers. But when these
bureaucratic failures reach epic proportions, in the millions, a pattern
emerges: they become forms of predatory bureaucracy, a collection of
private-sector bureaucratic techniques aimed to disguise injury as inef-
ficiency, to sidestep transparency, and to extract profits while conceal-
ing these goals within a rhetoric of assistance. Random errors should
reward homeowners and lenders equitably. But in loan modification
bureaucracies, rampant miscalculations typically worked in favor of the
lender—missing files never seemed to erase the debt balances of struggling homeowners, but often lost track of the mortgage installments
they had already made.

These predatory bureaucracies are not botched attempts to build
Weberian rational corporations akin to the corporations of the 1960s and
1970s but instead represent a new Wall Street–driven incarnation of
bureaucracy: predatory finance in the guise of private-sector efficiency. In
The Utopia of Rules: On Technology, Stupidity, and the Secret Joys of Bureaucracy,
David Graeber offhandedly suggests the term *predatory bureaucracy* when
outlining his vision of "total bureaucratization" as the "gradual fusion of
public and private power into a single entity, rife with rules and regula-
tions whose ultimate purpose is to extract wealth in the form of profits."[4]
While this is nothing new—Marxists have long pointed out the collusion
of government and private-sector bureaucracies in the service of capitalism—Graeber shows how today these links are intensified and disguised
even further. Here I develop Graeber's passing notion of predatory
bureaucracy to argue that corporate lenders seized tens of millions of

American homes by recasting an act of political violence as a technical and bureaucratic one.

I rely on the notion of predation, rather than mere profit-seeking, to mark a departure from postwar forms of industrial capitalism informed by a Protestant ethic, a move toward a Wall Street financial model. As David Harvey argues, this wave of financialization emerging after the mid-1970s has been exceptionally predatory in style, with its "stock promotions and market manipulations; Ponzi schemes and corporate fraud; asset stripping through mergers and acquisitions; the promotion of levels of debt incumbency that reduce whole populations, even in the advanced capitalist countries, to debt peonage."[5] My theory of predatory bureaucracy links the bureaucratic mechanisms of mortgage modifications to the forms of predatory lending and financialization that initiated the mortgage crisis in the first place.

A focus on predation also distinguishes the rapacity of private-sector corporate bureaucracies from the administrative power of state bureaucracies that have garnered the most anthropological attention. State bureaucracies, as anthropologists have shown, can and do marginalize citizens and funnel resources toward the wealthy. But that is not their stated intent. Analysts surveying state bureaucracies can therefore study how and why systems designed to augment citizen welfare often fail so miserably. In his probe of failing public welfare programs in Northern India, anthropologist Akhil Gupta, for instance, shows how the everyday practices of bureaucracies, along with endemic corruption, perpetuate structural violence against the poor as government programs exacerbate the very inequalities the programs set out to remedy.[6] In contrast, the predatory bureaucracies of corporate lenders are openly profit maximizing, unapologetically funneling capital toward the top. The question then becomes how these bureaucratic systems are seen as fit to deliver public assistance, to do the supposedly neutral work of the state to remedy social and economic inequities. And when they fail to deliver, how do the people most enmeshed in their daily operations make sense of these shortfalls?

IRRATIONAL OUTCOMES

Decisions in mortgage modification cases were often groundless. As new legal rulings emerged and guidelines changed, for example, employees described rapid shifts in how they handled foreclosure proceedings. Wanda Chavez, a Latina loan modification specialist in her mid-forties, described being called into her manager's office with a group of coworkers and instructed to "push applications down the waterfall," the industry term for moving applicants toward foreclosure. The following week, Chavez and her coworkers were corralled again and told that the guidelines determining modification eligibility had changed, and now they were instructed to halt the denials of loan adjustments they had implemented the week before. "I realized that the denials we had pushed through just the week before were probably illegal," Chavez told me. "Even worse, who made that cutoff was totally arbitrary." A TrustWorth Financial employee similarly described how many customers could be kicked out of programs like HAMP for haphazard reasons. "Say a death in the family doesn't apply," he said, "but unemployment does. Well, maybe in some instances a borrower had both happen. Well, they said the wrong thing on the phone call, so they get disqualified."

For Jason Silva, these uneven results of mortgage modification applications presented one of the chief challenges of his job. Jason estimated that well over half the successful modifications he saw were for people "working the system," people who "made out like bandits." He emphasized one particular case in which a couple, both real estate professionals, had purchased a massive estate with a pool on an estuary in Discovery Bay in 2008. They earned $89,000 on their purchase of the home because the husband was the broker. At the time they applied for a mortgage adjustment, their assets included five luxury cars, including a Hummer, and a speedboat. They made only seven payments on the house before they stopped paying, but were still in their home in 2012, banking over $4,000 a month in unpaid mortgage payments before Leviathan Bank awarded them a mortgage modification.

"[The] majority of people who got the mods," Jason told me, "knew how to work the system either by filing bankruptcy or actually knew a high level of how it worked to actually get it." He remembered seeing his first million-dollar mortgage loan approved for a modification. "We got that piece of paper, and I ran around the entire office with it, like, 'Look at this!'" The second million-dollar forgiveness loan Jason came across was a Century 21 real estate agent who had a home on the beach in Maui. He didn't make his payment for two and a half years and received a little over $2 million in principal forgiveness. When asked if the man had a qualifying hardship, Jason said, "The crazy part is you'd go online and visit his website, and he'd be talking about how he took trips to Australia to fish each and every year." In a similar vein, a friend of Jason's who owned a mortgage broker shop bought a McMansion with a custom swimming pool emblazoned with a Versace emblem in the deep end. He quit making his payments for five years and was granted a $250,000 principal forgiveness through a mortgage modification.[7]

In stark contrast, Jason saw some of the most deserving homeowners receive denials for modifications. In one of his toughest cases, Jason tried to reduce the mortgage payments of a sixty-eight-year-old retiree, but his health insurance and Medicare costs prevented him from meeting the standards. Debt-to-income ratios determined whether a homeowner could afford a modified payment, which could total no more than approximately 30 percent of his monthly income. The man had very little debt, only around $200 a month, but had to pay $600 toward Medicare costs. Addressing Jason by name, the man said, "Jason, I go to the store and I have to decide whether I am going to buy groceries or I'm going to buy my medication." "That just broke my heart, holy shit," Jason told me. "So I go to the head of our actual location, I say, 'Ken, what the hell is up with this guy? This is just wrong. What do I suggest for this guy to do? File bankruptcy, go behind so he can do this?' Pretty much his answer was, 'My hands are tied. We can't do anything about it.'"

Jason admitted to smuggling the man's information out of the office and calling him after-hours to encourage him to declare bankruptcy and stay in his home without paying until he was evicted. Jason had done this for a handful of cases. This kind of advice would have resulted in his immediate dismissal, but it also revealed a sense of his personal responsibility, even in a corporate bureaucracy meant to depersonalize and streamline the foreclosure process.

The inequitable outcomes of Leviathan Bank's modifications, which reduced the million-dollar debts of people living in luxury but pushed struggling elderly residents into destitution, chafed against Jason's notion of ethical business practices. "There was no rhyme or reason; nothing correlated," he said. "There was a lot of 'I can't believe this scumbag is getting this. I'm doing this because I know I have to.' [It] didn't make really any sense at all."

Because decisions were cloaked in mystery, when bureaucrats failed to reduce mortgage payments for worthy applicants, no one person could be held responsible. Designed to abdicate responsibility for outcomes and to increase profits, the postcrash bureaucratic systems put in place diffused authority and depersonalized the process of bank seizures. But for employees living and working in the context of widespread foreclosures throughout the Sacramento Valley, the sheen of a lender's objectivity often wore thin. Bureaucracies, as anthropologist Michael Herzfeld has shown in the context of Greek state bureaucracies, contribute to the social production of indifference, obscuring accountability and enabling bureaucrats to remain indifferent to the specific needs of applicants.[8] While this held true for modifications to a certain extent, the wildly illogical results of mortgage programs led employees to question the disastrous outcomes for homeowners and, at times, to feel personal responsibility for their role in applicants' dispossession.

ALGORITHMIC DISPOSSESSION

The heavy reliance on automated systems, which often generated seemingly illogical outcomes, enabled employees to abdicate responsibility for their employers' actions. These systems were designed to enable lending workers to perform their jobs without having access to their employers' internal information that determined how loan modifications were calculated. Even the agents with greater access to a homeowner's file described how management kept them in the dark as to why some homeowners but not others qualified for modifications. In contrast, homeowners were expected to lay bare the most intimate financial details of their lives to often untrained specialists.

Many lending employees described the net present value (NPV) test as a critical aspect of qualifying homeowners for a modification. The specifics of the equation were a guarded secret, but employees often described lenders and loan servicers as having misled homeowners by failing to emphasize that their ability to lower an applicant's payments hinged on profit projections according to the NPV. My respondents knew that the NPV ultimately aimed to increase a lender's profits and to protect against risks. As one worker explained, "On a personal level, I hated that, because it'd be, like, you know you're taking these people's houses away because of the net present value. But from a business standpoint, you can understand the bank was just looking at it, the numbers, and saying … it's more profitable for us to foreclose and sell the house, rather than to collect these mortgage payments." Many employees balanced their impulse for empathy against the knowledge of business practices based on these calculated strategies to maximize profits. For some, a kind of double consciousness developed in which employees learned to see things through what one respondent called a "business view."

The guarded algorithmic models used by corporate lenders to determine whether to seize a home reflected a widespread embrace of math-based data models governing a wide array of American institutions, including finance, education, insurance, and criminal justice—often with dubious consequences. In *Weapons of Math Destruction: How Big Data Increases Inequality and Threatens Democracy*, data scientist Cathy O'Neil criticizes how models formalize inequalities and eschew transparency in the process. Opaque and misunderstood, these models are ubiquitous, determining how Americans land a job, serve time in prison, secure health insurance, and gain access to loans.[9] Touting a greater emphasis on fairness and objectivity, these models often rely on data that is always incomplete or reflects ingrained biases. "Models are opinions," O'Neil points out, "embedded in mathematics."

Homeowners in Oak Park or similar low-income communities with high crime rates and lower property values would, for example, be less likely to receive mortgage modifications if a model is trained to decline applicants whose homes have less projected value over time. But the outcome—that black and Latino homeowners are disproportionately denied mortgage assistance—is discriminatory. There is no reason to believe that a resident of Oak Park who has responsibly paid her mortgage for over a decade is more likely to default on a modified payment plan than a white resident in an affluent neighborhood who bought his home as a savvy investment. In fact, the wealthy borrower might be more likely to walk away or strategically default to maximize his profits. If a human employee decided to favor the wealthy white homeowner, there would be recourse to challenge the decision as discriminatory. But when the black box of modeling makes the call, no one is held responsible. The algorithms exist in a universe beyond appeal, as O'Neil points out, deaf to logic, even when there is cause to question the data that fuels their conclusions.

Algorithmic models, O'Neil argues, with their biased assumptions and ensuing collateral damage, are simplifications that cannot substitute for human communication.[10] It is precisely this human connection, the absence of which is endemic within corporate modification bureaucracies, that both lending employees and homeowners craved. Homeowners and the midlevel employees entering their information into the data-processing systems that decided homeowners' fates had a dogged desire to make sense of the irrational denials the models doled out. Frustration reigned at both ends of the telephone line as outcomes failed to comply with common sense. Technological advances in mathematical modeling that enabled financiers to securitize mortgages and bet against them also facilitated the nonsensical outcomes of predatory bureaucracies in the aftermath of the crash, allowing corporate lenders to deny millions of struggling homeowners while abdicating any direct responsibility for the resulting mass dispossessions.

Contrary to homeowners' assumptions, getting a modification did not depend on how "upstanding" a borrower might be, nor were the programs crafted to right the wrongs of subprime lending. Rather, modification decisions were produced by algorithms programmed to make specific, calculated determinations that would maximize earnings for lenders. Government-sponsored modification programs such as HAMP required lenders and loan servicers to calculate if they would yield *more* from receiving modified payments than they would from pursuing foreclosure and, if so, to halt bank seizures. Widespread advertisements for mortgage assistance and the letters lenders sent to homeowners with distressed mortgages used terms such as *help, assistance,* and *qualified borrowers,* when in fact foreclosure decisions were made to profit lenders. Many applicants assumed that compiling the right paperwork, contacting the proper customer service representative, or presenting a more convincing case could save their homes, when in fact the algorithms determining their fate and the employees charged with pushing through these automated processes were programmed to work in the best interest of banks, not homeowners.

SCRUTINY AND SURVEILLANCE

Linda Jones, a white real estate professional in her fifties, humorous and heavyset with cropped, highlighted hair, had not expected to end up in the boiler room of Leviathan Bank. She hailed from an upper-middle-class family in San Diego; her father had been a successful engineer and senior manager at a lucrative firm. As a side business, he built and sold houses as real estate investments. Linda had learned about real estate from her father and for decades had worked for a handful of firms, real estate attorneys, and corporate lenders, including processing mortgage applications for TrustWorth Financial, doing what she described as back-end work. "I wasn't the one that screwed everything up," she told me, contrasting her role with that of her employer. "I was just getting paid by the hour."

Linda's veteran experience gave her, in 2006, the foresight to sell her San Diego house, which she had bought in 1999. Prices were at their peak, but Linda suspected they were unsustainable. "I remember when I went to sell my house," she said. "Someone right down the street had just bought a house. I am, like, 'It's time to get out.' And they are, like, 'No, it's going to keep going up.' They thought I was so foolish. I got a full-price offer on the first day." With the profits from her house, she decided to stop working for two years, but by the time she was ready to get back to work in 2008, the industry had already collapsed.

As Linda experienced a post-middle-class trajectory, she sensed the cognitive dissonance among the realities of the real estate job market, her fear that she would not be able to retire, and her new perception of herself as a downwardly mobile person. She quipped that her father earned a higher salary. Linda's earning power had no doubt been affected by her status as a single mother; she had divorced her husband when her children, now in their early thirties, were small. Even before the collapse of the mortgage industry, Linda had taken out a home equity line of credit and relied largely on credit cards to cover the expenses of food, clothing, and bills. Rather than acknowledging that structural changes within corporate industries had left her more vulnerable, she reconciled herself to her decline by explaining that "if you don't have anything, you work harder and do better." Blaming her own privilege for her financial instability, Linda reasoned, "Sometimes it skips a generation." This view allowed Linda to hold out the hope that her children would do better than she had, but it ran counter to the conventional belief that the social, financial, and cultural capital of one's childhood guaranteed a solid standing later in life.

In 2009, Linda moved to the Sacramento Valley, where living costs were cheaper than in San Diego. Facing a jobless landscape, she connected with a temporary employment agency that sent her, along with over one hundred unemployed former real estate employees, to work for Leviathan Bank as loan modification specialists. Leviathan indiscriminately hired anyone with any real estate experience, no matter how suspect, hiring workers sight unseen at $24 an hour. Encouraged by the pay rate—temp jobs typically garnered $15 an hour—Linda was soon dismayed by the rigid work environment. Staffers had to sort through reams of paperwork from applicants. Managers held staffers, for example, to a strict schedule, closely tracking breaks and arrival and departure times. Employees were prohibited from talking to one another or using their personal phones. People were fired daily for failing to comply with a long list of management rules. "After the first week, there were ten [new workers] gone," Linda said. "Like, if you were five minutes late, the second day you're done, bye-bye. I remember there was a gentleman that had cerebral palsy. You know how it is difficult to walk, and it was a long way from the parking lot to get inside, to get to the cafeteria, to get out to your breaks. He was trying to work around the first day, but you know he had a hard time, and he wasn't there the next day." The situation reflected the realities of call-center labor more than the stable, bureaucratic corporate hierarchies previously associated with lenders, and being surveilled and strictly monitored offended Linda's middle-class sensibilities.

The daily work routines often struck Linda as an elaborate hoax. She described unending online compliance training sessions and time wasted in endless team-building exercises where employees talked about their favorite foods and determined their personality types—do you communicate better one-on-one or in a group? (Linda discovered she preferred one-on-one.) But outside these monitored activities, interactions with coworkers were highly regulated. Because strict rules prevented employees from talking among themselves or using their phones, most sat in their cubicles and visited a handful of approved internet sites. "In retrospect, the job basically was just ridiculous," she said. "I think that they were in such hot water, [Leviathan Bank], that they needed to throw people and resources at the problem so that they can say, 'Look, we're starting to solve this problem. We've hired all these people.'" Linda imagined interrogating her bosses at Leviathan Bank, "'What were you doing with us down there, like, shuffling these papers around?' I mean seriously, I think they just threw them all up in the air. I think that was a part of their move. They kept reassigning, and then it was somebody else's turn."

This uneven balance of power characterized the relationship between institutions and individuals, as lenders subjected homeowners (and the boiler-room lending employees who sorted through their endless stream of documents) to intensified surveillance while also barring them from access to information. At Leviathan Bank and similar corporate lenders, postcrash, bottom-floor employees and delinquent borrowers were under intensifying forms of scrutiny, whereas financial institutions themselves enjoyed deregulation, wider latitude to operate, and increasing impenetrability. Similarly, employees in the collections department at Trust-Worth Financial detailed how the company strictly monitored their calls with homeowners, with once-a-week feedback sessions. Employee bonuses were based on call performance; any deviations from protocol threatened one's job security. Employees were evaluated on the dollars collected per hour and the average call handling time, or how long each agent spent with a customer. The system was structured so as to deter employees from engaging in the lengthy process of going over detailed financial information, which could have resulted in offering sounder advice. Homeowners were not the only formerly middle-class people now subjected to supervisory judgment through the application process; now, employees like Linda Jones, who were unaccustomed to the patronizing and controlling environment of call centers, found their interactions with Leviathan cementing their place within what had become a downward trajectory through the American class system.

Employees tasked with implementing what many described as nonsensical procedures struggled with staggering unemployment and industry reorganization. Even if workers had, precrash, followed a more conservative career path selling loans for a leading lender like Leviathan Bank rather than high-risk subprime products, this caution did not protect them from financial insecurity after the crash. This condition often piqued their sympathy for homeowners, but it also put lending employees in a position in which their livelihoods depended on their ability to follow the bureaucratic rules dictating loan modifications, even if they disagreed with their employers' approaches and the outcomes for homeowners. High-profile corporate lenders, facing widespread mortgage defaults and deficits, were downsizing. Layoffs plagued the ranks of even senior managers. Many lending employees lost their own homes to foreclosure and suffered long-term unemployment, positioning them in circumstances similar to those of homeowners seeking modifications.

The declining career trajectories of temporary staffers like Linda Jones and midlevel employees like Jason Silva influenced their perspectives, now that many industry professionals, similar to the homeowners they serviced, faced obstacles to traditional forms of middle-class security. The downsizing and outsourcing to temporary labor forces that characterized Leviathan Bank's mortgage-modification centers influenced how employees interpreted the social obligations between creditor and debtor after the crash. Corporate modification bureaucracies symbolized a broader historical trend in which traditional corporations, long known for stable long-term employment and the possibility of climbing the corporate ladder, unraveled as Wall Street investment firms, with their concomitant values, flooded into the market.

Wall Street financial institutions, as anthropologist Karen Ho has observed, seek short-term profits at any cost and, in doing so, dismantle corporate businesses built for long-term sustainability. Along the way, the process undermines job possibilities for employees. Ho is almost nostalgic for the corporate bureaucracies that preceded this change, showing how earlier organizations offered job stability, substantial benefits, and a clear path for advancement. The dismantling of these massive corporate administrations, Ho points out, disproportionately affected employees from working-class backgrounds and from ethnic communities that had been excluded from elite networks of financiers. Layoffs began just as outsiders began to make inroads into the corporate sector in the 1980s, when restructuring began.[11] Downsizing, once seen as a tragic loss of jobs, became a fashionable way to increase stock values for shareholders. Ho shows how managers at Wall Street firms learned to embrace their own layoffs as a natural part of the downsizing process, with the understanding that they would often be laid off and then rehired at another company. But lower- and midlevel employees would struggle with long-term unemployment and poverty.

RECIPROCITY SPURS AFFECTIVE LABOR

Paul Williams, a white midwesterner in his late twenties with a wiry frame and metal-rimmed glasses and a gentle demeanor, worked for TrustWorth Financial in a collections department tasked with collecting delinquent payments from homeowners and, if they failed to pay, then prequalifying them for modifications and sending their cases to the mortgage modification department. He had abandoned a short-lived teaching career in Asia and, with no experience in finance or mortgaging, was hired to work in the Spanish-language division of collections at TrustWorth Financial. If Paul could not recoup a borrower's scheduled payments, he would then refer the homeowner to another department to determine eligibility for a loan modification. The fact that a customer's first contact came from a collections agent suggests that TrustWorth tried to steer homeowners who qualified for reduced mortgage payments away from modifications.

If Paul failed to collect funds from a customer, he then helped the homeowner compile the documents to submit for a loan modification. After a few months, Paul noticed that clients he had prequalified for loan modifications would reappear in collections because their modifications had been denied for insufficient paperwork. "At first," he said, "I was very bright-eyed about it all, and I thought, 'You know, I'm helping people keep their homes.' But it was very demoralizing, because you knew a lot of them were getting set up for failure." Homeowners, he told me, would be rejected for loan modifications because they missed one pay stub in one hundred pages of faxed documents. He channeled his frustrations into phone calls with customers, meticulously walking them through the process of preparing paperwork for modification applications. Paul pointed out that if TrustWorth was just servicing the loan, the actual company that owned the mortgage would often allow only one or two application cycles per homeowner. Homeowners might be denied a modification based on errors or missing paperwork and then lose any chance to reapply.

Paul described how the job took an emotional toll on him and he became clinically depressed:

> To be honest, I got depressed from the job. I started taking Zoloft, because I was just, yeah, I was really down and out during those years, because I looked at all these people's stories and I really wanted to help them. But I just couldn't work the system.... I remember one phone call where a mother called and her son had just committed suicide, and I had to kind of walk her through it.... Sometimes you're the psychiatrist to people. Another lady, ... her husband had cheated on her and walked out on her, and she was, you know, trying to figure out what to do with her four kids and where to move and what to do with the house. And so, I mean, there were situations like that that I did take home with me.

Paul's lament that he could not "work the system" to help distressed homeowners draws on the same metaphor of the system that Jason Silva used to describe wealthy industry insiders who "worked the system" to achieve mortgage modifications. The ethos of who could work the system referred to one's ability to navigate specific bureaucratic techniques and also suggested a broader social context of inequalities. The notion of working the system reflects a symptom of what anthropologists Jean Comaroff and John Comaroff identify as "millennial capitalism," a pernicious manifestation of neoliberalism that foments predatory forms of economic activity, exacerbating inequalities while rendering class distinctions difficult to articulate.[12]

Like Paul, many employees felt the emotional strain of failing to help struggling homeowners, resulting in high levels of burnout and turnover. The employees who had the most success, Paul explained, were the coldest, with the "hardest shells," those who could separate themselves from the clients entirely. But this ideal proved hard to meet. Despite institutional measures aimed to depersonalize and render opaque the process of collections and mortgage appeals, collections agents and modification specialists working for big banks often told me stories of becoming sympathetic to homeowners. Lending employees mired in the often-heartrending details of homeowners' cases found the work emotionally challenging. When I asked Paul if he resented homeowners who were frequently angry at him on the phone, he surprised me by saying that he could understand their anger, because what was happening to them was tragic; Paul felt they "needed someone to absorb it." This made his job exhausting, but he felt it was a small effort on his part that might alleviate some profound suffering for them. This type of affective labor is often underestimated in scholarly renderings of bureaucrats who are seen as categorically indifferent to their clients' cases, a defining feature of disinterested functionaries. But in the emotionally loaded postcrash world of debt collections, modification denials, and looming evictions, transference and affective labor abound.

Paul criticized institutional measures that distanced homeowners from lending employees. If homeowners were missing documents for a loan modification, most of the time they would receive one reminder phone call on their voicemail. The message, however, usually did not explain what document was missing, but instead only instructed them to call back. When homeowners returned the call, they would have to answer a series of questions before the agent could discuss their case. Agents had to follow a script, what Paul called a "mini-Miranda," with a list of points that had to be covered. Making matters worse, by the time homeowners contacted the lender, most often their modification application had already been denied. "It was very selfish," Paul told me, "reading off of a script when you're dealing with people, and they're trying to talk about their situation financially, and why they can't pay their mortgage.... It wasn't really good for building rapport with people."

Paul's depression lifted once he left collections for loan origination, where he was approving new loans for clients with high credit scores. In contrast to the loan modification system, in loan origination, customer service representatives would go to great lengths, calling, emailing, and incessantly following up to acquire the necessary documents to complete the loan. "You can fax it, you can email it—any which way you please," Paul said. "We'll send you umpteen reminders before we deny your loan. We'll go out of our way to approve it. That's because that's where the money was." Linda Jones, the temporary employee at Leviathan Bank, had a similar view, describing her precrash work for Trust-Worth Financial in loan origination: "Originations is such a more positive thing. People are getting loans; people are, you know, they're making money. It's just positive, you know? Everybody in modifications is just miserable."

The weaponizing of bureaucracy for financial gain by big banks becomes even more pronounced when we compare mortgage modifications with these employees' experiences in mortgage sales. Whereas a loan originator would have at most twenty-five to thirty loans to oversee at a time, loan modification specialists juggled over a hundred clients simultaneously. In loan origination departments, the computer systems that tracked files worked seamlessly. That lenders could design and implement bureaucratic systems that successfully sold mortgages suggests that the mistakes of loan modification departments within the same corporations were profit driven rather than accidental. The lost paperwork, dropped calls, failure to invest in adequate technology, reliance on temporary and inexperienced workers, and general bureaucratic runaround that characterized loan modification systems point toward the use of administrative violence by the mortgage industry to extract profits from the most vulnerable borrowers. By convincing applicants that they were responsible for qualifying for mortgage assistance, predatory corporate bureaucracies induced concrete damages among millions of borrowers while abdicating responsibility for these losses and leading borrowers to feel they were caught in a system beyond human control.

Many employees viewed the insistence on faxing paperwork for modification applications as a way to slow down the process for agents overwhelmed by the number of customers they were required to manage and to create more work for the homeowner as a deterrent. While the lenders claimed that faxes were necessary for security reasons, employees often doubted this reasoning. One collection specialist at a prominent lender told me, "They said it was for security reasons, but I honestly think it was just because the loan processors had so much on their plates. But it was a burden on the borrowers, because they had to find a fax machine. I mean, this was already in the 2000s, you know? Who uses fax?"

Similarly, Jeff Talbot, a white entry-level employee at TrustWorth Financial, revealed that during an early phase of the modification program, he was instructed to tell customers that a loan processor would call them back, all the while knowing that any return contact was rare.

> When I first started in 2010, the system was different.... We just told them what to send in, and we told them that they would get a call back. Well, that system never happened, because there were so many people applying and so many people prequalifying that there were, you know, so many collection agents and so many borrowers that there weren't enough loan processors. They couldn't hire them fast enough. So, there was, you know, a crazy amount of loans for each loan processor that they had to try to process and qualify. You know, if you have a pipeline of a hundred loans, you're going to be happy if you can kick one back. So, I mean, they were kicking people back all the time. But then those people couldn't prequalify again.

A loan modification processor at Leviathan Bank told a similar story, explaining that confronted with a hundred new cases, he and his coworkers were unable to return calls. He admitted, "[Homeowners] would reach out later, and you'd have a hundred new people you'd have to contact, so delete that message and you have to ignore it. Just not enough time in the day to manage all of it."

The industry language universally adopted by corporate lending employees with whom I spoke was telling in this regard. Jeff used the term *warm transfer* to describe how the systems changed, explaining that when he started, they didn't speak to the new agent receiving the case before transferring a call. A warm transfer allows a customer service representative to relay the details of a homeowner's case to the new representative to provide continuity and to smooth a client's transition from one department to another. The absence of warm transfers, to Jeff, symbolized the inefficiencies and misrepresentations built into the mortgage modification system. This call-center lingo implies a degree of intimacy and human contact between lending employees and homeowners and correlates assistance for homeowners with a closeness to qualified representatives who could shepherd their cases through. This language persisted even as lenders took measures to prevent employees from becoming attached to specific homeowners for whom they might advocate. These very procedures suggested the potential for an implicit tie between homeowners and lending employees that had to be managed and contained with bureaucratic techniques.

Not all lending employees, however, were sympathetic to homeowners. One staffer I interviewed, Rick Smith, a white, thirty-year-old loan officer at TrustWorth Financial, suggested that homeowners often misinterpreted the meetings and phone calls as an invitation to "unload" too much personal information. He disliked having to give homeowners his real name, labeling it an unnecessary breach of privacy. As with the customer service representatives who resented the personal tone of homeowners' hardship letters, the ideal customer for Rick presented only the information he needed to process a loan modification appeal. As I spent more time with him, it became clear that his financial struggles were influencing his perspective of customers. He and his wife had bought a condominium at the height of the market, and at the time of our interview it was worth less than half of what they owed on it. They had decided to keep making payments rather than walk away. Rick described it as a moral decision and often commented that he and his wife just counted the number of years they had until the home was paid off rather than focusing on the money that they were losing.

Although lending employees like Rick Smith remained unsympathetic to homeowners defaulting on their mortgages, like his more sympathetic coworkers he imagined a direct tie between lenders and borrowers. In his view, homeowners had a duty to repay their mortgages and to shoulder the burdens of decreasing returns *because* of their long-standing moral and economic relationship with banks. These competing approaches to homeownership after the crash share a view that an implicit social contract underlies mortgaging—for sympathetic employees, it is lenders who owe borrowers mutual assistance in the aftermath of suspect lending practices; for unsympathetic agents, it is borrowers who owe lenders despite widespread economic upheaval.

INEFFICIENCIES OF PROFIT

Scholars and policy makers often assume that the private sector offers a respite from the chronic inefficiencies of government bureaucracy. Yet, employees most familiar with corporate modification administrations described them as plagued by cultures of dysfunction that, at times, bordered on corruption. Publicly funded but privately administered enterprises delivered assistance ineffectively, and conflicts of interest abounded. Because the government had outsourced publicly funded loan modifications to private lenders and loan servicers, homeowners often had no choice but to work with the very companies that had saddled them with suspect loans or had bought their securitized mortgages in the hopes of profiting from high-risk mortgages. Once on the phone with a lender, homeowners were often steered into lenders' proprietary loan modification systems rather than into government ones like HAMP, even though these private programs had less favorable terms and higher fees. In other instances, modification options were hidden from homeowners who would have qualified, as lenders' collections agents would contact them to recuperate payments on mortgages that homeowners could no longer afford. Underhanded financial advice, profit driven by design but framed in terms of "helping" homeowners, was rampant.

A reliance on temporary workers as a means to maximize profits meant that inexperienced workers often provided incorrect information to homeowners. Forbearance programs, for example, were temporary measures that allowed homeowners to stop making mortgage payments or to make lower payments for a specified period. But homeowners often failed to realize that the balance would be added to their future payments and their credit score would be negatively affected by participating in the plan. Some homeowners whom I interviewed believed that the new lower payments were permanent and that they had qualified for a government loan modification, only to find out months later that their payments were higher than before and that they could no longer refinance because they now had bad credit. Jeff told me that he would enter a customer's information and then enthusiastically tell the client that he or she had won a forbearance. "When I came off the training classroom, I didn't know anything," he said. "So, I'd get to the screen after twenty minutes, and I would say, 'Ooh, congrats! You got a forbearance!' and I didn't really know what that meant. 'Oh, you only have to pay $200 a month,' and that's where the conversation ended. That was terrible, because it set them up for complete disaster."

The persistent illusion of private-sector efficiency, however, allows corporate players to dominate the dispersal of public assistance and aid. Locating mortgage assistance in the private sector aligns with a broader U.S. trend of privatizing and profiting from disaster relief, the trend journalist Naomi Klein identifies as "disaster capitalism," in which corporations, mercenaries, and even some nongovernmental organizations and humanitarian organizations increasingly profit from crises as government contracts are funneled through the private sector.[13] Only a minuscule fraction of the $317 billion TARP bailout program reached homeowners, whereas corporate lenders including Bank of America and Citibank received loans for over $40 billion from the program. The dominance of these corporate players, who often bid for U.S. government contracts in disasters occurring around the world, strongly suggests that only a tiny percentage of the billions of dollars of aid, flowing either through domestic bailouts or international USAID, reaches the people in whose name funding is approved.

Hybrid forms of government-corporate bureaucracy, in which taxpayer funds support private-sector enterprises to deliver services and reap profits, were disorganized due to their profit-driven nature.[14] Analyzing how private contractors failed to disperse federal funds to homeowners after Hurricane Katrina, anthropologist Vincanne Adams describes the devastating shortcomings of the Road Home Program, a state-run plan meant to compensate residents for homes destroyed or damaged by the storm.[15] Louisiana's government received billions of dollars in federal funding and contracted with a subsidiary of a consulting firm, ICF International, which was tasked with managing the recovery funds meant to help homeowners.[16] As with mortgage assistance programs after the crash, with post-Katrina assistance New Orleans residents faced lengthy delays, rampant errors, and miscalculations that stranded them without the resources they needed to rebuild. Underpayment and denials were typical because ICF implemented, as Adams notes, "procedures for accounting and distribution that placed corporate interests above the grant recipients."[17] More than three years after the storm, ICF had failed to disburse nearly two-thirds of the funding, roping homeowners into endless bureaucratic battles that obstructed relief efforts, while ICF corporate executives reaped multimillion-dollar bonuses.[18] Adams aptly sees these outcomes as a direct result of the "inefficiencies of profit," in which profit-driven systems cause disastrous results for people those systems claim to help.[19] Like the Hurricane Katrina housing recovery program, HAMP funneled government relief funds through private for-profit companies, creating what Adams describes in New Orleans as "privately organized, publicly funded bureaucratic failures."

Many employees like Jason Silva, Linda Jones, and Paul Williams attributed the failures of mortgage assistance programs to benign bureaucratic incompetence, as I had at the start of my research. Jason attributed the botched modification applications to an outdated technological infrastructure that Leviathan Bank—what he saw as an "old large bank"—had imported from preexisting collections systems, repurposing technology once used to collect late mortgage payments to process mortgage modifications. Corporate dinosaurs, he surmised, were slow to change, unwilling to adapt to the new demands of mortgage modifications. After leaving Leviathan Bank, Jason Silva had also worked for a smaller Sacramento firm, Obsidian Financial*, that he believed had scammed homeowners, promising to shepherd their cases through to modifications for a fee. Employees were instructed to lie to homeowners about the potential for modifications. (David Sanchez, coincidentally, had been victimized by an Obsidian Financial scheme.) Jason contrasted the two experiences, mapping a continuum from the "scumbags" who participated in outright fraud (Obsidian) to the clueless and incompetent corporate cogs who refused to update their computer systems (Leviathan). More than once, Jason described explaining this to his friends and relatives who accused corporate lenders of malfeasance. "There is no conspiracy," he would tell them. "It's just idiots."

These views perfectly capture the power of predatory bureaucracies to conceal forms of administrative violence as inefficacy. In some instances, the practices of large banks mirror the scams and schemes of small firms like Obsidian Financial. For example, in a civil lawsuit filed in Massachusetts against Bank of America, employees claimed they were instructed to lie to homeowners, encouraged to meet foreclosure quotas, and rewarded with bonuses for pushing people into foreclosure. The former employees recounted, for example, being instructed to mislead borrowers by telling them that their records were incomplete and by purposefully holding financial documents for thirty days, at which point homeowners would have to reapply with updated information.[20]

Perhaps more pernicious were the muted forms of fraud and disregard Jason described at his own employer, Leviathan Bank; they were more dangerous precisely because they were camouflaged as well-intentioned ineptitude. In Jason's account, there was no one to blame. Even his immediate manager, a thirty-year veteran at Leviathan who worked his way up from a position as a teller, often commiserated with Jason about the illogical ramifications of mortgage modification denials. They were on the same side, the side against corporate bureaucracy—even as they turned the gears that ran the machine.

Employees openly acknowledged that the outcomes made no sense, and some even criticized the results as unjust, but they universally felt there was nothing anyone could do about it. Their stories revealed their sense of powerlessness to guide or resist what they described in varying contexts as "the system"—in concrete terms a bureaucratic structure but symbolically a broader reality that supported and normalized it. This rhetoric of "the system" externalized the responsibility for employees' actions, reflecting what anthropologist Jim Ferguson describes as an "anti-politics machine"—the power of administrative techniques and bureaucracy to obscure the political nature of their effects.[21] Whereas dispossessed homeowners were more likely to entertain the notion that the waves of foreclosures were purposefully orchestrated by lenders and loan servicers undertaking a massive land grab, most lending employees felt that mere ineptitude was to blame.

One could argue that the mortgage modification bureaucracies of corporate lenders embody Max Weber's vision of the rational, instrumental order of Western capitalism. Witness the orderly arrangements of endless cubicles, a structure developed to promote debt repayment, with strict hierarchies of workers and tasks divided by floor. Jason's objection to his inability to bend the rules to help deserving homeowners would seem a textbook illustration of Weber's iron cage, where the rules go too far and limit human freedoms in the service of efficiency. But modification bureaucracies of big banks merely mime the empty rituals of an earlier Weberian bureaucratic form without replicating them. These bureaucracies are in fact irrational and inefficient, failing to deliver mortgage adjustments that would allow people to honor their debts—one of the defining features of the Protestant ethos of Western capitalism according to a Weberian view. In an even starker departure from the industrial forms of capitalism Weber described, it is the ineptitude rather than the efficiency of these bureaucratic systems that serves capital. Predatory bureaucracies embody a postindustrial embrace of speculative capitalism that erodes trustworthiness to the point of blatant fraud, abandoning any aura of the Protestant ethic that informed its industrial precursor.

Robust profits, however, could be had in less detrimental ways. As David Sanchez pointed out, Leviathan Bank would have made nearly $100,000 in interest over the thirty-year life of his mortgage had it granted him a modification, but it could profit *more quickly* by foreclosing on and selling his home. Had the social value of keeping families in their homes, children in their schools, and neighborhoods together been quantified and factored into the net present value test, the outcomes of the foreclosure epidemic could have been radically different. For instance, Adam Byrne, a biracial white and Korean senior vice president of lending at a large California credit union, described sitting down with a committee of fellow employees and reviewing distressed mortgages on a case-by-case basis. He personally knew many of the homeowners and their families facing evictions and detailed the measures the credit union took to "do everything [it] could to keep people in their homes." Like the corporate employees, Adam described the emotional strain of implementing foreclosures when there were no other options. But his stress was mitigated by his view that he maintained personal relationships with homeowners; foreclosures were an absolute last resort, rather than the inevitable result of mismanagement, automated algorithms, short-term profit seeking, and error, as was often the case in corporate lending.

Failed modification programs erected after the crash expanded the scope of lenders' and loan servicers' suspect business practices instead of departing from them and offering restitution for the misdeeds of subprime lending. These workers' perspectives, while informed by abstract ideals about mortgage lending, arose most concretely from the daily realities of dissatisfying jobs and rapid downsizing in their industry. Like homeowners, many employees in the Sacramento Valley assumed that a lending relationship ideally entailed a certain degree of transparency, fairness, and mutuality, much like the patron-client relationship

Jason Silva described in his grandfather's grocery store. They therefore struggled with the distancing mechanisms, such as rigid scripts and call monitoring, implemented by lenders and loan services to streamline foreclosures and surveil employees and homeowners alike. Likewise, employees criticized the understaffing and deficient infrastructure that created chaos and wrongful evictions for some homeowners and allowed others to use insider knowledge to work the system. The profit-driven motives of the lenders seemed antithetical to the spirit of government-mandated assistance programs established to right the wrongs of industry carelessness and lack of oversight.

Most employees assigned to collect money from homeowners falling behind on their mortgages felt they should be able to help struggling homeowners or at least offer greater transparency than the ecologies of postcrash finance allowed. Bureaucratic techniques and algorithmic standards aimed to prevent preferential treatment and nepotism. But the practices chafed against homeowners' desires for individual attention and created massive inefficiencies that raised questions for lending employees about the fairness of the modification process. Lending employees detailed feelings of guilt and helplessness, even describing, at times, bouts of depression. The fact that sentiments of mutuality and connection persisted despite these bureaucratic structures and techniques indicates the deep embeddedness of the contemporary American notion that borrowers and lenders share responsibility for debts during times of widespread financial stress.

Those working inside corporate bureaucracies, like Jason Silva, and those living through the deleterious effects of their errors and biases, like David Sanchez, were united in the sense that Wall Street firms, with their drive toward ever-greater speculative debt finance, had restructured the possibilities of their now post-middle-class life trajectories. Of the employees who stayed in lending, many became acculturated to the profit-minded decisions of their corporate employers—the choice to use outdated technology or to decide foreclosures based on NPV rather than on hardship, for instance—and came to believe that these were the inevitable outcomes of "doing business." Questionable practices and millions of suspect home seizures, however, would not have qualified as "doing business" even within the profit-driven corporations of the 1960s and 1970s. Workers in corporate bureaucracies, many of them post-middle-class subjects, indicated feeling powerless over the very decisions they were generating and implementing, but many learned to accept what initially had struck them as unjust and unfair.

CHAPTER FIVE

We Shall Not Be Moved

The Shifting Moral Economies of Debt Refusal

After Leviathan Bank demanded David Sanchez's wife's signature on his modification paperwork months after she had passed away, David described "giving up." Giving up, however, did not entail capitulating, packing his boxes, and handing over the keys to Leviathan. Instead, it meant squatting in his home until he was evicted. Detailing his decision to stay in his house without paying, David told me, "I start reading in the paper the banks are foreclosing on people who were never behind or got into the mod program. There's billions of dollars not being used to help people. I'm sorry [but] people need help; they don't need excuses."

Nearly a year after Karen's death, David was still isolating himself, but had settled into a new routine without Karen, a daily life that included standing up to Leviathan's eviction threats. He had laughed off the recommendation of a Leviathan mortgage modification agent to find a roommate to increase his monthly income, telling the agent, "How can I get a roommate when I might get evicted any day?" Sitting in his living room surrounded by his cats and musical instruments, David insisted that the failures of mortgage modification bureaucracies were political ones. "The bank got bailed out," he told me, "and the money they were given was to help people. I mean they're raking it in on interest and whatever. And then the more I read, I find out it's not just America they did it to, but the whole world is in the same fix and the bankers are smiling the whole way. It's their business, their rules."

David believed that banks were reaping profits by collecting insurance money on foreclosed homes, piling on government funds from assistance programs, and then trying to squeeze homeowners for payments. His view, however, did not amount to a wholesale critique of capitalism. David emphasized this point: "I mean, there's nothing wrong with putting a deal together and making a few dollars. But [banks are] putting a deal together and raping somebody over and over and over again. How many times," he asked, "do big banks need to get paid?" But even with his feeling that corporate lenders had bamboozled homeowners, the initial decision to refuse to pay his mortgage hadn't come naturally to David. "I talked to my tax man and he said just stay a year or two and just walk away," David explained. "That didn't make sense to me. But I'm still here."

"Why didn't it make sense to you?" I asked.

"I was still believing that having credit was a good thing. It was a point of being a man, being honest, being a true American. Yes, I am a veteran. And that was all just built into our feelings and our thoughts that you do the right thing. I'm a straight arrow—I'm not broken and I'm straight. I'm a real person. I'm honest."

David expresses a markedly postwar view, one that David Harvey attributes to what he calls the New Generation that emerged from the populist, state-driven economic policies of the mid-twentieth century.[1] American manhood was shaped by time in military service and on the factory floor but also enabled by state-driven policies and widespread union membership that created an environment in which a working-class family could live on one breadwinner's salary. Debt repayment represented the honor intrinsic to being "a man" and a "real American," as people internalized a Protestant ethic of hard work. Homeownership, as evidence of one's ability to provide, was central to this masculinist subjectivity. As David said, "The truth that we were fed was hard work and you get your home and life goes on." But for David, it seemed that life, especially the life he had imagined with Karen, had abruptly ended. Now he puttered around his home, with the ghosts of dreams and selves deferred, waiting in defiance for the day Leviathan Bank dared evict him.

David articulated a post-middle-class awakening to what he called the "new rules" of debt repayment, in which lenders and borrowers no longer harbored a moral duty to repay—a view shared by a striking majority of my respondents. Confrontations with obtuse predatory bureaucracies radicalized many homeowners in the Sacramento Valley, inadvertently inspiring them to abandon debts in ways most would have considered unimaginable before the crash. Like David, Darren Lewis, the computer programmer, had never missed a credit card payment but eventually used mortgage modification delays to remain in his home for over a year without paying. Rachel Leibrock, the journalist who fell victim to dual tracking, titled her article about the experience "Default!"—at once a description of her experience and a call to homeowners to walk away from mortgages after suffering the abuses of corporate lenders. Judy Zaro, the retired government worker, had initially scoffed at falling behind on her payments but came to condone the practice of walking away from an underwater mortgage as a justifiable financial decision. Other homeowners engaged in more controversial forms of protest such as destroying homes before evictions and even threatening suicide, acts that inspired some ambivalence and even criticism among homeowners. Less common but equally significant were homeowners who participated in collective social movements to demonstrate against corporate lenders and the lasting damage done by widespread foreclosures. Homeowners, as well as some lending employees, described these acts as a mimetic response to lenders' violations of the implicit social contracts of postwar American debt ties; that is, lenders' acts of disloyalty revealed new rules that upended reciprocity and repayment in the Sacramento Valley.

WALKING AWAY

Taking David's advice, I drove out to meet Jim Foster, David's best friend for almost twenty years. Jim's rental home stood in a quiet, cookie-cutter suburb in northern Sacramento. His cul-de-sac backed up against an expanse of empty grassland, the last page in a frenzied chapter of precrash development. I walked up Jim's driveway, squeezing past his white Chevy pickup. Homemade signs Jim had printed out hung in his window and were taped to his door: "No Solicitation. DO NOT DISTURB. Disturbed Enough." and "BEWARE: Gun Owner Inside." Jim, a towering, heavyset Italian American Vietnam veteran in his sixties, had tan skin, short dark hair, and a deep laugh. He described himself as a "hippie Republican," the kind of socially progressive libertarian common in the rural enclaves of Northern California, and he was partial to jeans and oversized T-shirts boasting fantastical images of coyotes. A similar Native American motif was threaded throughout his house—dream catchers and blankets he had collected at powwows. He had no children, but he and his wife, Brenda, had adopted nine stray cats, who wandered the house with entitlement, perching on shelves and on the headrest of Jim's well-loved La-Z-Boy recliner.

In 2007, Jim and Brenda, a midlevel county employee, refinanced the house Brenda had owned for twenty-two years. They used the equity to pay off their credit cards and make improvements in preparation for selling the house to take advantage of rising home prices. "We're not the kind of people that go into something without knowing what we're doing," Jim said. After the crash, their mortgage was nearly double the value of their home. They tried to modify their mortgage with GMAC. By that point, eight of their neighbors were also facing mortgage default. Soon, foreclosure dominated the everyday chitchat on the block. One woman had already defaulted, bringing down property values even more and igniting the ire of the remaining residents. Her default started a "cascade" on the block, as Jim described it, with two more homeowners defaulting after spending a year trying to secure a modification. A few others filed bankruptcy. One neighbor, Jim said, "just bailed," without even applying for a mortgage modification. The last holdout on the block eventually agreed to a short sale and moved into a trailer. "Even if people could afford to make payments," Jim said, "the equity was gone, and walking away made more sense." After four failed modification attempts, Jim and Brenda decided on a short sale, marking the first time they had ever defaulted on a debt; before that moment, they had never even missed a payment.

Like David, Jim seemed to be confronting a new world order in which the values and life trajectories of previous generations were suddenly illegible in a financialized world. Jim, now on disability because of his arthritis, described his childhood as solidly middle class. His father, a steelworker who had fought in World War II, went to college on the GI Bill and began a career as an industrial engineer building factories. Jim's parents had purchased one of the first American tract homes, near Disneyland in 1961, a suburban development that served as the epitome of the postwar American Dream. After serving in Vietnam, Jim had enjoyed a career working for the county and had spent some years as a financial manager. Military service, factory and government work, and homeownership had shaped Jim's vision of an upright moral citizenship that included debt repayment. His views about the moral valence of mortgage default begin to shift, however, as his neighborhood disintegrated before his eyes. Good, hardworking neighbors whom Jim and Brenda had known for decades—a corrections officer, two teachers, a firefighter, and a handful of government employees—felt that the loss of home equity was not worth the financial sacrifice, and many decided to walk away. Jim initially chafed at this idea but came to see it as a fair response to the unfair practices of corporate lenders. "It was all political," Jim said of the foreclosure epidemic. "The government and the banks made out."

Jim and Brenda sold their camping trailer to fund a move to Oregon, where housing and taxes were cheaper than in Northern California. Brenda would commute five hours back to Sacramento for work, staying with friends during the week and heading home for the weekends. "Before," Jim told me, "the worst thing you could do was declare bankruptcy or lose your house. Now it's about self-preservation and survival. About taking care of your family. Morals have changed. I was embarrassed at first, didn't tell anyone in my family until the short sale was done. But now I don't feel that way. This is not the country I grew up in, not the country I went to Nam for." Jim grew up believing that fighting for America was honorable, the right thing to do. Now, it seemed, he was endlessly fighting against it.

In Jim's neighborhood, increasing openness to strategic default—when a homeowner makes a financial decision to walk away from an underwater mortgage he can theoretically afford to pay—reflected regional and national trends. According to legal scholar Brent White, who studied hundreds of cases of strategic default across the United States, homeowners' feelings of hopelessness and anger at lenders and the government were primary forces driving them to disregard preexisting feelings of shame in abandoning mortgage debts when they could afford to pay.[2] Political pundits and policy makers often described strategic default as a moral hazard capable of undermining the stability of financial institutions and the national economy.[3] Mainstream media narratives derided homeowners who defaulted on mortgages, often reflecting the views of policy scholars, government officials, and mortgage industry professionals who framed the absence of foreclosure stigma as a form of "contagion" that increased the likelihood of default throughout communities, as with the domino effect of walking away in the case of Jim's neighborhood.[4] These loaded metaphors, whose language associated with viral disease instantiates a biopolitical view of mortgage default, are not applied, however, to commercial real estate; in contrast, business owners often abandon insolvent real estate contracts without social consequence. Nor are they applied to lenders or mortgage industry professionals, whose practices often lack public transparency and thereby remain immune to public shaming.[5]

Refusing to pay mortgage debts, by either occupying one's home or abandoning it, was a typical response to the disregard of corporate modification bureaucracies, and one that was by no means limited to the Sacramento Valley. Anthropologist Anna Jefferson, in her extensive research on mortgage modifications at a Michigan housing counseling agency, shows how homeowners walked away from debts as a way to salvage circumscribed agency when confronting failed modifications and evictions. Analyzing Michigan homeowners' decisions to abandon debt repayment after being embroiled in Kafkaesque modification dramas, Jefferson posits that homeowners did so because they felt that lenders had "broken the social terms of debt relations."[6] Like California, Michigan suffered from one of the highest foreclosure rates in the nation; while some foreclosures were triggered by subprime lending, especially in segregated, deindustrialized cities such as Detroit, many more resulted from unemployment and reduced income, which I have identified as post-middle-class realities in the Sacramento Valley.[7] "Homeowners facing foreclosure," Jefferson offers, "recounted the frustrations of dealing with their lenders as evidence of deep personal affront, the corruption and moral depravity of corporations, and the breakdown of the social order."[8]

DIGITAL DOMAINS

An ad hoc movement of Sacramento residents encouraging one another to abandon debt responsibilities and to squat in their homes, strategies embraced by David and Jim, crystallized in online domains. Two of the most popular websites for Sacramento homeowners were Reddit and the Craigslist Housing Forum.[9] On Reddit, foreclosure-related discussion forums (called subreddits) included categories such as economy, personal finance, legal advice, and "WTF."[10] (According to Reddit, its registered users tend to be socially liberal and interested in politics, with the slim majority being college-educated eighteen- to thirty-four-year-olds.) Both Craigslist and Reddit ensure a high level of anonymity, as users' identifying information remains private. This anonymity was important for many of the homeowners I interviewed, especially those who were striving to become middle-class professionals, because members of this demographic tend to hide their financial anxieties from friends and family, and some even conceal their dire situations from spouses until eviction is imminent, as was the case with Judy Zaro, the senior who hid an impending eviction from her husband, who had suffered a stroke.[11] Having overcome her initial reticence to share her story, Rachel Leibrock, the journalist who chronicled her own foreclosure in an online feature article in her local newspaper, told me, "There was no outlet before. You didn't use to talk about how poor you are with other people.... With social media, ... there's a safety online that you don't get face to face; it feels safer to share your story."

Behind the safety of this anonymity, posters on the forums shared personal information, including mortgage troubles that emerged in conjunction with divorce, depression, suicidal thoughts, and chronic illness.[12] Alongside these confessions, users provided concrete figures describing their loans, personal savings, home prices, income, and standing consumer debt. They freely exchanged financial information ordinarily considered taboo in face-to-face social settings, especially among those in the United States aspiring to middle-class status. Digital forums thereby provided a diverse cross section of Sacramento Valley homeowners a semipublic stage from which they could question the value of applying for loan modifications and even urge mortgagors to disregard foreclosure notices until evicted.

One participant with the online name of Natomasucks (a riff on Natomas, the name of Sacramento's middle-class suburban development devastated by the housing crash) reposted an interview with loan executives that had appeared in the *Sacramento Bee* in which the executives recommend loan modifications instead of mortgage default.[13] The thread, titled "To Walk Away or Not Walk Away?," inspired a user named Coakl to reply, "Loan executives are looking out for their interests; Don't play their game.... These loan executives are trying to pull one last sub-prime trick: persuading millions of upside-down homeowners to ignore the market collapse and make payments." Posters pointed toward lenders' refusals to renegotiate mortgage contracts or to halt foreclosure proceedings for worthy candidates as evidence of the illegitimacy of some forms of mortgage indebtedness in the context of the crash. Walking away from underwater mortgages no longer suggested a dishonorable response to crushing debt but instead seemed a choice justified by the shifting landscape of credit-debt ties. Many posters agreed that lenders were misleading homeowners by claiming that modifications would be in their best interests. This discussion suggesting that default was preferable to working with lenders to make payments took place between 12:30 and 3:00 a.m., showing that online users whose days were filled with the responsibilities of work and family were motivated to participate in public debate even in the early morning hours.[14]

Whereas postwar middle-class sensibilities were often defined by an investment in the American Dream, many homeowners posting online presented this ideal as naïve and anachronistic, with its empty promises becoming useful only insofar as they justified the abandonment of debt responsibilities once considered fundamental to middle-class propriety. Many Sacramento respondents, such as the following, suggested that their fellow posters stop making payments but stay in their homes:

> JCASETNL: I bet he could just stay in it. Seriously. There's so many foreclosures in Sacramento.
>
> WHISKEY_MCSWIGGENS: I'm not sure how, but my neighbor … has been living in his house for over a year without paying mortgage payments and it's a bank-owned house. He's obviously going to lose the house at some point, but not until someone buys the house from the bank. OP [original poster] should look into how to do this.
>
> CHADCF: There is no 'how to do this.' It just involves not moving, until the Sheriff comes to kick you out. The bank isn't letting them stay there because they have some desire to not make people homeless, they do it because there are a ton of foreclosures and they have a huge backlog to deal with and if the house is upside down it's not like it's going to be any more profitable to move quickly.

Here, squatting without payment is articulated as a justified response to the unethical and immoral practices of financial institutions.

This tone of critique of corporate mortgage lenders, however, had its limits. Online users did not abandon wholesale the old forms of shame and stigma arising from economic hardship; in fact, many posters resisted democratizing these acts of debt refusal to make them available to all individuals facing foreclosure. Forums could erupt in outright attacks on posters who advocated for mortgage default without feeling ashamed, especially if they were not suffering from financial hardship. In one example, a user on Reddit calling himself tvisforbabyboomers instigated a firestorm when he described his lack of humiliation upon initiating strategic mortgage default:

> My wife and I are foreclosing **on purpose**. We live a middle class lifestyle and *can* afford our house, but our mortgage is "no longer sustainable." ... Our house is $150,000 underwater.... We *do not* feel guilty about not paying our mortgage to our bank because when we asked for refinance assistance months ago, they said "google it" (seriously, they did). Furthermore, our mortgage is probably insured, so they will end up getting money anyway. Besides, it is business.... The banks got bailed out, wall street got bailed out ... and I'm middle class, this is *my* bail out.... **De-Occupy your home.**[15] (boldface and italics in the original)

Tvisforbabyboomers politicized his decision by drawing on an Occupy Wall Street discourse that fingers the government and banks for the crisis and asserts that walking away is a business decision on par with the unscrupulous practices of lenders. Other commentators, however, attacked tvisforbabyboomers, accusing him of indulging in an "entitlement mentality." They derided borrowers' unwillingness to pay despite lack of hardship, suggesting that these unscrupulous homeowners were unlike themselves, who had been "hit hard by the crisis" and forced into mortgage default because of uncooperative lenders.

Some digital domains dedicated to foreclosure, however, resisted reinforcing these normative judgments, joining mortgagors in a populist-inflected counterpoint to dominant narratives of homeowner immorality. This allowed homeowners to set aside deeply rooted financial reciprocity models and to see themselves as victims of, rather than obligated to, their lenders. For example, America Underwater, an activist blog launched jointly by leftist organizations Rebuild the Dream and The New Bottom Line, encouraged homeowners with underwater loans to upload an image of themselves holding a sign that showed the amount they owed accompanied by a story describing their situation.[16] Inspired by the use of Tumblr among Occupy activists, the blog was aimed at unseating Edward DeMarco, the director of the Federal Housing Finance Agency, for failing to help deserving homeowners. On it, a diverse group of homeowners—men and women of white, African American, and Latino descent, including teens, baby boomers, seniors, and retirees—created a collective narrative that sought to link their individual mortgage debts to mishandling by the mortgage industry and government housing officials, to whom they ascribed responsibility for foreclosures.

Yet the lack of physical copresence mattered. In attempting to mobilize the online publics emerging from the U.S. mortgage crisis, activists confronted obstacles that confirmed that the functioning of online publics, as literary critic Michael Warner points out, depends on participants remaining strangers who address their appeals to a general public.[17] In the posts on America Underwater, for example, many homeowners used their signs to maintain anonymity by obscuring their faces, hinting at a desire to participate from a distance. The impulse to obscure one's identity on activist blogs also suggests that participants recognized how the same types of visibility that can serve as a source of social empowerment and political mobilization could be used to subject individuals to new modes of surveillance.[18] Instead of converting social isolation into an experience of physical copresence, as in a protest on Wall Street or a march on Washington, self-generated publics offer critical alternative narratives and moral orientations to indebtedness.[19] That said, within this space, homeowners revise cultural conceptions of the morality of abandoning overwhelming debt burdens, and they bring these understandings to bear in their various other social spheres.

GUTTING THE PLACE

Home damage as a means of evening the score with abusive corporate lenders was so prevalent in the Sacramento Valley that, after 2008, a cottage industry dedicated to cleaning foreclosed homes emerged, with online instructional videos and business plans offering unemployed residents career opportunities. Typical acts of destruction included removing appliances, cabinets, carpets, doors, light fixtures, plumbing, smoke detectors, toilets, and window coverings; smashing walls and ceilings and breaking windows; and pouring concrete into pipes to render them useless. Less common but story-worthy destruction included dumping tuna fish or cat food in the house to attract stray animals; covering the carpet with water, urine, or even excrement; building booby traps by, for instance, leaving fans dangling by wires; and scrawling messages ("Fuck BofA!") on the interior walls. These damages spurred online threads dedicated to sharing photos taken by cleaning crews, the more egregious, the more highly viewed—one post of a room filled, nearly waist high, with used wads of toilet paper garnered over one hundred comments. Lest we think these protests were isolated acts of deranged homeowners and not a conscious form of dissent, one Sacramento real estate agent said that this type of damage could be found exclusively during and following the 2008 foreclosure epidemic.

Homeowners who embraced debt refusal often empathized with the rage fueling homeowners' impulse to destroy a home before eviction, but they disparaged these as acts as unethical. Property destruction, in other words, was an extreme against which post-middle-class homeowners could mark a modicum of respectability even as they abandoned the traditional forms of financial responsibility associated with middle-class lifestyles. Jim, for instance, contrasted his decision to walk away with that of his neighbor and friend Manuel Medina, who "trashed" his home before his family's eviction.

The only Mexican American family on the block, Manuel and his wife and four children had been in their house for almost twenty years when they were evicted. In the decade before the crash, their household had expanded as two of his daughters married and their husbands moved in, along with Manuel's mother from Mexico. Aside from Manuel's elderly mother, they all worked full time, Manuel at a local nursery, and they all picked up second jobs to remodel the house to make it more comfortable for their multigenerational household.

When they missed a mortgage payment in 2009, Leviathan Bank quickly foreclosed. A court ruled it a wrongful foreclosure, but the Medinas were so far into the eviction process that it could not be reversed. (Manuel believed, and Jim agreed, that the foreclosure, different in its pace from those of his white neighbors, had been racially motivated.) In response, the Medinas gutted their home before they were evicted—removing the toilets, kitchen cabinets, doors, light fixtures, copper pipes, countertops, and appliances, including the water heater. "I warned Manuel," Jim told me, "that he could be up against a felony for destruction of property, but he was so mad, he didn't care." The Medinas reasoned that they had remodeled and had purchased the fixtures and appliances, so why leave them behind? Some things could be resold or repurposed in new homes, while others were taken to prevent lenders from profiting from their sweat equity.

But these acts of destruction garnered widespread criticism. In everyday conversations and online, people psychologized the acts of protest, accusing homeowners who vandalized their properties as being "low-class," undeserving of homeownership to begin with, irrational, and deviant. The most fervent criticism emerged among Sacramento residents who were in the market to purchase foreclosed homes and flip them for a profit. Rhonda Baker, a white preschool teacher in her late forties who ran an in-home daycare, had started a side business with her husband in 2010 buying and flipping bank-owned homes. They owned a home in the middle-class neighborhood where I lived during my fieldwork and were using the cash from their real estate business to remodel a vacation home in Lake Tahoe that they had purchased (also a foreclosure). Rhonda often complained that the condition of the foreclosed homes made the process so stressful it almost outweighed the financial benefits. "You should see what some of these people do to the places," she told me as we stood in her sun-drenched backyard watching toddlers race tricycles and chase her pet rabbit, the size of a breadbox, into a cluster of bushes. "The people who wreck them up are like animals. And then we have to go in there and clean up their messes, try to piece it back together." Many critics' comments ran along similar lines: "I love my home. Even if I was losing it, I would never destroy it."

Hesitant to portray homeowners in an unsympathetic light, even I initially shied away from including these often sensationalist stories. Elderly residents duped by slick brokers incite empathy; disgruntled homeowners smearing human feces on their walls rouse disgust. But the damage done to homes by property owners is important, because it inspires the moral repugnance of Sacramento Valley residents who were spared in the foreclosure epidemic and were looking to profit from a downturn in prices. For them, the violence of bank seizures and the stories of homeowners who occupied the homes, with their failed marriages, cancer diagnoses, and depression, were erased. Stories of busted kitchens and purposefully mildewed carpets circulated more widely than tales of ruined marriages, wiped-out family savings, and stress-related illness following bank seizures. Urban myths detailing property revenge naturalized evictions as inevitabilities, the landscape for a wave of new real estate investment. In these moral tales, the value of property—universalized, as if it could be emptied of its political context and social meaning—remains sacrosanct.

A double standard emerged, however, in which the violence of banks implementing questionable home seizures and neglecting Sacramento properties was duly erased, while the vengeful destruction of homes by their owners came under a spotlight. The beat-up condition of blighted foreclosed homes—foreclosures, now owned by banks, that were in violation of city codes—was often indiscernible from that of homes damaged by evicted tenants. Corporate lenders, unaccustomed to managing so many properties, often allowed homes to fall into disrepair, driving down neighborhood property values and triggering blight. Yet the destruction of properties by banks was rarely, if ever, recognized as a form of violence. These vacant homes amassed city violations for neglected yards, insect and animal infestations, and infrastructural issues, while also attracting vagrants who would strip the houses of copper wire to sell or break into abandoned properties to use drugs. Real estate agents selling bank-owned properties and cleanup crews were often hard-pressed to determine whether damage had been done by spiteful homeowners or had simply resulted from lenders' neglect in the years following foreclosure, during which time the homes had languished as vacancies. Here, a homeowner's violence toward his home does not repudiate the rule of law and market practices, but counterfeits it.[20] How was it that Manuel Medina could be accused of "stealing" his own toilet? Could not Leviathan Bank, with its wrongful foreclosure on his home, be considered to have "stolen" his entire house?

FIND ME IN MY HOME

If destroying a home uses property as a means of retribution, homeowners also turned destruction inward as an act of protest. Stories about suicide attempts and threats during or immediately following foreclosure proceedings after 2008 have been widely noted by scholars and policy makers; one study even links a slight rise in the U.S. suicide rate after 2008 directly to foreclosures.[21] In California, for example, a Pasadena woman shot herself after setting her house on fire because of her foreclosure.[22] Another California cash-for-keys worker, who would offer homeowners up to $1,000 to move "peacefully" without wrecking their homes, reported finding dead bodies in the homes on three occasions. "They would most often hang themselves," he recalled, "so it's the first thing you see when you walk in the door." In a handful of cases, bodies had sat for years while houses decayed, only to be discovered by new owners after buying the properties sight unseen (the typical way bank-owned properties were sold).

In the Michigan housing counseling agency where anthropologist Anna Jefferson volunteered during her research on mortgage modifications, counselors often discussed the suicide attempts or threats of homeowners they were assisting. Staff members had to complete training and learn how to refer at-risk clients to mental health services. It was not uncommon for a homeowner to remark to housing counselors that if lenders came to seize the home, they would find the homeowner's body hanging in the house.[23] Some homeowners followed through on their threats. Were these suicides the result of a generalized depression, illuminating the overlay of economic hardships and mental anguish, one depression inciting another? Not entirely. Jefferson shows how suicide threats were prompted by the ongoing harassment and abuse from corporate lenders as homeowners appealed for assistance. One housing counselor commented to Jefferson: "It's not just because 'Oh, my house is in foreclosure, now I'm going to do this'—it's *because of the lenders*. They call them every day and harass them.... These lenders just play so many games, you know."[24] These forms of abuse were exacerbated by financial hardship, but, Jefferson convincingly argues, the warning of self-annihilation, the threat of leaving their body in the house as a burden to the lender, serves as a form of revenge, a final commentary, an act of protest.[25]

These acts of self-annihilation offer an example of Emile Durkheim's canonical study of suicide, in which the French sociologist examines suicide not as an individual or psychological failing but as a social one.[26] Durkheim argues that "anomic suicide" occurs when social institutions are weak and people maintain fragile, distant ties to those institutions. Anomic suicide grows from "anomie," Durkheim's theory of the instability that occurs as standards and values break down. Linking anomic suicide to an individual's disintegration from social institutions reflects Durkheim's overarching goal of understanding the persistence of cohesion in nineteenth-century Western societies. It is not widespread poverty that inspires suicides during an economic downturn but the upheaval of the social order that leaves people uncertain of their place in a changing world. In studying the juxtaposition of personal debt and an epidemic of suicide in contemporary Botswana, historian Julie Livingston likewise finds that people emphasized a decay of social institutions as a driver of suicide. Livingston highlights how neoliberal and state rhetoric falsely promised people self-determination, and when poverty persisted, many people embraced suicide.[27] In a similar vein, it was not bankruptcy or evictions that spurred U.S. homeowners to threaten, or even attempt, suicide but the breakdown of imagined forms of financial reciprocity between borrowers and lenders that had provided social context and status for lower-middle-class and middle-class residents for decades. The failed promise of stability and security prompted self-destruction. The dissolution of these ties, evidenced through the harassment, disrespect, and abuse by modification and collections agents for corporate lenders, triggered in homeowners a sense of disorientation and a desire to materialize the violence of this process, even if that violence was turned inward as an act of protest.

RELIGIOUS COLLECTIVES OF REFUSAL

Lisa Davis, a quick-witted, blonde, blue-eyed thirty-six-year-old, originally from a small farming community in the Central Valley, had taken a slow path to activism, as she described it. She had attended college in San Francisco, where she met her husband. After they married, they joined the Peace Corps, serving together in Suriname. Upon returning to the United States, they moved to Sacramento, and Lisa's husband enrolled in graduate school at the University of California at Davis. Lisa also decided to return to school, for her teaching credential. After graduating, she found work at a highly ranked public school, and her husband secured a government job. In 2007, after their first child was born, they bought a house in a neighborhood that had resurged since the late 1990s and that still offered affordable homes for working- and middle-class families. They chose a mortgage broker who was a family friend, and they agreed to a loan that, despite this personal connection, Lisa later regretted. She told me:

> We went in there thinking that we wanted a conventional loan—a good percentage down and a thirty-year fixed rate. He said we'd qualify for more. We said no. He wanted us to take $50,000 more than we wanted. I explained that we weren't looking to flip the house. He convinced us to put

zero percent down and use that 10 percent to fix up the house. So we took it, nothing down and thirty-year fixed-rate loan. At least we had that thirty-year fixed.

Following the advice of the broker, who was motivated by the higher fee he would receive for the subprime loan, Lisa and her husband remodeled their new home, adding landscaping and skylights and hiring professionals to paint the exterior. The extra cash on hand also was useful when they had a second child two years after buying their home and Lisa transitioned to a part-time teaching position.

After the housing crash, Lisa was laid off from her teaching job (her part-time status having left her vulnerable), and her husband suffered a three-year salary freeze. Their healthcare premiums had gone up three times in three years. As they came to grips with foreclosure in 2011, Lisa fixated on not having stuck to her original plan to put 10 percent down on the mortgage. She recalled, "I kept thinking, 'What did we do that was irresponsible that got us into this position? You don't get something for nothing, you dummy. We should have put that 10 percent down!'"

Lisa and her husband visited a HUD loan counselor, who told them that they did not qualify for a HAMP modification because they had $8,000 in their savings account. Lisa pointed out to me that HAMP did not ask about the number of children in the family or the number of people being supported on the family's salary. "You have to be even more desperate to qualify," she explained. To qualify for the HAMP modification, the couple spent down their savings by paying on the mortgage. Still, Lisa recalled returning in 2012 to the HUD counselor, who looked at their information and told them, "There's nothing I can do; you're losing your house."

Against her best efforts to contain her emotions, Lisa told me that she had broken down during a church event. She described her church as a middle- to upper-middle-class, liberal, and predominantly white Unitarian congregation where people were friendly and supportive, but it was still considered taboo to discuss financial difficulties. Yet, after she testified to the loss of her home, many parishioners reached out with similar stories. Many were government employees who were experiencing furloughs, some were losing their jobs, and many others could no longer afford their healthcare premiums. One family of four had become homeless after their foreclosure, eventually moving to Los Angeles so the father could take a job as a cashier at Disneyland. Even parishioners who did not struggle with foreclosure were affected, because many had taken in extended family members after their evictions.

Lisa recounted the sense of camaraderie that emerged as parishioners began sharing their economic hardships. For Lisa, the face-to-face outpouring of stories similar to hers transformed grief into outrage. She joined a national interdenominational coalition of activists working through their churches and synagogues to advocate for homeowners' rights and social justice. Having a newfound purpose, she said, made her "feel less helpless, but also more irate." The organization's model of activism centered on storytelling; advocates organized listening sessions and then created campaigns around the issues that arose during these meetings. Stories offered powerful political tools, and the religious communities provided a ready-made network for organizing.

Lisa's pastor, for example, used her story when he was invited to testify in front of the state legislature in 2012 to promote the California Homeowner Bill of Rights. This legislation, which came into law in 2013, supports mortgagors facing foreclosure by guaranteeing a single point of contact at their lender and restricting the practice of dual tracking, the illegal practice of foreclosing while homeowners are making modified payments that had plagued Rachel Leibrock.[28] Lisa also participated in small acts of resistance, moving her money out of Vertex National Bank and into a local credit union, for instance, and confronting the bank manager at Vertex while doing so. Like Lisa, a few others who lost their homes in lower-middle-class or middle-class neighborhoods found that their foreclosure experiences inspired forms of social activism, most typically through venues and social networks with which they were familiar.

COMMUNITY MOBILIZATION

It was a bright spring day in Oak Park, but fluorescent lights hummed overhead and linoleum floors squeaked as sneakered African American and Latino residents took their seats. An elected county official, a thin, white, tired-looking man in his fifties, stood at the podium detailing his administration's achievements. He was the first of three government officials slated to speak, following a lineup of community activists, but one of the other two government representatives had not turned up, and the organizers, unfazed, assumed he would be a no-show. Diego Ventana, the church janitor introduced in chapter 2, who had raised six children and lost his home to foreclosure, stood to the left of the podium, wearing a bright yellow Alliance of Californians for Community Empowerment (ACCE) T-shirt.

Losing interest in the politician's stump speech, I let my attention wander to the posters that volunteers had hastily taped to the wall just minutes before the event. One placed strategically behind the speaker had been especially laborious to make: a blown-up black-and-white map of the neighborhood with an explosion of red stickers showing areas of blight. Esmeralda Bolt, a stunning, charismatic Latina single mom in her early thirties who had been briefly married to a professional basketball player, was the ACCE community organizer in charge of the event. In a yellow ACCE T-shirt matching Diego's, she directed the local news crews she had convinced to cover the meeting to set up their cameras along the corridor of the meeting room. Commenting on her ability to get press attention, she told me, "I'm a big believer in putting what you want out there." She once told me, "You have to let everyone know what it is you're trying to get. I've manifested a lot of things that way."

An elderly African American resident in her Sunday hat hobbled in on her walker in the middle of the county official's speech. Esmeralda helped her into a chair in the front row; the young black man occupying that seat instinctively moved to the aisle floor. Minutes later, when the county official finished his speech, the elderly woman raised her hand and pressed him on what specifically he would do to stop the epidemic of blight, to keep the drug users and vagrants out of the house across the street from her own.

"We're working on it," he said.

"We want it in writing," she replied.

Diego took to the podium and invited the county official, along with the other government representative who had showed up, to sign a handwritten document hung on the wall with duct tape, a contract promising to commit resources to address blight in Oak Park.

The official laughed, but he soon realized that the activists were not joking. "I can't just sign anything, I have to know what I'm signing," he said, trying to brush it off.

"Read it," the woman called from the front row.

The official crouched down to read the document, quipping, "I'll only sign it if he does," pointing to the other guest who was waiting to speak.

The official, who struck me as sympathetic and overburdened, signed the document—a symbolic win for activists. It was a seemingly inconsequential moment in a long history of neighborhood discrimination, but it highlights how Oak Park residents relied on long-standing community organizations to manage the deleterious impact of the foreclosure epidemic, even using it to address problems like blight, which predated but were exacerbated by subprime lending. Whereas homeowners struggling with mortgage modifications in lower-middle-class or middle-class neighborhoods adopted forms of debt refusal or retribution, long-standing community organizations in Oak Park like ACCE allowed many residents to direct their frustrations toward collective action. If homeowners in higher-income areas learned, through protracted encounters with bureaucracies, to see lenders' disregard and failed modifications as a form of individual abandonment, community advocates in Oak Park, who were mainly excluded from mortgage modification bureaucracies, framed housing struggles as a collective civil rights issue. These grassroots meetings in churches and community centers encouraged residents to understand the structural inequities driving what some had initially viewed as personal financial failings. It was precisely this scaffolding that would have taken individual acts of squatting and strategic default among middle-class homeowners in wealthier neighborhoods and mobilized them to send a message to financial institutions and government agencies.

The histories of community organizations like ACCE served to ensure their success. Uniting Lisa Davis's church-based activism with the ACCE events in Oak Park was the presence of civic organizations that had long-standing community ties. In contrast, activists who launched a Sacramento Occupy Homes group—an offshoot of the Occupy Wall Street movement—after reading about Occupy efforts on social media had a tougher time mobilizing residents. The collective, a handful of predominately white and Jewish middle-class Sacramento activists, was spearheaded by a legal aid lawyer and a retired cellist for the city symphony. The tenor of the group was more measured than that of the robust Occupy networks two hours south in the San Francisco Bay Area. Unlike ACCE, which typically focused on government and policy solutions, Occupy Homes targeted lenders. In one of its more memorable direct actions, Occupy Homes organized a sit-in at Bank of America to protest its pilfering of federal funds for mortgage modifications while failing to dole out assistance. (At one meeting, members debated who should handcuff themselves to the Wells Fargo sign at a later protest.) These acts of civil disobedience aimed to attract press scrutiny of corporate lenders, thereby shifting dominant public narratives about mortgage default. Most of my homeowner respondents knew little about Occupy Homes or had never heard of it, even though they shared its fundamental criticisms of corporate lenders. Unlike ACCE, which provided a civil-society scaffolding for homeowners to mobilize their grievances into action, Occupy Homes was a new collectivity, ungrounded in any particular social institution like a church, and did not have the same infrastructure or reach with which to catalyze individual acts of debt refusal into collective action.

MORAL ECONOMIES OF DEBT REFUSAL

Homeowners' various rituals of debt refusal—from squatting to walking away from mortgages to organizing community protests—call into question a broader U.S. moral economy attached to indebtedness. Resistance to bank seizures challenges the underlying assumptions about the moral turpitude of so-called deadbeats. Homeowners such as best friends David Sanchez and Jim Foster were doing everything right, according to the ideologies of the American Dream: working hard, serving their country in the military, and conforming to standards of "good debt" established by previous generations. But lending institutions failed them, so they learned to play by what they called the new rules, whereby they also abandoned the commitments born out of credit-debt ties. More than a tit for tat, efforts of refusal and defiance reflected a general uneasiness about what many Sacramento Valley residents viewed as a breakdown in the social order, in which a drive for profits reigned supreme despite the human costs.

Widespread forms of debt refusal in the face of failed mortgage modifications in the Sacramento Valley, along with hard-hit postindustrial states like Michigan, show how late-liberal financial markets remain beholden to moral economies. Theories of moral economy have long offered anthropologists a way to understand the limits of capitalist exploitation—how much can a system abuse the bodies and mental capacities of workers before they refuse to comply? The economy is always a moral system, as historian E. P. Thompson argues in his work on eighteenth-century food riots in England, during which peasants insisted on a fair price for food instead of allowing prices to be set by a free market that worked against them. Peasants protested, Thompson points out, not as a direct, visceral response to hunger, but rather in defense of traditional rights reflective of communal notions of fairness. As anthropologist Didier Fassin points out in his reading of Thompson, peasants revolt not because their resources are scarce but because "the implied commitments of rights and obligations are not met."

Their revolt reminds us, Fassin writes, that another form of exchange is possible.[29]

Yet mass riots and revolts, like the legendary 1850 squatters' riots that marked the founding of Sacramento, were nonexistent after 2008. Neutralized by mammoth bureaucratic techniques and a tendency for homeowners, especially those in formerly middle-class neighborhoods, to individualize strategies of refusal, these impulses to revolt were, most often, channeled into private forays online, the abandonment of mortgage payments, and the quiet occupations of homes. The imagined mutuality between residents and corporate banks no doubt played a significant role in shaping the muted, often private acts of defiance that arose after 2008. Just as the dense sociality of markets raised different expectations for mutuality depending on racial, class, and neighborhood histories, responses to breaches in these systems of reciprocity were shaped by people's relative social positions. Refusals were incorporated into daily life in ways that echo James Scott's canonical study of moral economies in historical agrarian societies in Burma and Vietnam, where peasants assumed a degree of mutuality between themselves and their patrons, which influenced how they resisted abuses of power. Breaches in these dense reciprocal networks catalyzed resistance—not typically in the form of a rebellion or revolution but rather in what Scott famously calls everyday forms of resistance, a "constant struggle between the peasantry and those who seek to extract labor, food, taxes, and rents and interest."[30] In the Sacramento Valley, beliefs in financial reciprocity between mortgage lenders and homeowners inspired residents to expect assistance from banks and to protest when lenders failed to come through, but these visions of mutuality also relegated resistance to a universe of daily life instead of promoting a political revolution in debt ties.

Scholars tend to associate moral economies with peasants and subsistence farmers, exploring the conflict between pastoral notions of economic fairness and global capitalist markets that strain these values with an incessant drive for profit. The rural origins of the Sacramento

Valley, still present in its daily rhythms, intensified its residents' notions of fairness and traditions of small-town respect, but these practices cannot fully explain why many homeowners self-righteously abandoned debt repayment. Residents lived near farmland but were by no means dependent on corporate lenders for subsistence and survival, as Scott's peasants had been with their patrons. What Sacramento Valley residents did share with these earlier peasant societies was the experience of seismic economic shift. Whereas peasants confronted the encroachment of industrialization, Sacramento Valley residents realized that postwar forms of industrial work, consumption, leisure, and property ownership had been replaced by financialized late-liberal markets in which the Protestant values and commitments undergirding social economic life were increasingly anachronistic. Relocating these moral economic narratives, so often linked to pastoral ideals of land and belonging, to the realities of and responses to contemporary finance shows how even these modern hypercapitalist markets are destined to remain complexly embedded in shifting American moral ecologies.

Drawings

Homeowners draw their relationships with mortgage lenders.

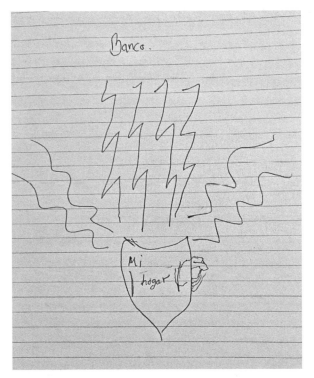

Drawing by Miguel Santos, a Mexican American unemployed carpenter and father of four, who lost his Oak Park home to Leviathan Bank after signing on for a subprime mortgage through his cousin. (Text translates as "Bank" and "My home.")

Drawing by Jennifer Rhodes, a white housing counselor at a nonprofit helping residents to apply for mortgage modifications and the single mother of two daughters. Rhodes was foreclosed on by TrustWorth Financial in 2010.

Drawing by Ted Mather, a white IT assistant in his mid-thirties applying to modify his underwater mortgage on a home in Oak Park. "You don't have any control; you pick a lender you trust, and they sell your mortgage to a worse lender."

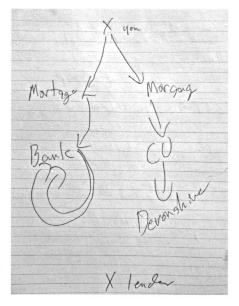

Drawing by Darren Lewis, a white computer programmer in his early forties, foreclosed on by Vertex National Bank. Darren described his drawing as "Charlie Brown trying to kick the football, and Lucy moving it every time. In back of Lucy is a pit of money."

Drawing by Irma Machado, a Mexican American seasonal farmworker, who secured a mortgage for a home in Oak Park from Washington Mutual for over $200,000 with no down payment and no income verification and then was offered a line of equity with IndyMac. After she and her husband were evicted, the house sold for $40,000 at auction. Text translates as "Bank" and "You."

CONCLUSION

You Can't Go Home Again

Brooke Young and I were walking to pick up her six-year-old from his Spanish-English bilingual public school near her rental home in San Jose. It was a bright, sunny day in January, the light reflecting off a collection of glass chimes in her front yard. The sound drowned out the ambient buzz of the freeway, hidden behind a stucco wall that formed the southern boundary of the neighborhood. The scent of lawn trimmings lingered. To walk side by side on the narrow sidewalk we squeezed close together as she pushed a stroller carrying her sleeping newborn son past trim hedges and planter boxes, moving into the street when a well-worn Toyota family van blocked the sidewalk.

After resisting mortgage default for months, a process detailed at the start of this book, Brooke and her husband, Jarred, had defaulted on their underwater mortgage and found a rental just three blocks from their home. Letting go of her house triggered grief like the loss of a loved one, she told me, but giving up on their debt also offered tremendous relief. She seemed lighter, more her old self. Financial trouble had forced them to delay having a second child, a gut-wrenching decision as Brooke neared forty. Just two months after moving, she became pregnant. Brooke was now approaching the final week of her unpaid maternity leave and would soon return to teaching her middle school class.

We left her house a little earlier than I had expected, and Brooke asked if we could take a detour. As we walked a few blocks out of our way, I realized that her daily route to pick up her son included a stop in front of the home she and her husband had lost to foreclosure. We stood on the opposite side of the street and stared. The modest two-bedroom, one-bathroom house still stood vacant six months after Brooke's family had moved out. Without their wooden bench and lawn decorations clustered in the front yard, the house's pink paint and white trim seemed contrived rather than cozy. Thinking back to packing Brooke's garage, I was overcome by the irony of rushing to vacate her house, trashing things that could not be packed in time, only to have the house sit vacant for months, epitomizing the perversity of the entire ordeal. Brooke described how the new owners had pulled her favorite oak tree from the front yard and torn up the vegetable garden that she and her son had planted in the back. They had also made some nice changes, she admitted, opening up the kitchen and remodeling the bathroom, renovations that Brooke had wanted to make but could never afford. "The new owners," Brooke said, "are most likely preparing it for renters." Brooke told me that there had been an open house, and although she had considered going to sate her curiosity, she decided against it, concluding that it would have been too painful. Instead, she had adopted this daily ritual of stopping by the house to assess the changes from afar, occasionally peeking through the windows.

Many Sacramento Valley homeowners I spoke to confessed to a similar fixation on the homes they had lost, often continuing to drive by even months after they had moved out. Their visits to their former homes struck me as a kind of "searching behavior," a stage of grief psychologists identify in which the bereaved move from numbness to a stage of yearning.[1] For homeowners, these searching moments generated an unlikely mix of judgmental indignation, as they criticized the poor tastes of the new owners or investors, coupled with a low-level embarrassment at their lingering attachments, exposing the tender spots left by bank seizures. As people described to me their compulsion to return, they treated the subject as if I had stumbled upon them snooping through an ex-lover's social media profile, a blend of nosiness and resentment leading them down a rabbit hole of nostalgia. These hauntings reminded me of Marcel Mauss's line, "Things sold still have soul. They are still followed around by their former owner, and they follow him also."[2]

It seemed to me that homeowners were trying to recuperate more than their houses, holding onto something intangible that had been misplaced in the move. To me, standing beside Brooke and staring into her uninhabited former home, it seemed we were peering into a life trajectory that had been foreclosed upon, a version of her that had been lost. On the surface, life moved on. Housing markets recovered. People cut their losses and set out to rebuild their savings. Some even planned to buy another home, while many more, like Brooke, religiously swore off mortgaging and soberly committed to a lifetime of renting. But the nagging question of recovery remained: Who was I then, and could I ever be as well or even better off now?

Open wounds festered just beneath the surface. David Sanchez spent his golden years of retirement widowed and alone, on the brink of eviction, instead of riding off into the sunset with his wife, Karen. Judy Zaro, the senior tricked into taking on a subprime home equity loan, woke up every day in a cramped senior-living apartment with her ailing husband in a dismal snow-banked town in the Midwest, worlds away from her best friends and support network in Sacramento. Joy and Nancy Moore-Jones, the blind couple in Oak Park, scrambled to make their rent payments by taking part in ill-advised pyramid schemes to supplement their disability income, using the money to pay rent on a home they had lost through fraud. Even Jason Silva, the Leviathan Bank lending employee, abandoned his lucrative career in real estate for one in the tech sector, deciding to start over at the bottom of a company doing work that he felt was less morally problematic.

At the start of their struggles, these Sacramento Valley residents described impending foreclosures with an undercurrent of hope. They believed they were entering a transitional stage rather than a terminal one. But by the end of their foreclosure struggles, people were grappling with post-middle-class existence—mourning the death of a set of aspirations, expectations, and attachments. Their experiences heightened ongoing, growing financial insecurities brought about by neoliberal policies that closed factories, normalized massive layoffs, privatized pension funds, and stranded families with insurmountable debts. After the crash, my respondents were beaten down by predatory corporate bureaucracies that extended these logics, privatizing public assistance. Already stretched thin, using consumer credit to meet the basic needs of housing, childcare, food, and education, these families now faced even greater hurdles to the security and stability that earlier generations had enjoyed. As Vietnam veteran Jim Foster described it, the image he had once had of the United States, one nurtured by a childhood in the burgeoning suburbs within eyesight of Disneyland and by a young adulthood in military service, had become unrecognizable.

Homeownership had not only served as an investment strategy for these Sacramento Valley residents, but it had symbolized *going somewhere* and *becoming something;* it was a sign that their hard work was paying off. If they played by the rules and made prudent choices, they believed, they could expect fair results from financial markets. The temporality of long-term mortgage payments required the vision that a homeowner's future included stability, that life for future generations would continue to improve. But this perspective had been nurtured by an environment of oft-invisible government regulation and state subsidies, which together would scaffold an American middle class, especially the white men in its growing ranks, by providing federal mortgages, education through the GI Bill, and jobs through public works and infrastructure programs.

Evictions, once the purview of the poor, have now become a typical experience for post-middle-class families in the Sacramento Valley. My respondents likewise described standing in unemployment lines, turning to payday lenders to make it through the month, and occasionally relying on food banks—all symbols of poverty historically foreign to the ranks of Sacramento Valley residents with college educations and professional careers, but experiences that have become increasingly common. The refrain "I never thought I would end up here" echoed across my conversations with teachers, police officers, office managers, government workers, and real estate professionals who were often worse off than their parents, with no immediate signs of regaining any sustainable upward momentum. Corporate lenders cemented homeowners' downward mobility, subjecting applicants to unprecedented forms of surveillance, protracted delays, and senseless runaround. Homeowners were dehumanized and disenfranchised by administrative techniques, no matter how much the mortgage modification commercials suggested that wasn't the case. In a 2012 survey of California housing counselors working at fifty nonprofit agencies, 88 percent reported that Bank of America, for example, almost always delayed responses, lost documents, and gave homeowners inconsistent information. Its modification practices were so pernicious that, in 2012, the Department of Justice acted against the corporate giant for defrauding HAMP.[3] The mismanagement that plagued Bank of America's modification bureaucracies was widespread.[4] In the survey, housing counselors, for example, described how JPMorgan Chase, Wells Fargo, and Citibank made significant errors as well, with all servicers delaying decisions and responses and losing documents.

Through my research, I came to see the possibilities for my own life trajectory through a different lens. Just as I was fighting my way into the professional class, homeownership in urban centers became prohibitively expensive. Most of the families I had grown up with in the Bay Area were, like mine, forced to move following the tech boom that brought Google and Facebook and inflated housing prices, relocating either to growing peri-urban developments in central California or to other states altogether. The market-rate apartments neighboring the government-subsidized low-income units where I grew up in San Jose are now worth nearly $800,000. According to the *San Jose Mercury News*, in the Bay Area, a family of four living on a salary of approximately $105,000 in 2016 qualified as low income largely due to these unprecedented housing costs.[5] Our generation is faced with skyrocketing expenses to cover daily life; we now must support parents without retirement funds or whose funds were wiped out by fluctuations in the market, pay rising healthcare costs, and fund college educations for our children that will outpace our salaries and leave us with insurmountable debts. Yet my grandfather, a French Canadian immigrant with no opportunity to attend college, who worked as a live-in butler and, later, a unionized dockworker in San Francisco, could support a family of four, buy a modest home in the coastal suburbs, and enjoy a comfortable retirement. Witnessing the recent dispossession of my relatives across California, I remain painfully aware that I am lucky, in this new American reality, to have a steady job with health benefits and retirement options.

Publicly sponsored but privately administered mortgage modification programs took advantage of American homeowners' anachronistic attachment to the possibility of living "the good life" despite the rapidly deteriorating forms of economic and social existence that have characterized the neoliberal era. A flood of mortgage modification commercials implied that the losses triggered by the crash were not the new normal but merely an economic hiccup in a grander trajectory of middle-class stability. The mere possibility of forbearance or assistance indicated that this chapter of loss in homeowners' lives could come to a close. Of course, these mortgage modification bureaucracies put the onus on individual homeowners to "save their homes"—the commercials and billboards throughout the Sacramento Valley implied that inaction guaranteed eviction but determination would warrant success. Homeowners who failed to amend their mortgages and save their homes, according to the narratives spun by corporate lenders and mortgage servicers, could be blamed for failing to fax the correct paperwork or contact the appropriate service representative.

Contrary to their branding, mortgage modification programs were not established to restore the possibility that struggling Americans could achieve the good life. Quite the opposite. These programs were established to force lenders and loan servicers to consider the possibility that forbearance might reap higher profits than foreclosure and, if so, to halt evictions. Ads failed to mention that profit-seeking algorithms and net present value (NPV) tests determined outcomes, recklessly misleading homeowners to believe that a fairy-tale ending was within their reach.

As a result, mistrust and skepticism of government and mainstream financial institutions have become cornerstones of post-middle-class subjectivity in the Sacramento Valley. After the 2008 crash, Congress signed off on billions of dollars in bailout funds, but the money ended up in the hands of corporate lenders that, in the decades leading up to the crash, had acquired an amount of debt more substantial than the combined gross domestic products of every country in the world combined.[6] As the system crumbled, David Graeber points out, Americans were shockingly open to alternative solutions. An overwhelming majority of Americans surveyed believed that the banks should not be rescued, despite the potential economic consequences, but that citizens with underwater mortgages should be saved.[7] "My tax dollars are going to rescue Wall Street," more than one homeowner griped, "but where is my help?" By "awarding the arsonists," as former secretary of the Treasury Timothy Geithner described his own institution's actions of funneling bailout funds to Wall Street, these so-called recovery efforts left millions of Americans wary of the government and big banks. Many had arrived at the stark realization that the rules of mortgaging—and of finance more broadly—had changed: the social contract they imagined, which united creditors and debtors, citizens and government, had become a one-sided affair. Now, disillusionment has replaced blind faith in major financial institutions and government agencies for many homeowners on both the political left and the right.

This shift toward disaffection reached sparked a wave of populist sentiment that defined the 2016 presidential election cycle, bringing the socialist candidate Bernie Sanders and the reality television icon Donald Trump to the forefront of the presidential race. While Sanders's record of promoting working-class interests galvanized supporters on the left, Trump too fashioned himself as a protector of the white working class. Trump's campaign captured the loyalties of foreclosed-upon homeowners like Jim and Brenda Foster, whose distrust of the government prompted them to vote for a real-estate baron whose very business model epitomized the practices that had stranded them in foreclosure. They were inspired by Trump's campaign promise to dismantle, as one campaign spot put it, "a global power structure ... that [has] robbed our working class and put that money into the pockets of a handful of large corporations."

In his first months in office, however, Trump reneged on policy promises to protect working families, while relying on racialized discourse to demonize immigrants for the hardships of working- and middle-class Americans. For example, Trump pledged to "do a number" on the Dodd-Frank Act, which had reined in Wall Street financial abuse after the 2008 crash, and gutted the Consumer Financial Protection Bureau, which had by the summer of 2017 fined corporations $11.9 billion and redistributed that money to consumers. Trump's administration rolled out a tax bill that analysts argued would favor companies and the ultrawealthy over the middle class. Perhaps most tellingly, Trump appointed as Treasury secretary Steven Mnuchin, a hedge fund CEO who earned a hefty portion of his $300 million net worth pushing through suspect foreclosures on behalf of OneWest, formerly IndyMac, the mortgage lender that defrauded Joy and Nancy Moore-Jones. OneWest was named in a series of lawsuits over questionable foreclosures under Mnuchin's direction and paid out millions of dollars for wrongful evictions.[8]

Trump's justification for having betrayed his campaign promises drew on a rhetoric of preventing government overreach into the market. But homeowner assistance programs failed to deliver the promised benefits to those facing foreclosure because those programs were relegated to the private sector. They were not public enough. It was the *private* bureaucracies that failed to stave off the unending losses by denying homeowners the loan modifications that would allow them to keep paying on mortgages and stay in their homes. The government was the problem only insofar as it declined to carry Americans' toxic mortgages as the Home Owner's Loan Corporation had done during the Great Depression. Yet these details often remained obscure to the homeowners I interviewed who found themselves in the thick of loan modification applications and foreclosures; their experiences were dominated by ongoing confrontations with an endless bureaucratic maze of misinformation that raised questions, both practical and philosophical, about debt repayment. Homeowners like Jim and Brenda, who suffered from the erosion of oversight of the lending and mortgage industries, were desperate to find someone they could trust to "make America great again," as the Trump campaign slogan promised. After feeling such intense abandonment and invisibility, these homeowners are finding that Trump's promise to restore a country that many felt they had lost is fostering deregulation that risks triggering even more predation and volatility in mortgage markets.

No doubt those who will suffer most as the financial sector is once again left unchecked will be those most vulnerable to predatory financial schemes: the elderly, minority homeowners historically excluded from credit, and residents in low-income neighborhoods. In the Sacramento Valley, these residents were more likely to sign up for high-cost subprime loans and faced direr consequences than their middle-income counterparts did. Homeowners straddling the poverty line were more likely to be victimized by predatory lending and faced additional obstacles to securing loan modifications, such as living in areas with low property values. Yet these residents were less likely than middle-class borrowers to feel entitled to assistance from lenders and more likely to rely on community networks for assistance, turning to local activists or friends, for instance, instead of expecting payback for their having been victimized by illegal lending practices. Street smarts and negotiation skills aided these low-income homeowners, but their reliance on personal networks to resolve financial problems also opened them to con artists posing as loan modification agents.

Major financial crises like that of 2008, David Harvey points out, typically lead to a reorganization of capital that can spawn new forms of class power. Writing as the crisis unfolded, Harvey argued that the "powers that held sway" would clean up the mess at the expense of the American people unless deterred by a "surge of political opposition."[9] Harvey's prescient pessimism was well founded. Although political opposition did surge in the form of Occupy Wall Street and activist movements centering on debt, it did not gain enough momentum to dismantle the forces that had fostered the crisis in the first place. Graeber, an economic anthropologist and also the Occupy Wall Street activist credited with originating the slogan "We are the 99%," laments that the "conversation stopped dead, popular rage against bailouts sputtered into incoherence."[10] In the Sacramento Valley, disdain for the bailout, as Harvey and Graeber predicted, did not capsize the system. Collective action was much harder to come by than individual outrage.

The failures of corporate mortgage modification bureaucracies, however, did generate more than mass dispossessions: they inspired forms of debt refusal inconceivable before the 2008 crash. In the Sacramento Valley, a unifying sense of disengagement from debt repayment arose from the pervasive feeling that homeowners had been defrauded by lending institutions and then falsely promised loan modifications that never materialized. The rise of modification programs, in other words, has remade everyday perspectives on the social obligations of debt in significant ways. Many Northern California homeowners with distressed mortgage debt after the 2008 crash have questioned traditional credit-debt ties, transforming the failure to pay debt from an abdication of responsibility into a righteous reaction to lenders' disloyalty. The discourses of financial reciprocity that rose from the debris of the foreclosure epidemic indicate the possibility for mobilization. The trick, then, is connecting the dots between individual experiences such as those of David Sanchez, Judy Zaro, Joy and Nancy Moore-Jones, and Rachel Leibrock with all the others—an effort I have begun in modest terms in this book. If harnessed, the prevailing impulse to imbue the market with expectations for mutuality can serve as a critical lever to marshal demands for a more just economy.

The fact that corporate lending employees shared homeowners' visions of fairness and financial reciprocity in mortgage agreements suggests the persistence of a powerful and pervasive cultural ideology. United by experiences in a growing post–middle class, homeowners and lending employees often shared a vision of financial fairness. Although institutions designed the loan modification process to prevent specialists from bonding with applicants, lending employees, faced with downsizing and institutional reorganization, still found themselves forming sentimental attachments to certain cases and determining value along moral and social lines rather than merely according to financial calculations. Moral economies persisted even in the byzantine administrative mazes of post-Weberian bureaucracies. But despite their attempts to tilt the playing field in favor of deserving applicants, many modification specialists found that the so-called game of mortgage modification ultimately failed to help the right homeowners, ensuring that millionaires rested easy in their Maui beachfront properties or floated along in infinity pools perched over a Sacramento Valley estuary, whereas elderly retirees in modest homes decided between a can of Campbell's soup and their blood-pressure medication.

In the context of the 2008 financial crisis, homeowners and lending employees posited market transactions as embedded in dense forms of sociality—a significant finding for anthropological theories of debt. Everyday confrontations within mortgage modification programs generate expectations of sociality that scholars have typically associated with exchange in so-called gift economies.[11] The flourishing of expectations of reciprocity and relief, articulated in different ways by homeowners and the service representatives processing their appeals, shows that non-commodified forms of debt and sociality proliferate within late-liberal financial markets. Ironically, as Wall Street investment firms commodified mortgage debt and then securitized and sold it on secondary derivatives markets, the links between borrowers and lenders became opaque. But rather than render obsolete the social contracts implicit in debt ties, rampant financialization has led to a pervasive sense that lenders enter into a reciprocal relationship with borrowers that guarantees lenders' profit margins. My respondents emphasized the moral duty of lenders to offer forbearance to mortgagors who had established enduring ties by "choosing" certain lenders and making payments on time. By carefully examining how people parse mortgage modification applications and foreclosures, I have shown the embeddedness of seemingly straightforward financial transactions. Monetized exchange and nonmonetized forms of reciprocity coexist and are interdependent.[12] Abstract financial instruments and corporate bureaucracies shape and are shaped by the social world. Reciprocity and mutuality, values associated with noncommodified spheres of intimate exchange, travel circuitous and promiscuous routes, reframing the meaning of even the most ordinary bureaucratic ephemera.

For mortgagors in lower-middle-class and middle-class neighborhoods in the Sacramento Valley, mortgaging was a lifelong tie that implied a relationship, not simply a faceless financial transaction. Because a home was not solely a commodity or a securitized payment stream to its owner, but an object of profound sentimental attachment, homeowners applied to their lenders the standards and expectations of duty and forgiveness fostered in social contracts of domestic realms. The profound ways in which homes are invested with fantasies about kinship and belonging meant that homeowners embroiled in loan modifications would expect individualized attention and forbearance as an inalienable right. Such expectations of mutuality and respect, imbued with postwar Keynesian economic policies, remain in the American popular imagination but are quickly eroding. These postwar systems were far from perfect; forms of racial and class exclusion such as redlining and gender inequalities were endemic. Yet, seizing on these preexisting assumptions of fairness and reciprocity and making visible how these ideals have been undermined could fortify from below these impulses regarding idealized American moral economies. Instead of mourning the demise of these beliefs, social and political movements could capitalize on these expectations of fairness in economic dealings.

New forms of capitalist production and market technologies coconstitute the everyday realities in which people work, live, and strive to find connection. This is an optimistic finding in many respects, because if the meaning of finance is socially embedded, as society changes and values shift, dominant modes of economic exchange will follow. Financial instruments such as subprime loans and corporate bureaucracies predated the crisis but did not gain such widespread popularity until norms shifted, allowing scams and schemes to become mainstream. Apolitical financial tools—mortgages, securities, corporate bureaucracies—were weaponized against those middle-class families that had once defined the boundaries of social and economic inclusion.

While mass dispossessions after 2008 crystallized new realities for residents of the Sacramento Valley, most homeowners profoundly misunderstood the incentive structures and inner workings of contemporary financialized mortgage markets, even if they were knowledgeable about the process of mortgage lending and repayment. This lack of awareness made informed consent next to impossible. Financial literacy after the 2008 crash must be reconceived beyond the basic terms and concepts of interest rates and repayment plans. Financial institutions and go-betweens such as brokers and agents exploited customers' outdated visions of Main Street lending in which banks put themselves at risk when leveraging mortgages. Homeowners entered into complex financial relationships with secondary mortgage markets about which they knew little or nothing at all. The insult came in the miscommunication: homeowners believed mortgages were conservative investments and trusted banks to determine whether borrowers qualified, whereas mortgage lenders no longer used these metrics to assess qualifications and sought to sell high-risk loans that turned quick profits and generated higher fees. These knowledge gaps were even more extreme among elderly homeowners and those in low-income communities. Lenders and loan servicers deployed a misguided rhetoric of trust, loyalty, and even intimacy in their materials promoting mortgages and then kept up the charade with advertisements offering help for distressed mortgages once the market had collapsed. That homeowners could rarely decipher the true profit motives of loan modification bureaucracies suggests a need for more in-depth financial education and protections. Consumers, especially those most vulnerable to scams and schemes, need better tools with which to decipher the new rules of the lending game.

As of 2018, federal mortgage modification programs are wrapping up, processing the last million or so applications. The end of the mortgage modification drama, however, will likely begin another chapter for predatory techniques. Unless subjected to regulatory checks, the rapacious bureaucratic methods of profit extraction developed in the wake of the mortgage crash will be replicated again and again as private interests and contractors lobby to control the dispersal of billions in federal aid. If history is any indication, Californians will confront disasters—natural and manmade. Residents will face bureaucratic roadblocks in the aftermath of these tragedies when trying to secure insurance payouts and federal relief, and these experiences will damage the implicit social contracts that govern everyday life.

To be sure, the social institution of U.S. mortgaging, as well as the rights and responsibilities it entails, has been radically transformed by the failure of postcrash mortgage modification programs to deliver on the promise of relief. Most important, bureaucratic fiascos have shaped the futures and subjectivities of those homeowners and lending employees caught in the crosshairs of the foreclosure crisis. Unlike some Sacramento Valley residents who lost their homes after 2008, none in my story were forced to take shelter in their car or tent, faced prolonged weeks of hunger, or hanged themselves in their entryway. But they were all considerably worse off than they had been before 2008. To weather a crisis takes courage, and many people discovered they had the mettle to handle the disappointment of foreclosure. But the administrative violence they experienced in the process became too great an insult to ignore. As both homeowners and lending employees criticized modification failures, they reconsidered debt obligations in ways that might challenge the profit-based system of financial mortgaging. In the context of that sense of unfairness, homeowners and lending employees alike developed a vision of debt refusal that could, if captured correctly, have radical consequences for reimagining a renewed American moral economy. Like millions of Americans, Brooke and her family can't go home again, but perhaps new, unknown destinations hold greater promise.

Acknowledgments

This book would not have been possible without the generosity of the people in the Sacramento Valley, families who found the courage to share their stories. People graciously included me in their social and kin networks and although I cannot mention most them by name, I can openly thank my friends and colleagues in the Valley for their time, insights, and hospitality: Bill Burg, Amelia Garduno, Jesus Hernandez, Anné Klint, Rachel Leibrock, Justin McCoy, and Dan and Emel Wadhwani.

As I started this project, I took a leap of faith that was only possible because of the enthusiasm of friends and colleagues who cheered me on. Emily Martin was a champion of this project from the first moment to the last. Fred Myers likewise encouraged me both with his friendship and by helping me to hone my analytical engagements with debt. Faye Ginsburg was a tireless reader and supporter in all things. Bruce Grant offered invaluable advice and feedback.

Other colleagues in the Department of Anthropology at New York University also contributed to my research during various stages, especially Tom Abercrombie, Jane Anderson, Sonia Das, Arlene Dávila, Cheryl Furjanic, Teja Ganti, Helena Hansen, Aisha Khan, Sally Merry, Anne Rademacher, Rayna Rapp, Susan Rogers, Renato Rosaldo, Bambi Schieffelin, and Angela Zito. Susan Antón's support as chair was much appreciated, and Tom Carew's support as dean spurred my confidence.

The pioneering work of Kate Dudley and Chris Walley offered a model for how to develop and pursue projects that were personally meaningful, analytically rigorous, and politically important. I have been lucky to have them as supporters, advocates, and coconspirators for this project.

I also thank Sylvia Yanagisako, who has been a mentor and friend since I discovered anthropology as a wide-eyed undergraduate. I have been motivated by her brilliance and reassured by her sharp sense of humor, and she has always reminded me to make explicit the feminist roots of my inquiries. Sylvia brought me into the Gens Network, where my thinking was enriched and challenged by collaborators and friends: Hannah Appel, Jessica Cattelino, Hilary Chart, Karen Ho, Eleana Kim, Lisa Rofel, Caroline Schuster, Anna Tsing, and Mei Zhan. Engaging with economic anthropology and the anthropology of finance more broadly, Gustav Peebles, Rachel Heiman, Bill Maurer, and Caitlin Zaloom offered invaluable intellectual guidance.

Throughout various stages of research and writing, generous financial funding made this work possible. Seed funding from the Furman Center for Real Estate and Urban Policy at NYU and the guidance of Ingrid Gould Ellen, whose work continues to offer a gold standard for research, and the University Research Challenge Fund at NYU jump-started my research. Long-term field research was supported by the National Science Foundation, and the generous funding paled in comparison to the help and guidance from my exceptional program officers, Jeff Mantz and Deb Winslow. A fellowship from the American Council of Learned Societies supported archival research and writing.

Special thanks to Margaret Levi and Sally Schroeder at the Center for Advanced Study in the Behavioral Sciences at Stanford University for offering the precious gift of uninterrupted time to think and write in a peaceful setting. I was lucky to have ongoing conversations with Margaret about the morality of economic action to enrich my thinking, as did her no-nonsense approach to the analytically rigorous work of social justice. I'm grateful to her and my colleagues at CASBS for encouraging me to think more broadly and engage big questions—especially Hector Amaya, Tara Behrend, Brooke Blower, Steve Feld, Mark Greif, Miyako Inoue, Jonathan Jansen, Paul Jargowsky, Roberta Katz, Eric Klinenberg, Allison Pugh, and Eitan Wilf.

The faculty and staff in the Department of Anthropology at the University of California at Davis hosted me as a visiting scholar during my time in the field, and the Anthropology Department at Stanford University invited me to spend time in the writing stages.

The unyielding support of University of California Press executive editor Naomi Schneider helped me to transform my research into a book, as she offered an infinite wealth of patience and encouragement. Benjy Malings provided technical support to make the book a reality in the final stages. Denise Tanyol was a tireless editor, confidante, and reader. In addition to her eagle eye, wit, and unprecedented breadth of knowledge, she was good company in the trenches. Kristen Tate's sharp insight into the manuscript encouraged me to find a connection to the material when I had lost my way. Alison Jacques and Barbara Armentrout offered skillful manuscript editing in the final stages.

I appreciate the efforts of my talented research assistants, Desiree Barron, a bright star who made time to contribute to this project as she finished her dissertation, and Sam Rolfe, who first wowed me with his analytical gifts during my undergraduate course and has since bloomed into a scholar and social advocate in his own right.

I am indebted to colleagues who read drafts of various articles that made their way into chapters and offered invaluable feedback, especially Don Brenneis (who kindly read the entire rough draft), Lucas Bessire, Niko Besnier, Catherine Besteman, Dominic Boyer, Josh Cohen, Hugh Gusterson, Kevin O'Neill, Lawrence Ralph, and Carolina Reid. Through informal conversations with colleagues, I learned much about bureaucracy and the politics of indebtedness—particularly Julie Bettie, Mathew Hull, Carla Jones, Jovan Lewis, Sean Mallin, Sherry Ortner, Katie Porter, Janet Roitman, Richard Sennett, Parker Shipton, and Susan Woodward. Dale Maharidge is one of the few fellow travelers who could understand every nuance of this project and its meaning for me, from the streets of Sacramento to the high-rises of New York City. I was lucky to have his guidance at the beginning and the end.

Around the time I finished this book, my colleague, friend, and former doctoral advisor Mary Steedly passed away. She was a ferocious storyteller who stirred my faith in the merits of telling everyday tales from the places we know best. I'm thankful to have learned from her and hope to continue to honor her spirit in the work I do.

One of the best parts of conducting research for this book was reconnecting with family and close friends in California. Love and support from Michelle Comeau, Sally Espinoza, Linda Kunsemiller, Shawn Kunsemiller, Carla Najera, Ana Matosantos, Alisa Lehman, Lisa Pope-McDonald, Tim McDonald, Ervin Stout, Amelia and Mike Vitarelli, and Niko Watry Wrencher made it a true homecoming. Special thanks to my mom, Lori "Mae" Gray, for her encouragement during our daily phone calls. Her honesty, sense of humor, and deep sensitivity to injustice continue to inspire me. Finally, I am forever indebted to Matt Lehman, my partner in all things, for helping to make this project happen and to our boys, Bohdy and Damian, for teaching me the true meaning of home.

Glossary

APPRAISAL: a required step in the process of assessing the value of a home and setting the terms for a mortgage loan. A licensed appraiser comes to the property and inspects its size, condition, function, and quality.

BAILOUT: a common term for the Emergency Economic Stabilization Act of 2008, a law passed in response to the subprime mortgage crash that allowed the U.S. secretary of the Treasury to spend up to $700 billion to purchase toxic mortgages and supply cash to banks.

BANKRUPTCY: a court procedure that protects an individual or company from debt collectors, wiping out the majority of one's debts. During the bankruptcy process, the court will force the repossession of some assets, but others will be protected. Declaring bankruptcy results in bad credit for a set number of years.

CREDIT SCORE: a number assigned to a person indicating that individual's supposed ability to repay a loan. One needs a certain credit score to qualify for a loan, rental home, or credit card.

DEFAULT: the failure to pay back a loan.

DERIVATIVES MARKET: a financial market for derivatives, which are financial instruments derived from other forms of assets, including future contracts or options. Derivatives are used to speculate and hedge against market changes. In the lead-up to the 2008 crash, a type of derivative called a credit default swap allowed investors and mortgage lenders to bet against the housing market and thus to profit even if the mortgages they sold failed.

EVICTION: expelling a resident from a property.

FINANCIALIZATION: a shift from industrial capitalism to the predominance of a financial sector.

FIXED-RATE MORTGAGE: a mortgage loan with an interest rate that remains stable, allowing a borrower to accurately predict future payments.

FORECLOSURE: the seizure of a home by a lender or loan servicer to pay off an unpaid debt. Foreclosures typically happen when a homeowner falls behind on home loan payments.

FORECLOSURE AUCTION: the sale of a foreclosed property on the courthouse steps to the highest bidder.

HAMP: the Home Affordable Modification Program, a temporary government program introduced in 2009 to help struggling homeowners avoid foreclosure by modifying mortgage payments to a level that borrowers can afford.

HOUSING BOOM: a real estate bubble triggered by a rapid increase in housing prices brought about by a complex interplay of factors that often includes, among other things, lax lending standards and relaxed regulatory systems.

INTEREST: money paid regularly at a particular rate, or interest rate, for the use of money lent, or for delaying the repayment of a debt.

INVESTOR: a person or organization that puts money into a financial arrangement or a property in order to achieve a profit.

LIEN: the legal right of a creditor to sell the collateral of the property of a debtor who fails to pay. A property that is the subject of a lien cannot be sold without the consent of the creditor.

LOAN MODIFICATION SPECIALIST: a mortgage specialist or often a lending employee who works to modify the mortgages of homeowners facing default.

LOAN OFFICER OR LOAN ORIGINATOR: a person who works for a bank or other financial institution selling loans.

LOAN SERVICER: a company that handles billing and collects payments from a borrower. A loan servicer is often not the original lender.

MORTGAGE: a legal agreement by which a bank or other creditor lends money so a buyer can purchase a property. The creditor charges interest and takes possession of the property should the borrower default or otherwise fail to make agreed-upon payments.

MORTGAGE APPLICATION: a document submitted by an individual applying to borrow money to purchase a property.

MORTGAGE-BACKED SECURITY OR MORTGAGE SECURITY: a type of asset-backed security that is secured by a collection of mortgages.

MORTGAGE MODIFICATION: a process by which a lender or loan servicer changes the terms of a mortgage.

NET PRESENT VALUE (NPV) TEST: a measurement of the profitability of an investment, calculated by subtracting the present values of cash outflows from the present values of cash inflows over a period of time.

NOTARY: a person certified to draw up and certify contracts and deeds.

PREDATORY LENDING: a practice that imposes unfair or abusive loan terms on a borrower. Often deceit or coercion is used to convince a borrower to take on a loan that she or he does not need or cannot afford.

PRIME: borrowers, rates, or holdings in the lending market that are considered to be of high quality. Prime borrowers are deemed the most creditworthy, and the prime rate is a lower rate at which a lender will lend money to high-quality borrowers.

REAL ESTATE BROKER: a person who acts as an intermediary between sellers and buyers in the purchase of real estate. In the Sacramento Valley, brokers often secured mortgage loans for buyers.

REDLINING: a practice of denying services, either directly or through selectively raising prices, to residents of certain areas based on the racial or ethnic composition of those areas.

REFINANCE: to pay off an old loan by taking on a new loan with new terms, typically at a lower interest rate.

SECOND MORTGAGE: the taking out of another loan, which uses the home as collateral, on a home that is already mortgaged.

SECONDARY MARKET: a market on which investors buy from and sell securities or assets to other investors.

SECURITIZATION: using an illiquid asset or group of assets such as mortgages, auto loans, and credit card debt, and selling their cash flows, or payments, to third-party investors as "securities."

SHORT SALE: a sale of real estate in which the total proceeds from the sale will fall short of the debts secured by liens against the property. This type of sale is accomplished by getting all lien holders to agree to accept less than the amount owed on the debt.

SUBPRIME MORTGAGE LOAN: a loan offered to prospective borrowers with less-than-perfect credit records. These mortgages feature higher interest rates and less favorable terms for the borrower in order to compensate the lender for accepting greater risk in lending. Often, subprime mortgages are adjustable-rate mortgages whose interest rates change, outside a borrower's control.

TEASER RATE: an introductory interest rate charged to a borrower during the initial stages of a loan. The rate, which can be as low as 0 percent, expires after a set period, at which point a higher-than-normal rate will apply.

UNDERWATER MORTGAGE: a mortgage loan with a higher balance than the current value of the home, preventing the homeowner from selling without incurring an out-of-pocket loss or refinancing.

UNDERWRITER: a specialized loan officer who analyzes and assesses the creditworthiness of potential borrowers to see if they qualify for a loan.

Notes

INTRODUCTION

1. RealtyTrac, "2014 Year-End U.S. Foreclosure Market Report," 2015, accessed December 17, 2017, www.realtytrac.com/news/foreclosure-trends /1–1-million-u-s-properties-with-foreclosure-filings-in-2014-down-18-percent-from-2013-to-lowest-level-since-2006/; Matthew Hall, Kyle Crowder, and Amy Spring, "Variations in Housing Foreclosures by Race and Place, 2005–2012," *Annals of the American Academy of Political and Social Science* 660, no. 1 (2015): 217–37.

2. Ben Casselman, Patricia Cohen, and Doris Burke, "The Great Recession Knocked Them Down. Only Some Got Up Again," *New York Times,* September 12, 2018.

3. Jesse McKinley, "Residents of Sacramento's Tent City to Move to Fairground," *New York Times,* March 25, 2009, www.nytimes.com/2009/03/26/us /26sacramento.html.

4. Pulitzer Prize–winning journalist, author, and longtime Sacramento resident Dale Maharidge pointed out to me that the tent city existed long before the 2008 crisis. In fact, few of the residents were actually victims of the financial crisis.

5. In 2010, with the passage of the Dodd-Frank Act, the Troubled Asset Relief Program would be reduced to approximately $475 billion.

6. For more details on the specific firms that received bailout funds, see "9 Wall Street Execs Who Cashed In on the Crisis," *Mother Jones,* January-

224 / *Notes to Pages 9–13*

February 2010, www.motherjones.com/politics/2010/01/wall-street-bailout-executive-compensation/.

7. As opposed to lenders, which originate mortgages, loan servicers manage the loans thereafter. They process payments, keep track of the principal and interest, and initiate foreclosures if payments are delinquent. Although original lenders may also service their mortgages, loans were increasingly managed by third-party servicers during the crash because of widespread mortgage securitization.

8. Office of the Special Inspector General for the Troubled Asset Relief Program (SIGTARP), *Quarterly Report to Congress,* April 26, 2017, www.sigtarp.gov/Quarterly%20Reports/April_26_2017_r1_Report_to_Congress.pdf.

9. I borrow the term *predatory bureaucracy* from anthropologist and Occupy Wall Street activist David Graeber, who mentions it parenthetically while describing "total bureaucratization." David Graeber, *The Utopia of Rules: On Technology, Stupidity, and the Secret Joys of Bureaucracy* (New York: Melville House, 2015), 17.

10. Vincanne Adams, *Markets of Sorrow, Labors of Faith: New Orleans in the Wake of Katrina* (Durham, NC: Duke University Press, 2013), 49.

11. Naomi Klein, *The Shock Doctrine: The Rise of Disaster Capitalism* (New York: Macmillan, 2007).

12. Journalist Antony Loewenstein shows the global reach and scale of disaster capitalism, demonstrating how international relief efforts in response to crisis have garnered private profits for Western corporations in a range of contexts from Papua New Guinea to Haiti to Afghanistan to the United States. Antony Loewenstein, *Disaster Capitalism: Making a Killing Out of Catastrophe* (New York: Verso Books, 2015), 7.

13. Timothy Geithner's mother was a liberal and his father a Republican who worked as a program officer for the Ford Foundation in India and Thailand, where Geithner spent years of his childhood. Having grown up abroad, he describes being struck by the severe impact of U.S. economic policies and ethnocentrism of his compatriots with regard to international issues.

14. Timothy F. Geithner, *Stress Test: Reflections on Financial Crises* (New York: Broadway Books, 2015).

15. Geithner, *Stress Test,* 389.

16. Brent White, "Underwater and Not Walking Away: Shame, Fear and the Social Management of the Housing Crisis," *Wake Forest Law Review* 45 (October 27, 2010): 971, Arizona Legal Studies Discussion Paper No. 09–35, last revised

May 9, 2015, https://papers.ssrn.com/sol3/papers.cfm?abstract_id=1494467. White references specific shows such as Fox's "The Deal: Walk Away from Your Home" on *Your World with Cavuto;* "YouWalkAway.com" on Salem Radio Networks' *The Mike Gallagher Show;* and "The U.S. Mortgage Meltdown" on CBS's *60 Minutes.*

17. As Janet Roitman attests, a range of pundits from opposing theoretical and political camps, from neo-Marxists to neo-Keynesians, succumb to the same logical fallacy by promoting a narrative of "crisis." Their reports trace a chain of events during which the "housing market fell" and homeowners lost equity and defaulted on their mortgages. The critical question of why housing prices began to fall, Roitman suggests, is preemptively excluded. Janet Roitman, *Anti-Crisis* (Durham, NC: Duke University Press, 2013), 57.

18. For example, Paula Chakravartty and Denise Ferreira da Silva, "Accumulation, Dispossession, and Debt: The Racial Logic of Global Capitalism—An Introduction," *American Quarterly* 64, no. 3 (2012): 361–85; Shawn Shimpach, "Realty Reality: HGTV and the Subprime Crisis," *American Quarterly* 64, no. 3 (2012): 515–42; Roitman, *Anti-Crisis.*

19. Sherry B. Ortner, *New Jersey Dreaming: Capital, Culture, and the Class of '58* (Durham, NC: Duke University Press, 2003), 51.

20. Jacob Hacker, *The Great Risk Shift: New Economic Insecurity and the Decline of the American Dream* (New York: Oxford University Press, 2008).

21. Hugh Gusterson and Catherine Besteman, eds., *The Insecure American: How We Got Here and What We Should Do about It* (Berkeley: University of California Press, 2010), 7.

22. Angus Burgin, *The Great Persuasion: Reinventing Free Markets since the Depression.* (Cambridge, MA: Harvard University Press, 2012).

23. Katherine S. Newman, *Falling from Grace: Downward Mobility in the Age of Affluence* (Berkeley: University of California Press, 1988).

24. Rachel Heiman, *Driving after Class: Anxious Times in an American Suburb* (Oakland: University of California Press, 2015), 1.

25. Marianne Cooper, *Cut Adrift: Families in Insecure Times* (Berkeley: University of California Press, 2014).

26. Karen Ho, *Liquidated: An Ethnography of Wall Street* (Durham, NC: Duke University Press, 2009).

27. Thomas Piketty, *Capital in the Twenty-First Century* (Cambridge, MA: Harvard University Press, 2014), 294.

28. Piketty, *Capital in the Twenty-First Century,* 297.

29. Piketty, 297.

30. On race and class discrimination in U.S. housing, see LeeAnn Lands, *The Culture of Property: Race, Class, and Housing Landscapes in Atlanta, 1880–1950* (Athens: University of Georgia Press, 2009); Amanda Seligman, *Block by Block: Neighborhoods and Public Policy on Chicago's West Side,* Historical Studies of Urban America (Chicago: University of Chicago Press, 2005); Andrew Wiese, *Places of Their Own: African American Suburbanization in the Twentieth Century* (Chicago: University of Chicago Press, 2004). On deindustrialization, see Arjun Appadurai, *Modernity at Large: Cultural Dimensions of Globalization* (Minneapolis: University of Minnesota Press, 1996); Gusterson and Besteman, *The Insecure American;* Aiwha Ong, *Neoliberalism as Exception: Mutations in Citizenship and Sovereignty* (Durham, NC: Duke University Press, 2006); Christine Walley, *Exit Zero* (Chicago: University of Chicago Press, 2013).

31. Debbie Gruenstein Bocian, Wei Li, Carolina Reid, and Roberto G. Quercia, *Lost Ground, 2011: Disparities in Mortgage Lending and Foreclosures,* Center for Responsible Lending, November 2011, www.responsiblelending.org/mortgage-lending/research-analysis/Lost-Ground-2011.pdf.

32. William Apgar and Allegra Calder, "The Dual Mortgage Market: The Persistence of Discrimination in Mortgage Lending," in *The Geography of Opportunity,* ed. Xavier De Souza Briggs, 101–27 (Washington, DC: Brookings Institute Press, 2005).

33. Ortner, *New Jersey Dreaming.*

34. Julie Bettie, *Women without Class: Girls, Race, and Identity* (Berkeley: University of California Press, 2014), 7.

35. Franz Boas, "The Indians of British Columbia," *Popular Science Monthly* 32 (1888): 631; Bronislaw Malinowski, *Argonauts of the Western Pacific: An Account of Native Enterprise and Adventure in the Archipelagoes of Melanesian New Guinea* (1922; repr., New York: Dutton, 1961); Marcel Mauss, *The Gift: The Form and Reason for Exchange in Archaic Societies,* trans. W. D. Halls (1925; repr., London: Routledge, 1990).

36. Mauss, no apologist for capitalism, was a communist but believed in a bottom-up revolution not dictated by an omnipotent state government.

37. Marilyn Strathern, *The Gender of the Gift: Problems with Women and Problems with Society in Melanesia* (Berkeley: University of California Press, 1988). See also Christopher Gregory, *Gifts and Commodities* (London: Academic Press, 1982). Bill Maurer in his work on mobile money later challenges the notion that "money corrodes social bonds and moral reasoning in service of instrumental logics of transactional exchange." Bill Maurer, "The Anthropology of Money," *Annual Review of Anthropology* 35, no. 1 (2006): 15–36.

38. Laura Bear, Karen Ho, Anna Tsing, and Sylvia Yanagisako, "Generating Capitalism," Theorizing the Contemporary (conversation), *Cultural Anthropology* (blog), March 30, 2015, https://culanth.org/fieldsights/650-generating-capitalism; and more recent work by Hannah Appel, "Toward an Ethnography of the National Economy," *Cultural Anthropology* 32, no. 2 (2017): 294–322. Much of this work builds on and engages Karl Polyani's notion of embeddedness. Polyani, *The Great Transformation: The Political and Economic Origins of Our Time* (1944; repr., Boston: Beacon Press, 2001).

39. See Jessica Cattelino's approach to this question, centering her inquiry around forms of exclusion and inclusion in American Indian struggles. Jessica Cattelino, "The Double Bind of American Indian Need-Based Sovereignty," *Cultural Anthropology* 25, no. 2, (2010): 235–62. In a similar spirit, Caroline Schuster, in her study of microcredit borrowers and lenders in Paraguay, argues that it matters "how and for whom social reciprocity takes hold in capitalist markets." Caroline Schuster, *Social Collateral: Women and Microfinance in Paraguay's Smuggling Economy* (Berkeley: University of California Press, 2015).

40. James C. Scott, *The Moral Economy of the Peasant: Rebellion and Subsistence in Southeast Asia* (New Haven, CT: Yale University Press, 1977).

41. As David Graeber highlights, money has a "capacity to turn morality into a matter of impersonal arithmetic—and by doing so, to justify things that would otherwise seem outrageous or obscene." David Graeber, *Debt: The First 5,000 Years* (Brooklyn: Melville House, 2011), 14.

42. An ethnographic approach best shows how historical social contexts matter. For example, neoliberalism within American financialized capitalism is distinct from the flexible forms of neoliberalism developed within contemporary Chinese capitalism—and also reveals how omnipresent forms of capitalist exploitation are only seemingly preordained; rather, they arise from the real choices people make each day.

43. Pseudonyms have been used for homeowners, lending employees, and activists unless otherwise noted. In four cases I have combined moments from two different ethnographic tableaus for ease of storytelling; these composite scenes have left all the specific details of homeowners' and lending employees' stories intact, such as their employment histories, mortgaging particulars, life events, and backgrounds.

44. To establish a comparative perspective, I observed and analyzed five cases of homeowners involved in mortgage refinancing—loan renegotiation for mortgagors who are not delinquent—to supplement my findings.

45. Of my respondents in lending, approximately one-quarter were no longer employed by corporate banks. In each case, my respondents had worked for banks within the past three years. I considered how changes in public discourse and the fleeting nature of memory influenced their views.

46. Joan Didion, "California Notes," *New York Review of Books,* May 26, 2016, www.nybooks.com/articles/2016/05/26/california-notes/.

47. Lila Abu-Lughod, "Can There Be a Feminist Ethnography?," *Women and Performance: A Journal of Feminist Theory* 5, no. 1 (1990): 7–27.

48. George Packer, "Don't Look Down: The New Depression Journalism," *New Yorker,* April 29, 2013, www.newyorker.com/magazine/2013/04/29/dont-look-down.

49. George Packer, *The Unwinding: An Inner History of the New America* (New York: Farrar, Straus and Giroux, 2014); Dale Maharidge and Michael Williamson, *Someplace Like America: Tales from the New Great Depression* (Berkeley: University of California Press, 2013); Barbara Garson, *Down the Up Escalator: How the 99 Percent Live in the Great Recession* (New York: Doubleday, 2013).

1. DREAM IT, OWN IT

1. By the turn of the twentieth century, agriculture had come to dominate the economic landscape of the Sacramento Valley region, a movement enabled by the expansion of rail lines and the development of refrigerated train cars that could carry California's crops to the East Coast. By the 1890s, 75 percent of all the fruit shipped to the East Coast came from the Sacramento Valley. In 1905, the growth of the agricultural industry drove the establishment of the University of California at Davis as a "university farm school." The agricultural boom attracted migrants from across the country, as well as from Japan, Mexico, and China. In the next decades, large-scale industrial agriculture was matched by manufacturing and the growth of canneries in Sacramento.

2. Louis Hyman, *Debtor Nation: The History of America in Red Ink* (Princeton, NJ: Princeton University Press, 2011), 1.

3. Lendol Calder, *Financing the American Dream: A Cultural History of Consumer Credit* (Princeton, NJ: Princeton University Press, 1999); Hyman, *Debtor Nation.*

4. Brett Williams, *Debt for Sale: A Social History of the Credit Trap* (Philadelphia: University of Pennsylvania Press, 2004).

5. Louis Hyman, "Ending Discrimination, Legitimating Debt: The Political Economy of Race, Gender, and Credit Access in the 1960s and 1970s," *Enterprise and Society* 12, no. 1 (March 2011): 201.

6. Dianne Harris, *Little White Houses: How the Postwar Home Constructed Race in America* (Minneapolis: University of Minnesota Press, 2013).

7. Hyman, "Ending Discrimination, Legitimating Debt," 224.

8. Cf. Kathryn Marie Dudley, *End of the Line: Lost Jobs, New Lives in Postindustrial America* (Chicago: University of Chicago Press, 1994); Graeber, *Utopia of Rules;* Gusterson and Besteman, *Insecure American;* Walley, *Exit Zero.*

9. Andrew Ross, *Creditocracy and the Case for Debt Refusal* (New York: OR Books, 2013), 11.

10. The rich history of the Punjabi Mexican American community in Northern California is outlined in Karen Leonard's *Making Ethnic Choices: California's Punjabi Mexican Americans* (Philadelphia: Temple University Press, 1992).

11. Sandra described feeling lucky that she found a way to stay in the business when most of her peers faced unemployment after 2008. "I ran into one former colleague when I was at the House of Pancakes," Sandra said. "She was our waitress."

12. Louise Story, "Home Equity Frenzy Was a Bank Ad Come True," *New York Times,* August 15, 2008, www.nytimes.com/2008/08/15/business/15sell .html.

13. Luigi Guiso, Paola Sapienza, and Luigi Zingales, "Moral and Social Constraints to Strategic Default on Mortgages," NBER Working Paper 15145 (Cambridge, MA: National Bureau of Economic Research, 2009), www.nber .org/papers/w15145.

14. Brian Faith, "New Nationwide Survey Provides Comprehensive Look at Sentiment toward Housing," Federal National Mortgage Association (Fannie Mae), news release, April 6, 2010, www.fanniemae.com/portal/media /corporate-news/2010/4989.html.

15. Cf. Rachel Heiman, Carla Freeman, and Mark Liechty, "Charting an Anthropology of the Middle Classes," in *The Global Middle Classes: Theorizing through Ethnography,* ed. Rachel Heiman, Carla Freeman, and Mark Liechty (Santa Fe, NM: School for Advanced Research Press, 2012), 8. In fact, by 2002, Harvard University's Civil Rights Project named Sacramento one of the most racially integrated cities in the United States.

16. Kathryn Marie Dudley, *Debt and Dispossession: Farm Loss in America's Heartland* (Chicago: University of Chicago Press, 2000), 5.

17. Brent White, "Take This House and Shove It: The Emotional Drivers of Strategic Default." Arizona Legal Studies Discussion Paper No. 10–17 (Tucson: University of Arizona, James E. Rogers College of Law, last revised May 15, 2010), https://papers.ssrn.com/sol3/papers.cfm?abstract_id=1603605.

18. David Harvey, *The Enigma of Capital and the Crises of Capitalism* (New York: Oxford University Press, 2011), 149.

19. Harvey, *Enigma of Capital*.

20. Saskia Sassen, *Expulsions: Brutality and Complexity in the Global Economy* (Cambridge, MA: Belknap Press, 2014).

21. Struggles over land rights coincided with a surge in white supremacist policies. Between 1850 and 1854, the all-white California legislature segregated African American and white schools and banned African Americans, Chinese, and Native Americans from testifying in cases involving white plaintiffs and defendants.

22. Karen Ho, *Liquidated: An Ethnography of Wall Street* (Durham, NC: Duke University Press, 2009), 183.

2. PUT OUT

1. Statistics for zip codes 95817 and 95820 based on RealtyTrac data with projected trends for 2012, compiled and reprinted in Alliance of Californians for Community Empowerment and The California Reinvestment Coalition, *The Wall Street Wrecking Ball: What Foreclosures Are Costing Sacramento Neighborhoods* (Los Angeles: ACCE, September 2011), 7.

2. Carol B. Stack, *All Our Kin: Strategies for Survival in a Black Community* (New York: Basic Books, 1975), 107.

3. Christi Baker, Kevin Stein, and Mike Eiseman, *Foreclosure Trends in Sacramento and Recommended Policy Options: A Report for the Sacramento Housing and Redevelopment Agency* (San Francisco: California Reinvestment Coalition, 2008), http://sacramento.granicus.com/MetaViewer.php?view_id=22&clip_id=1526&meta_id=147291.

4. Baker, Stein, and Eiseman, *Foreclosure Trends in Sacramento;* Vicki Been, Mary Weselcouch, Ioan Voicu, and Scott Murff, "Determinants of the Incidence of Loan Modifications," NYU Law and Economics Research Paper Series No. 11–37 (New York: NYU School of Law, last revised December 8, 2012), https://ssrn.com/abstract=1941915; G. Thomas Kingsley and Kathryn L. S. Pettit, *High-Cost and Investor Mortgages: Neighborhood Patterns* (Washington, DC: Urban Institute, 2009), http://webarchive.urban.org/uploadedpdf/411941_highcost.pdf.

5. Servicers fail to report all data. Servicers' failure to collect key data is a violation of HAMP contracts, thwarts transparency, and obscures whether antidiscrimination laws are being followed. This is yet another example of

servicer noncompliance with HAMP. Moreover, 43 percent of loan modification records in four California MSAs do not include the race or ethnicity of the borrower. Servicer nonreporting accounted for 10 percent of all records lacking race and ethnicity data. Kevin Stein and Kristina Bedrossian, *Race to the Bottom: An Analysis of HAMP Loan Modification Outcomes by Race and Ethnicity* (San Francisco: California Reinvestment Coalition, July 2011).

6. According to Hernandez, a large body of evidence based on the Home Mortgage Disclosure Act, passed in 1975, "has shown racial discrimination in the mortgage industry over the last twenty years, in particular against black and Hispanic borrowers." Jesus Hernandez, "Redlining Revisited: Mortgage Lending Patterns in Sacramento 1930–2004," *International Journal of Urban and Regional Research* 33, no. 2 (2009): 291–313.

7. Hernandez points out that the legacies of these programs shifted Oak Park's demographics from 6.5 percent nonwhite residents in 1950 to nearly half minority residents by 1970. Hernandez, "Redlining Revisited." See also Guy Stuart, *Discriminating Risk: The U.S. Mortgage Lending Industry in the Twentieth Century* (Ithaca, NY: Cornell University Press, 2003); David Freund, "Marketing the Free Market: State Intervention and the Politics of Prosperity in Metropolitan America," in *The New Suburban History*, ed. Kevin M. Kruse and Thomas J. Sugrue (Chicago: University of Chicago Press, 2006).

8. Stuart, *Discriminating Risk*, 12.

9. Hernandez, "Redlining Revisited," 302.

10. For a complementary study that shows how notions of reciprocity were central to mortgage lending within poor neighborhoods in Spain, see Jamie Palomera, "Reciprocity, Commodification, and Poverty in the Era of Financialization," *Current Anthropology* 55, no. 9 (2014): S105–15.

11. Carolina Reid, "Sought or Sold? Social Embeddedness and Consumer Decisions in the Mortgage Market," Working Paper 2010–09 (San Francisco: Federal Reserve Bank of San Francisco, December 2010), www.frbsf.org /community-development/files/wp2010–09.pdf.

12. In a 2008 investigation, the Center for Responsible Lending (CRL) cited a number of lawsuits across the nation filed against IndyMac. In Savannah, Georgia, IndyMac approved a mortgage based on the falsified Social Security income of Ben Butler, an eighty-year-old retiree. In Brooklyn, New York, IndyMac steered Simeon Ferguson, an eighty-six-year-old retiree suffering from dementia, into a "stated income" mortgage requiring that the file *not* contain any documentation. In Washington, DC, Willie Lee Howard, a sixty-five-year-old construction worker who had grown up in a sharecropping family in North

Carolina, received a cold call from IndyMac; he explained that he could not read or write, but the loan application IndyMac subsequently prepared for him said he had sixteen years of education. For another senior in Georgia, Elouise Manuel, IndyMac went even further, requiring the broker to redact her Social Security income information. See Mike Hudson, *IndyMac: What Went Wrong? How an "Alt-A" Leader Fueled its Growth with Unsound and Abusive Mortgage Lending,* CRL Report (Durham, NC: Center for Responsible Lending, June 30, 2008), www.responsiblelending.org/mortgage-lending/research-analysis/indymac_what_went_wrong.pdf. Hudson cites Scott Vaughan (attorney at law), letter to Clarice Paschel, IndyMac, October 8, 2007; Ferguson v. IndyMac Bank, U.S. District Court for the Eastern District of New York, filed February 14, 2008; Manuel v. American Residential Financing, Inc. et al., Superior Court of Gwinnett County, State of Georgia, April 3, 2008.

13. According to Hudson, *IndyMac,* in one $354 million pool of mortgages IndyMac sold as securities in 2006, over 90 percent of the loans used "stated income," with no documentation such as pay stubs or tax returns to corroborate income. IndyMac employees called these pervasive and fraudulent loans "Disneyland loans" after IndyMac granted a mortgage loan to a Disneyland cashier whose income was listed as $90,000 a year.

14. The underwriter was interviewed by representatives of the Center for Responsible Lending.

15. Hudson, *IndyMac: What Went Wrong?,* 6.

16. Kath Weston, *Families We Choose: Lesbians, Gays, Kinship* (New York: Columbia University Press, 1997).

17. Sylvia Yanagisako, *Producing Culture and Capital: Family Firms in Italy* (Princeton, NJ: Princeton University Press, 2002).

18. Reid, "Sought or Sold?," 9.

19. Reid.

20. Philippe Bourgois, *In Search of Respect: Selling Crack in El Barrio* (Cambridge: Cambridge University Press, 1996).

21. Peter Goodman and Gretchen Morgenson, "Saying Yes, WaMu Built Empire on Shaky Loans," *New York Times,* December 27, 2008, www.nytimes.com/2008/12/28/business/28wamu.html.

22. With option ARMs, interest rates adjusted monthly, and once the unpaid interest hit a specific amount, the loan would become fixed rate, with much higher payments. Consumer advocates warned against option ARMs because of the dangers of deceiving borrowers.

23. In 2012, Joel Blanford, a WaMu loan officer working in the subprime divisions of two California offices, was found guilty of bribing a loan coordinator to falsify documents, providing fraudulent employment information about borrowers to allow himself to reap more than $1 million in commissions between 2003 and 2005. Erin Ivie, "San Ramon Man Sentenced to 30 Months in Prison for Defrauding Employer," *East Bay Times,* February 25, 2013.

24. Drew DeSilver, "Killinger Got $25M in WaMu's Final Year," *Seattle Times,* April 12, 2010.

25. They also capitalized on the media attention on foreclosures in Oak Park to generate public awareness of long-standing social ills affecting the neighborhood. ACCE, for example, orchestrated an antiblight campaign. As blight and abandoned properties became salient issues in the local news, activists organized a community meeting to address blight in Oak Park. They invited the press, government officials, and key policy makers and forced them to address the city's failure to pursue negligent owners who did not comply with the city code.

26. Dan Immergluck and Geoff Smith, "The External Costs of Foreclosure: The Impact of Single-Family Mortgage Foreclosures on Property Values," *Housing Policy Debate* 17, no. 1 (2006): 57–79.

27. Debbie Gruenstein Bocian, Keith S. Ernst, and Wei Li, "Race, Ethnicity and Subprime Home Loan Pricing," *Journal of Economics and Business* 60, no. 1 (2008): 110–24.

28. Baker, Stein, and Eiseman, "Foreclosure Trends in Sacramento"; Sewin Chan, Michael Gedal, Vicki Been, and Andrew Haughwout, "The Role of Neighborhood Characteristics in Mortgage Default Risk: Evidence from New York City," Working Paper, Furman Center for Real Estate and Public Policy (New York: New York University, 2012); Kingsley and Pettit, *High Cost and Investor Mortgages.*

29. Been, Weselcouch, Voicu, and Murff, "Determinants of the Incidence of Loan Modifications."

30. Chan, Gedal, Been, and Haughwout, "Role of Neighborhood Characteristics."

31. Matthew Desmond, *Evicted: Poverty and Profit in the American City* (New York: Broadway Books, 2017).

32. Hudson Sangree and Phillip Reese, "Homeownership in Sacramento Plummets to Lowest Level in 40 Years," *Sacramento Bee,* May 12, 2014.

33. Piketty, *Capital in the Twenty-First Century.*

3. ROBBING PETER TO PAY PAUL

1. Jerry Anthony, "Home Burdens: The High Cost of Homeownership," in *Broke: How Debt Bankrupts the Middle Class,* ed. Katherine Porter (Palo Alto: Stanford University Press, 2012), 65–84.

2. While there is a significant lack of data due to loan servicers' failure to report the race and ethnicity of applicants, as is mandated by HAMP, what little evidence exists points to worse outcomes for Latino and African American homeowners in California. Kevin Stein and Kristina Bedrossian, *Race to the Bottom: An Analysis of HAMP Loan Modification Outcomes by Race and Ethnicity* (San Francisco: California Reinvestment Coalition, July 2011).

3. Walley, *Exit Zero.*

4. Joseph Howell, *Hard Living on Clay Street: Portraits of Blue Collar Families* (Prospect Heights, IL: Waveland Press, 1972).

5. Providing this intimate knowledge not only makes homeowners feel scrutinized, but there is evidence that doing so increased their risk of bank seizure. In a study of 2007 bankruptcy data, contact with lenders and mortgage servicers actually *increased* the likelihood that a lender would initiate foreclosures among homeowners filing for bankruptcy. Working with bankruptcy data from 2007, Jerry Anthony shows that lenders were more likely to initiate foreclosure actions against households that had received foreclosure notices before bankruptcy if those households had contacted their lenders. Anthony surmises that this trend suggests that mortgage companies learned information while negotiating with struggling homeowners that led them to decide to pursue seizures. Anthony, "Home Burdens," 82.

6. Portions of my analysis appeared in Noelle Stout, "Petitioning a Giant: Debt, Reciprocity, and Mortgage Modification in the Sacramento Valley," *American Ethnologist* 43, no. 1 (2016): 1–14.

7. The PSA was produced by the Ad Council for HUD and for the Department of the Treasury.

8. Janet Roitman, *Fiscal Disobedience: An Anthropology of Economic Regulation in Central Africa* (Princeton, NJ: Princeton University Press, 2005), 73.

9. Graeber, *Debt: The First 5,000 Years,* 120.

10. Yanagisako, *Producing Culture and Capital,* 12. Yanagisako shows how kinship, often understood by Marxist feminist scholars as important to the offstage social reproduction of capitalism—creating and maintaining a workforce—actually plays a center-stage role in the production of industrial capitalist markets.

11. Viviana Zelizer, *The Social Meaning of Money* (New York: Basic Books, 1994), 2. See also Gustav Peebles, "The Anthropology of Credit and Debt," *Annual Review of Anthropology* 39 (2010): 225–40; Kaitlin Zaloom, *Out of the Pits: Traders and Technology from Chicago to London* (Chicago: University of Chicago Press, 2006).

12. Georg Simmel, *The Philosophy of Money,* trans. Tom Bottomore and David Frisby (New York: Routledge Classics, 1978).

13. Lauren Berlant, *Cruel Optimism* (Durham, NC: Duke University Press, 2011).

14. Here I use Rachel's real name, with her permission, in order to link her story with her cutting-edge journalism on the topic of foreclosure.

15. Rachel Leibrock, "Default!," *Sacramento News & Review,* December 16, 2010.

16. Of the major mortgage servicers, Bank of America was the worst, with 75 percent of counselors reporting that dual tracking "always" and "almost always" occurred. JPMorgan Chase, Wells Fargo, and Citibank were close behind.

17. Kevin Stein and Sarah Brett, *Chasm between Words and Deeds VIII: Lack of Bank Accountability Plagues Californians* (San Francisco: California Reinvestment Coalition, April 2012).

18. Lindsay A. Owens, "Intrinsically Advantageous? Reexamining the Production of Class Advantage in the Case of Home Mortgage Modification," *Social Forces* 93, no. 3 (2014): 1185–1209.

19. Stein and Brett, *Chasm between Words and Deeds,* 7.

20. Numerous articles in the press have documented robo-signing practice; see Associated Press, "'Robo-signing' of Mortgages Still a Problem," CBS News, July 18, 2011, www.cbsnews.com/news/robo-signing-of-mortgages-still-a-problem; David Segal, "Debt Collectors Face a Hazard: Writer's Cramp," *New York Times,* October 31, 2010.

21. Office of SIGTARP, *Quarterly Report to Congress,* 68.

22. Kathryn Marie Dudley, *Debt and Dispossession: Farm Loss in America's Heartland* (Chicago: University of Chicago Press, 2000), 46.

23. Dudley, *Debt and Dispossession,* 54.

24. Similarly, anthropologists have observed how fundamental assumptions embedded in mortgaging are historically contingent and culturally specific. Parker Shipton, *Mortgaging the Ancestors: Ideologies of Attachment in Africa* (New Haven, CT: Yale University Press, 2009), for example, describes Luo skepticism at the prospect of using land, which is tied to ancestors, to

acquire credit in Western Kenya. Bill Maurer, *Pious Property: Islamic Mortgages in the United States* (New York: Russell Sage Foundation, 2006), likewise traces the history of Islamic home financing, which prohibits the payment of interest, in the United States.

25. See, for example, David Graeber, "On Social Currencies and Human Economies," *Social Anthropology* 20, no. 4 (2012): 417.

26. Michel Foucault, "Lives of Infamous Men," in *The Essential Works of Foucault, 1954–1984,* vol. 3, *Power,* ed. James Faubion, trans. Robert Hurley (1977; New York: New Press, 2001), 157–77.

27. Graeber, *Debt: The First 5,000 Years,* 45.

28. If you buy a used bicycle from a seller on Craigslist, there is no expectation that you will maintain a relationship beyond that transaction. In fact, if you continued to text the seller after the sale with friendly conversation, you might be deemed a threat, as if you were unable to parse the implicit rules of exchange. Had you bought the bicycle from a big-box retailer such as Target and then tried to stay in touch with the cashier, your behavior would be even more troubling. By paying for the bicycle, you've ended the encounter and both parties are meant to move on.

29. Marcel Mauss, *The Gift: The Form and Reason for Exchange in Archaic Societies,* trans. W. D. Halls (1925; repr., London: Routledge, 1990).

30. Mary Douglass, preface to Mauss, *The Gift,* vii. If someone gives you a scarf for your birthday, for example, and you reimburse him or her the exact amount for the cost of the scarf, it would be an insult, a refusal of the social tie made through the act of giving.

31. Marilyn Strathern, *The Gender of the Gift: Problems with Women and Problems with Society in Melanesia* (Berkeley: University of California Press, 1988); Gregory, *Gifts and Commodities.*

32. Annette Weiner, *Inalienable Possessions: The Paradox of Keeping-While-Giving* (Berkeley: University of California Press, 1992), 25.

33. Anna Tsing, "Sorting Out Commodities: How Capitalist Value Is Made through Gifts," *HAU: Journal of Ethnographic Theory* 3, no. 1 (Spring 2013): 21–43.

34. Tsing, "Sorting Out Commodities," 22.

35. Igor Kopytoff, "The Cultural Biography of Things: Commoditization as Process," in *The Social Life of Things: Commodities in Cultural Perspective,* ed. Arjun Appadurai (Cambridge: Cambridge University Press, 1986), 64–94.

36. Brent White, "Take This House and Shove It: The Emotional Drivers of Strategic Default," Arizona Legal Studies Discussion Paper No. 10–17

(Tucson: University of Arizona, James E. Rogers College of Law, last revised May 15, 2010), https://papers.ssrn.com/sol3/papers.cfm?abstract_id=1603605.

37. Owens, "Intrinsically Advantageous?," 1188.

38. Owens argues that middle-class applicants were at a particular disadvantage relative to working-class residents because shame prevented them from discussing their predicaments with their social networks. The working-class Californians in Owens's study learn crucial information by asking neighbors, family members, and friends for advice. The setting in the Sacramento Valley where foreclosures were widespread among middle-class neighborhoods was markedly different; middle-class homeowners began with feelings of shame but as the scope of the crisis expanded, they turned to social networks for advice.

39. Owens, "Intrinsically Advantageous?"; J. Michael Collins and Collin O'Rourke, "Financial Education and Counseling, Still Holding Promise," *Journal of Consumer Affairs* 44, no. 3 (Fall 2010): 483–89; J. Michael Collins and Carolina Reid, "Who Receives a Mortgage Modification? Race and Income Differentials in Loan Workouts," Community Development Investment Center Working Paper 2010–07 (San Francisco: Federal Reserve Bank of San Francisco, 2010).

40. Rebecca L. Sandefur, "Access to Justice: Classical Approaches and New Directions," in *Access to Justice,* ed. Rebecca L. Sandefur (Bingley, UK: Emerald, 2009).

41. Owens, "Intrinsically Advantageous?"

42. Kevin T. Leicht, "Borrowing to the Brink: Consumer Debt in America" in *Broke: How Debt Bankrupts the Middle Class,* ed. Katherine Porter (Palo Alto: Stanford University Press, 2012), 202.

43. Elizabeth Warren and Deborah Thorne, "A Vulnerable Middle Class: Bankruptcy and Class Status," in Porter, *Broke.*

44. Warren and Thorne, "A Vulnerable Middle Class," 25.

45. Katherine Porter, "Bankruptcy and Financial Failure in American Families," in Porter, *Broke,* 4–5.

46. Porter, "Bankruptcy and Financial Failure," 5.

47. Porter, 5.

48. Annamaria Lusardi, Daniel Schneider, and Peter Tufano, "Financially Fragile Households: Evidence and Implications," Netspar Discussion Paper No. 03/2011–013.2011 (Tilburg, Neth.: Netspar, 2011), https://papers.ssrn.com/sol3/papers.cfm?abstract_id=1809708##.

49. Brett Williams, *Debt for Sale: A Social History of the Credit Trap* (Philadelphia: University of Pennsylvania Press, 2004).

50. Graeber, *Debt: The First 5,000 Years,* 121.

4. CAN'T WORK THE SYSTEM

1. Statistic from Nelson Schwartz, "Voices of Foreclosure Speak Daily about Desperation and Misery," *New York Times*, November 16, 2010.

2. Contrasting the circulation of paper files with electronic filing systems emerging in Pakistan, Hull predicts that the digital databases would more likely lead to abuse, as was the case with corporate lenders. Matthew Hull, *Government of Paper: The Materiality of Bureaucracy in Urban Pakistan* (Berkeley: University of California Press, 2012), 255.

3. Jessica Silver-Greenberg and Michael Corkery, "Loan Complaints by Homeowners Rise Once More," *New York Times*, February 18, 2014.

4. Graeber, *Utopia of Rules*, 17.

5. Harvey, *Enigma of Capital*, 245.

6. Akhil Gupta, *Red Tape: Bureaucracy, Structural Violence, and Poverty in India* (Durham, NC: Duke University Press, 2012).

7. These modifications were secured through the Department of Justice, not HAMP, which covered loans originated through Fannie Mae and Freddie Mac.

8. Michael Herzfeld, *The Social Production of Indifference: Exploring the Symbolic Roots of Western Bureaucracy* (Chicago: University of Chicago Press, 1992).

9. Cathy O'Neil, *Weapons of Math Destruction: How Big Data Increases Inequality and Threatens Democracy* (New York: Penguin Random House, 2017).

10. O'Neil, *Weapons of Math Destruction*, 20.

11. Karen Ho, "Corporate Nostalgia?," in *Corporations and Citizenship*, ed. Greg Urban (Philadelphia: University of Pennsylvania Press, 2014), 272.

12. Jean Comaroff and John Comaroff, "Millennial Capitalism: Notes on a Second Coming," in *Millennial Capitalism and the Culture of Neoliberalism* (Durham, NC: Duke University Press, 2001), 1–56.

13. Naomi Klein, *The Shock Doctrine: The Rise of Disaster Capitalism* (New York: Macmillan, 2007).

14. For example, see Donald Brenneis, "Reforming Promise," in *Documents: Artifacts of Modern Knowledge*, ed. Annelise Riles (Ann Arbor: University of Michigan Press, 2006), 41–70; Gupta, *Red Tape*; Herzfeld, *Social Production of Indifference*; Matthew Hull, "The File: Agency, Authority, and Autography in a Pakistan Bureaucracy," *Language and Communication* 23, nos. 3–4 (2003): 287–314; Matthew Hull, "Documents and Bureaucracy," *Annual Review of Anthropology* 41 (2012): 251–67; Annelise Riles, *Documents: Artifacts of Modern Knowledge* (Ann Arbor: University of Michigan Press, 2006).

15. Adams, *Markets of Sorrow*.

16. According to the *New Orleans Times-Picayune*, six months after the program accepted its first applications, the program granted awards to only 215 out of a total of 100,000 applicants. J. Meitrodt, "Understaffed and Overwhelmed; the Firm Administering Louisiana's Road Home Program Has Consistently Underestimated the Magnitude of the Task, Records Show," *New Orleans Times-Picayune* (January 28, 2007): 1.

17. Adams, *Markets of Sorrow*, 35.

18. Timothy Green and Robert Olshansky (2012), "Rebuilding Housing in New Orleans: The Road Home Program after the Hurricane Katrina Disaster," *Housing Policy Debate* 22, no. 1 (2012): 75–99.

19. Adams, *Markets of Sorrow*, 90.

20. David Dayen, "Bank of America Whistle-Blower's Bombshell: 'We Were Told to Lie,'" *Salon,* June 18, 2013.

21. Focusing on bureaucratic development programs in southern Africa, Ferguson shows how these development bureaucracies recast political questions of land and jobs as technical issues in need of "development" intervention, squashing political resistance in the process. James Ferguson, *The Anti-Politics Machine: Development, Depoliticization, and Bureaucratic Power in Lesotho* (Minneapolis: University of Minnesota Press, 1994).

5. WE SHALL NOT BE MOVED

1. David Harvey, *A Brief History of Neoliberalism* (New York: Oxford University Press, 2005), 46.

2. White, "Take This House and Shove It."

3. See, for example, Paul Langley, "Debt, Discipline and Government: Foreclosure and Forbearance in the Subprime Mortgage Crisis," *Environment and Planning* 41 (2009): 1404–19; Brent White, "The Morality of Strategic Default," UCLA Law Review Discourses, Arizona Legal Studies Discussion Paper No. 10–15 (Tucson: University of Arizona, James E. Rogers College of Law, May 22, 2010), https://ssrn.com/abstract=1597835.

4. Chan et al., "Role of Neighborhood Characteristics," 2. The authors observe that homeowners are more likely to default if they know someone who has defaulted or if they live in an area where mortgage defaults occur.

5. Importantly, these discourses of strategic default were also raced and classed, as white, middle-class homeowners were more often described as "strategically" defaulting while their lower-income counterparts were

described as wayward financial subjects, ignorant of the consequences of their actions.

6. Anna Jefferson, "Narratives of Moral Order in Michigan's Foreclosure Crisis," *City and Society* 25, no. 1 (2013): 101.

7. Jefferson, "Narratives of Moral Order," 96.

8. Jefferson, 101.

9. Craigslist discussion forums also harbor a robust community, with more than 200 million users and 100 topical forums. Reddit, a site with over 1 million registered users, is divided into more than 100,000 subreddits, or topic threads. When Reddit's page "What Businesses Should Know" (http://frog-dog.com /articles/detail/reddit_what_businesses_should_know/, December 26, 2012) was accessed on April 1, 2014, the site reported that it garnered 34.9 million unique views each month. When this same page was accessed in September 2018, although the page was still dated December 26, 2012, it reported "150 million page views per month and 18 million unique users per month." As of February 2018, Alexa Internet ranked Reddit as the third most-visited website in the United States, with 542 million monthly visitors (234 million unique users).

10. Portions of my analysis of online domains appeared in Noelle Stout, "#Indebted: Disciplining the Moral Valence of Mortgage Debt Online," *Cultural Anthropology* 31, no. 1 (2016): 81–105.

11. Owens, "Intrinsically Advantageous?"

12. The anonymity of the sites is not absolute, and users might post otherwise private financial information in ways that raise pressing questions about the use of these data. Deville, for example, shows how an online loan company uses "leaky data" to determine the risk of a borrower and therefore the interest rate the borrower is charged. These data include information such as the browser and the device with which users access the site, the time of day they log on, and their Facebook activity. Joe Deville, "Leaky Data: How Wonga Makes Lending Decisions," Charisma Consumer Market Studies, May 20, 2013, www.charisma-network.net/finance/leaky-data-how-wonga-makes-lending-decisions.

13. The article the forum participants were discussing was Jim Wasserman, "Underwater Mortgages—To Pay or Walk Away?," *Sacramento Bee,* March 8, 2009.

14. For professionals working in office jobs, these online sessions were appealing because they could take place surreptitiously during work hours, and for homeowners with jobs in the service industries, online searches and participation were unrestricted to business hours and could commence after long workdays.

15. Tvisforbabyboomers, "I got hit hard by the crash and I'm going through a foreclosure," r/Frugal, reddit, April 2012, www.reddit.com/r/Frugal /comments/sm8kr/i_got_hit_hard_by_the_crash_and_im_going_through /c4f8xe9/, accessed April 1, 2014.

16. A progressive organization founded by Van Jones, an Obama advisor and CNN *Crossfire* host, Rebuild the Dream draws on mass media and digital technologies to campaign for social issues. See www.rebuildthedream.com /support_for_homeowners.

17. Michael Warner, *Publics and Counterpublics* (New York: Zone Books, 2002).

18. Evgeny Morozov, *The Net Delusion* (London: Allen Lane, 2011); Heather A. Horst and Daniel Miller, eds., *Digital Anthropology* (London: Bloomsbury); Deville, "Leaky Data."

19. These online publics generate novel orientations toward debt that suggest a distinct but important extension of the face-to-face debates taking place in town hall meetings and around Occupy's tents pitched on Wall Street.

20. John L. Comaroff and Jean Comaroff, "Law and Order in the Postcolony: An Introduction," in *Law and Order in the Postcolony,* ed. John L. Comaroff and Jean Comaroff (Chicago: University of Chicago Press, 2006), 5.

21. Jason N. Houle and Michael T. Light, "The Home Foreclosure Crisis and Rising Suicide Rates, 2005 to 2010," *American Journal of Public Health* 104, no. 6 (June 2014): 1073–79.

22. Anna Gorman, "Eviction Ends in Tragedy," *Los Angeles Times,* October 15, 2008, http://articles.latimes.com/2008/oct/15/local/me-deadwoman15.

23. Jefferson, "Narratives of Moral Order," 103.

24. Jefferson, 103.

25. Jefferson, 103.

26. Emile Durkheim, *Suicide: A Study in Sociology* (1897; repr., New York: Free Press, 1979).

27. Julie Livingston, "Suicide, Risk, and Investment in the Heart of the African Miracle," *Cultural Anthropology* 24, no. 4 (2009): 652–80.

28. Ironically, had federal programs not been relegated to the private sector in the first place, California would not have had to legislate against predatory mechanisms.

29. Didier Fassin, "Moral Economies Revisited," *Annales* 64 (2009): 1237–66, 1247.

30. James Scott, *Weapons of the Weak: Everyday Forms of Peasant Resistance* (New Haven, CT: Yale University Press, 1985), xvi.

CONCLUSION

1. For an insightful exploration of these themes, see Kathryn Schulz, "When Things Go Missing: Reflections on Two Seasons of Loss," *New Yorker,* February 13 and 20, 2017, 66–75.

2. Here, Mauss is conveying how noncommodified forms of exchange make their way into industrial markets. Mauss, *The Gift,* 66.

3. At the time of publication, a separate case is proceeding on behalf of homeowners against Bank of America that claims that the lender is an "unlawful racketeering RICO enterprise, denying a streamlined HAMP modification process mandated by Congress."

4. Wells Fargo fared slightly better in one regard, with only half of counselors reporting that representatives gave inconsistent misinformation.

5. Annie Sciacca, "In Costly Bay Area, Even Six-Figure Salaries Are Considered 'Low Income,'" *San Jose Mercury News,* April 22, 2017. http://www .mercurynews.com/2017/04/22/in-costly-bay-area-even-six-figure-salaries-are-considered-low-income.

6. Graeber, *Debt: The First 5,000 Years,* 16.

7. Graeber, 16.

8. Andrew Ross Sorkin, "Unlikely Fund-Raiser for Trump and Party," *New York Times,* May 10, 2016.

9. Harvey, *Enigma of Capital,* 12.

10. Graeber, *Debt: The First 5,000 Years,* 17.

11. Gregory, *Gifts and Commodities;* Malinowski, *Argonauts of the Western Pacific;* Mauss, *The Gift;* Strathern, *Gender of the Gift;* Weiner, *Inalienable Possessions.*

12. Gregory, *Gifts and Commodities;* Christopher Gregory, "On Money Debt and Morality: Some Reflections on the Contribution of Economic Anthropology," *Social Anthropology* 20, no. 4 (2012): 380–96; Alessandra Simoni, Guilherme Cardoso, Luisa Pessoa de Oliveira, and Rodrigo Bulamah, "Pigs and Mobile Phones: A Conversation with Marilyn Strathern," *Revista Proa* 2, no. 1 (2016): 1–12; Strathern, *Gender of the Gift;* Weiner, *Inalienable Possessions.*

References

Aalbers, Manuel B. "The Financialization of Home and the Mortgage Crisis." *Competition and Change* 12, no. 2 (2008): 148–66.

Abu-Lughod, Lila. "Can There Be a Feminist Ethnography?" *Women and Performance: A Journal of Feminist Theory* 5, no. 1 (1990): 7–27.

Adams, Vincanne. *Markets of Sorrow, Labors of Faith: New Orleans in the Wake of Katrina*. Durham, NC: Duke University Press, 2013.

Alliance of Californians for Community Empowerment and The California Reinvestment Coalition. *The Wall Street Wrecking Ball: What Foreclosures Are Costing Sacramento Neighborhoods*. Los Angeles: ACCE, September 2011.

Allison, Anne. *Precarious Japan*. Durham, NC: Duke University Press, 2013.

Anthony, Jerry. "Home Burdens: The High Cost of Homeownership." In *Broke: How Debt Bankrupts the Middle Class*, edited by Katherine Porter, 65–84. Palo Alto, CA: Stanford University Press, 2012.

Apgar, William, and Allegra Calder. "The Dual Mortgage Market: The Persistence of Discrimination in Mortgage Lending." In *The Geography of Opportunity*, edited by Xavier De Souza Briggs, 101–27. Washington, DC: Brookings Institute Press, 2005.

Appadurai, Arjun. *Modernity at Large: Cultural Dimensions of Globalization*. Minneapolis: University of Minnesota Press, 1996.

Appel, Hannah. "Occupy Wall Street and the Economic Imagination." *Cultural Anthropology* 29, no. 4 (2014): 602–25.

———. "Toward an Ethnography of the National Economy." *Cultural Anthropology* 32, no. 2 (2017): 294–322.

Baker, Christi, Kevin Stein, and Mike Eiseman. *Foreclosure Trends in Sacramento and Recommended Policy Options: A Report for the Sacramento Housing and Redevelopment Agency by the California Reinvestment Coalition.* San Francisco: California Reinvestment Coalition, April 11, 2008, 5–10. http://sacramento.granicus.com/MetaViewer.php?view_id=22&clip_id=1526&meta_id=147291.

Bear, Laura, Karen Ho, Anna Tsing, and Sylvia Yanagisako. "Generating Capitalism." Theorizing the Contemporary (conversation). *Cultural Anthropology* (blog), March 30, 2015. https://culanth.org/fieldsights/650-generating-capitalism.

Been, Vicki, Mary Weselcouch, Ioan Voicu, and Scott Murff. "Determinants of the Incidence of Loan Modifications." NYU Law and Economics Research Paper Series No. 11–37. New York: NYU School of Law, last revised December 8, 2012. https://ssrn.com/abstract=1941915.

Benson, Peter. *Tobacco Capitalism: Growers, Migrant Workers, and the Changing Face of a Global Industry.* Princeton, NJ: Princeton University Press, 2011.

Berlant, Lauren. *Cruel Optimism.* Durham, NC: Duke University Press, 2011.

Bettie, Julie. *Women without Class: Girls, Race, and Identity.* Berkeley: University of California Press, 2014.

Boas, Franz. "The Indians of British Columbia." *Popular Science Monthly* 32 (1888): 631.

Bocian, Debbie Gruenstein, Keith S. Ernst, and Wei Li. "Race, Ethnicity and Subprime Home Loan Pricing." *Journal of Economics and Business* 60, no. 1 (2008): 110–24.

Bocian, Debbie Gruenstein, Wei Li, Carolina Reid, and Roberto G. Quercia. *Lost Ground, 2011: Disparities in Mortgage Lending and Foreclosures.* Chapel Hill: Center for Responsible Lending, November, 2011. https://www.responsiblelending.org/mortgage-lending/research-analysis/Lost-Ground-2011.pdf.

Bourgois, Philippe. *In Search of Respect: Selling Crack in El Barrio.* Cambridge: Cambridge University Press, 1996.

Brennan, Denise. *What's Love Got to Do with It? Transnational Desires and Sex Tourism in the Dominican Republic.* Durham, NC: Duke University Press, 2004.

Brenneis, Donald. "Reforming Promise." In *Documents: Artifacts of Modern Knowledge,* edited by Annelise Riles, 41–70. Ann Arbor: University of Michigan Press, 2006.

Burgin, Angus. *The Great Persuasion: Reinventing Free Markets since the Depression.* Cambridge, MA: Harvard University Press, 2012.

Calder, Lendol. *Financing the American Dream: A Cultural History of Consumer Credit.* Princeton, NJ: Princeton University Press, 1999.

Cattelino, Jessica. "The Double Bind of American Indian Need-Based Sovereignty." *Cultural Anthropology* 25, no. 2 (2010): 235–62.

Chakravartty, Paula, and Denise Ferreira da Silva. "Accumulation, Dispossession, and Debt: The Racial Logic of Global Capitalism—An Introduction." *American Quarterly* 64, no. 3 (2012): 361–85.

Chan, Sewin, Michael Gedal, Vicki Been, and Andrew Haughwout. "The Role of Neighborhood Characteristics in Mortgage Default Risk: Evidence from New York City." Working Paper, Furman Center for Real Estate and Public Policy. New York: New York University, 2012.

Coleman, Gabriella. "Ethnographic Approaches to Digital Media." *Annual Review of Anthropology* 39 (2010): 487–505.

Collier, Jane. *From Duty to Desire: Remaking Families in a Spanish Village.* Princeton, NJ: Princeton University Press, 1997.

Collins, J. Michael, and Collin O'Rourke. "Financial Education and Counseling, Still Holding Promise." *Journal of Consumer Affairs* 44, no. 3 (2010): 483–89.

Collins, J. Michael, and Carolina Reid. "Who Receives a Mortgage Modification? Race and Income Differentials in Loan Workouts," Community Development Investment Center Working Paper 2010–07. San Francisco: Federal Reserve Bank of San Francisco, 2011.

Comaroff, John L., and Jean Comaroff. "Law and Order in the Postcolony: An Introduction" In *Law and Order in the Postcolony,* edited by John L. Comaroff and Jean Comaroff, 1–56. Chicago: University of Chicago Press, 2006.

———. "Millennial Capitalism: Notes on a Second Coming." In *Millennial Capitalism and the Culture of Neoliberalism.* Durham, NC: Duke University Press, 2001.

Cooper, Marianne. *Cut Adrift: Families in Insecure Times.* Berkeley: University of California Press, 2014.

Culhane, Marianne B. "No Forwarding Address: Losing Homes in Bankruptcy." In *Broke: How Debt Bankrupts the Middle Class,* edited by Katherine Porter, 119–36. Palo Alto, CA: Stanford University Press, 2012.

Dayen, David. "Bank of America Whistle-Blower's Bombshell: 'We Were Told to Lie.'" *Salon,* June 18, 2013.

DeSilver, Drew. "Killinger Got $25M in WaMu's Final Year." *Seattle Times,* April 12, 2010.

Desmond, Matthew. *Evicted: Poverty and Profit in the American City.* New York: Broadway Books, 2017.

Deville, Joe. "Leaky Data: How Wonga Makes Lending Decisions." Charisma Market Studies, May 20, 2013. www.charisma-network.net/finance/leaky-data-how-wonga-makes-lending-decisions, accessed April 1, 2014.

Didion, Joan. "California Notes." *New York Review of Books,* May 26, 2016. www
.nybooks.com/articles/2016/05/26/california-notes/.

Dudley, Kathryn Marie. *Debt and Dispossession: Farm Loss in America's Heartland.*
Chicago: University of Chicago Press, 2000.

———. *End of the Line: Lost Jobs, New Lives in Postindustrial America.* Chicago:
University of Chicago Press, 1994.

Durkheim, Emile. *Suicide: A Study in Sociology.* 1897. Reprint, New York: Free
Press, 1979.

Faith, Brian. "New Nationwide Survey Provides Comprehensive Look at Sentiment Toward Housing" (news release). Federal National Mortgage Association (Fannie Mae), April 6, 2010. www.fanniemae.com/portal/media
/corporate-news/2010/4989.html.

Fassin, Didier. "Moral Economies Revisited." *Annales* 64 (2009): 1237–66.

Ferguson, James. *The Anti-Politics Machine: Development, Depoliticization, and
Bureaucratic Power in Lesotho.* Minneapolis: University of Minnesota Press,
1994.

Fortun, Kim. *Advocacy after Bhopal: Environmentalism, Disaster, New Global Orders.*
Chicago: University of Chicago Press, 2001.

Foucault, Michel. "Governmentality." In *The Foucault Effect: Studies in Governmentality,* edited by Graham Burchell, Colin Gordon, and Peter Miller,
87–104. Chicago: University of Chicago Press, 1991.

———. "Lives of Infamous Men." In *The Essential Works of Foucault, 1954–1984,*
vol. 3, *Power,* edited by James Faubion and translated by Robert Hurley, 157–
77. New York: New Press, 2001.

———. *Security, Territory, Population: Lectures at the College de France, 1977–78.*
Translated by Graham Burchell. New York: Palgrave Macmillan, 2007.

Freeman, Carla. *High Tech and High Heels in the Global Economy: Women, Work, and
Pink-Collar Identities in the Caribbean.* Durham, NC: Duke University Press,
2000.

Freeman, Carla, and Mark Liechty. "Charting an Anthropology of the Middle
Classes." In *The Global Middle Classes: Theorizing Through Ethnography,* edited
by Rachel Heiman, Carla Freeman, and Mark Liechty. Santa Fe, NM:
School for Advanced Research, 2012.

Freund, David. "Marketing the Free Market: State Intervention and the Politics of Prosperity in Metropolitan America." In *The New Suburban History,*
edited by Kevin M. Kruse and Thomas J. Sugrue. Chicago: University of
Chicago Press, 2006.

Garson, Barbara. *Down the Up Escalator: How the 99 Percent Live in the Great Recession.* New York: Doubleday, 2013.

Geithner, Timothy F. *Stress Test: Reflections on Financial Crises.* New York: Broadway Books, 2015.

Ginsburg, Faye. "Rethinking the Digital Age." In *The Media and Social Theory,* edited by David Hesmondhalgh and Jason Toynbee, 127–44. London; New York: Routledge, 2008.

Goodman, Peter S. "Eminent Domain as Underwater Mortgages Fix: Why Some Cities Are Considering Unorthodox Measure." *Huffington Post,* October 1, 2012. www.huffingtonpost.com/2012/10/01/eminent-domain-mortgages_n_1917391 .html.

Goodman, Peter, and Gretchen Morgenson. "Saying Yes, WaMu Built Empire on Shaky Loans." *New York Times,* December 27, 2008. www.nytimes.com /2008/12/28/business/28wamu.html.

Gorman, Anna. "Eviction Ends in Tragedy." *Los Angeles Times,* October 15, 2008. http://articles.latimes.com/2008/oct/15/local/me-deadwoman15.

Graeber, David. *Debt: The First 5,000 Years.* New York: Melville House, 2011.

———. "On Social Currencies and Human Economies." *Social Anthropology* 20, no. 4 (2012): 417.

———. *The Utopia of Rules: On Technology, Stupidity, and the Secret Joys of Bureaucracy.* New York: Melville House, 2015.

Green, Timothy, and Robert Olshansky. "Rebuilding Housing in New Orleans: The Road Home Program after the Hurricane Katrina Disaster." *Housing Policy Debate* 22, no. 1 (2012): 75–99.

Gregory, Christopher. *Gifts and Commodities.* London: Academic Press, 1982.

———. "On Money Debt and Morality: Some Reflections on the Contribution of Economic Anthropology." *Social Anthropology/Anthropologie Sociale* 20, no. 4 (2012): 380–96.

Guiso, Luigi, Paola Sapienza, and Luigi Zingales. "Moral and Social Constraints to Strategic Default on Mortgages." NBER Working Paper 15145. Cambridge, MA: National Bureau of Economic Research, 2009. www.nber .org/papers/w15145.

Gupta, Akhil. *Red Tape: Bureaucracy, Structural Violence, and Poverty in India.* Durham, NC: Duke University Press, 2012.

Gusterson, Hugh, and Catherine Besteman, eds. *The Insecure American: How We Got Here and What We Should Do about It.* Berkeley: University of California Press, 2010.

Hacker, Jacob. *The Great Risk Shift: New Economic Insecurity and the Decline of the American Dream*. New York: Oxford University Press, 2008.

Hall, Matthew, Kyle Crowder, and Amy Spring. "Variations in Housing Foreclosures by Race and Place, 2005–2012." *Annals of the American Academy of Political and Social Science* 660, no. 1 (2015): 217–37.

Han, Clara. *Life in Debt: Times of Care and Violence in Neoliberal Chile*. Berkeley: University of California Press, 2012.

Harris, Dianne. *Little White Houses: How the Postwar Home Constructed Race in America*. Minneapolis: University of Minnesota Press, 2013.

Hart, Keith, and Horacio Ortiz. "Anthropology and the Financial Crisis." *Anthropology Today* 24, no. 6 (2008): 1–3.

Harvey, David. *A Brief History of Neoliberalism*. New York: Oxford University Press, 2005.

———. *The Enigma of Capital and the Crises of Capitalism*. New York: Oxford University Press, 2011.

Heiman, Rachel. *Driving after Class: Anxious Times in an American Suburb*. Oakland: University of California Press, 2015.

Heiman, Rachel, Carla Freeman, and Mark Liechty. "Charting an Anthropology of the Middle Classes." In *The Global Middle Classes: Theorizing through Ethnography*, edited by Rachel Heiman, Carla Freeman, and Mark Liechty. Santa Fe, NM: School for Advanced Research Press, 2012.

Hernandez, Jesus. "Redlining Revisited: Mortgage Lending Patterns in Sacramento 1930– 2004." *International Journal of Urban and Regional Research* 33, no. 2 (2009): 291–313.

Herzfeld, Michael. *The Social Production of Indifference: Exploring the Symbolic Roots of Western Bureaucracy*. Chicago: University of Chicago Press, 1992.

High, Holly. "Re-reading the Potlatch in a Time of Crisis: Debt and the Distinctions That Matter." *Social Anthropology* 20, no. 4 (2012): 363–79.

Ho, Karen. "Corporate Nostalgia?" In *Corporations and Citizenship*, edited by Greg Urban. Philadelphia: University of Pennsylvania Press, 2014.

———. *Liquidated: An Ethnography of Wall Street*. Durham, NC: Duke University Press, 2009.

Horst, Heather A., and Danny Miller, eds. *Digital Anthropology*. London: Bloomsbury, 2012.

Howell, Joseph. *Hard Living on Clay Street: Portraits of Blue Collar Families*. Prospect Heights, IL: Waveland Press, 1972.

Hudson, Mike. *IndyMac: What Went Wrong? How an 'Alt-A' Leader Fueled Its Growth with Unsound and Abusive Mortgage Lending*. CRL Report. Durham, NC:

Center for Responsible Lending, June 30, 2008. www.responsiblelending
.org/mortgage-lending/research-analysis/indymac_what_went_wrong.pdf.

Hull, Matthew. "Documents and Bureaucracy." *Annual Review of Anthropology*
41 (2012): 251–67.

————. "The File: Agency, Authority, and Autography in a Pakistan Bureaucracy." *Language and Communication* 23, nos. 3–4 (2003): 287–314.

————. *Government of Paper: The Materiality of Bureaucracy in Urban Pakistan.*
Berkeley: University of California Press, 2012.

Hyman, Louis. *Debtor Nation: The History of America in Red Ink.* Princeton, NJ:
Princeton University Press, 2011.

————. "Ending Discrimination, Legitimating Debt: The Political Economy
of Race, Gender, and Credit Access in the 1960s and 1970s." *Enterprise and
Society* 12, no. 1 (2011): 200–232.

Immergluck, Dan, and Geoff Smith. "The External Costs of Foreclosure: The
Impact of Single-Family Mortgage Foreclosures on Property Values."
Housing Policy Debate 17, no. 1 (2006): 57–79.

Jefferson, Anna. "Narratives of Moral Order in Michigan's Foreclosure Crisis." *City and Society* 25, no. 1 (2013): 92–112.

Kingsley, G. Thomas, and Kathryn L. S. Pettit. *High-Cost and Investor Mortgages:
Neighborhood Patterns.* Washington, DC: Urban Institute, 2009.

Klein, Naomi. *The Shock Doctrine: The Rise of Disaster Capitalism.* New York:
Macmillan, 2007.

Kopytoff, Igor. "The Cultural Biography of Things: Commoditization as Process." In *The Social Life of Things: Commodities in Cultural Perspective,* edited by
Arjun Appadurai, 64–94. Cambridge: Cambridge University Press, 1986.

Lands, LeeAnn. *The Culture of Property: Race, Class, and Housing Landscapes in
Atlanta, 1880–1950.* Athens: University of Georgia Press, 2009.

Langley, Paul. "Debt, Discipline and Government: Foreclosure and Forbearance in the Subprime Mortgage Crisis." *Environment and Planning* 41 (2009):
1404–19.

————. *The Everyday Life of Global Finance: Saving and Borrowing in Anglo-Amer-
ica.* Oxford: Oxford University Press, 2008.

————. "Financialization and the Consumer Credit Boom." *Competition and
Change* 12 (2008): 133–47.

Leibrock, Rachel. "Default!" *Sacramento News & Review,* December 16, 2010.
www.newsreview.com/sacramento/default/content?oid=1890749.

Leonard, Karen. *Making Ethnic Choices: California's Punjabi Mexican Americans.*
Philadelphia: Temple University Press, 1992.

Livingston, Julie. "Suicide, Risk, and Investment in The Heart of the African Miracle." *Cultural Anthropology* 24, no. 4 (2009): 652–80.

Loewenstein, Antony. *Disaster Capitalism: Making a Killing Out of Catastrophe.* New York: Verso Books, 2015.

Lovell, Anne, Samuel Bordreuil, and Vincanne Adams. 2010. "Public Policy and Publics in Post- Katrina New Orleans: How Critical Topics Circulate and Shape Recovery Policy." *Kroeber Anthropological Society* 100, no. 1: 104–28.

Lusardi, Annamaria, Daniel Schneider, and Peter Tufano. "Financially Fragile Households: Evidence and Implications." Netspar Discussion Paper No. 03/2011–013.2011. http://ssrn.com/abstract=1809708.

Maharidge, Dale, and Michael S. Williamson. *Someplace Like America: Tales from the New Great Depression.* Berkeley: University of California Press, 2013.

Malinowski, Bronislaw. *Argonauts of the Western Pacific: An Account of Native Enterprise and Adventure in the Archipelagoes of Melanesian New Guinea.* 1922. Reprint, New York: Dutton, 1961.

Maurer, Bill. "The Anthropology of Money." *Annual Review of Anthropology* 35, no. 1 (2010): 15–36.

———. *Pious Property: Islamic Mortgages in the United States.* New York: Russell Sage Foundation, 2006.

Mauss, Marcel. *The Gift: The Form and Reason for Exchange in Archaic Societies.* Trans. W. D. Halls. 1925. Reprint, London: Routledge, 1990.

McKinley, Jesse. "Residents of Sacramento's Tent City to Move to Fairground." *New York Times,* March 25, 2009. www.nytimes.com/2009/03/26/us/26sacramento.html.

Meitrodt, J. "Understaffed and Overwhelmed; the Firm Administering Louisiana's Road Home Program Has Consistently Underestimated the Magnitude of the Task, Records Show." *New Orleans Times-Picayune,* January 28, 2007.

Miyazaki, Hirokazu. *The Method of Hope: Anthropology, Philosophy, and Fijian Knowledge.* Stanford, CA: Stanford University Press, 2004.

Morozov, Evgeny. *The Net Delusion.* London: Allen Lane, 2011.

Nash, June. "Consuming Interests: Water, Rum, and Coca-Cola from Ritual Propitiation to Corporate Expropriation in Highland Chiapas." *Cultural Anthropology* 22, no. 4 (2007): 621–39.

Newman, Katherine S. *Falling from Grace: Downward Mobility in the Age of Affluence.* Berkeley: University of California Press, 1988.

Newman, Katherine S., and Victor Tan Chen. *The Missing Class: Portraits of the Near Poor in America.* Boston: Beacon Press, 2007.

Office of the Special Inspector General for the Troubled Asset Relief Program (SIGTARP). *Quarterly Report to Congress,* April 26, 2017. www.sigtarp.gov /Quarterly%20Reports/April_26_2017_r1_Report_to_Congress.pdf.

O'Neil, Cathy. *Weapons of Math Destruction: How Big Data Increases Inequality and Threatens Democracy.* New York: Penguin Random House, 2017.

Ong, Aiwha. *Neoliberalism as Exception: Mutations in Citizenship and Sovereignty.* Durham, NC: Duke University Press, 2006.

Ortiz, Horacio. "Anthropology—of the Financial Crisis." In *Handbook of Economic Anthropology,* 2nd ed, edited by J. Carrier, 585–96. Cheltenham: Edward Elgar, 2012.

Ortner, Sherry B. *New Jersey Dreaming: Capital, Culture, and the Class of '58.* Durham, NC: Duke University Press, 2003.

Owens, Lindsay A. "Intrinsically Advantageous? Reexamining the Production of Class Advantage in the Case of Home Mortgage Modification." *Social Forces* 93, no. 3 (2014): 1185–209.

Packer, George. "Don't Look Down: The New Depression Journalism." *New Yorker,* April 29, 2013. www.newyorker.com/magazine/2013/04/29/dont-look-down.

———. *The Unwinding: An Inner History of the New America.* New York: Farrar, Straus and Giroux, 2014.

Palomera, Jamie. "Reciprocity, Commodification, and Poverty in the Era of Financialization." *Current Anthropology* 55, no. 9 (2014): S105–15.

Peebles, Gustav. "The Anthropology of Credit and Debt." *Annual Review of Anthropology* 39 (2010): 225–40.

Piketty, Thomas. *Capital in the Twenty-First Century.* Cambridge, MA: Harvard University Press, 2014.

Polyani, Karl. *The Great Transformation: The Political and Economic Origins of Our Time.* 1944. Reprint, Boston: Beacon Press, 2001.

Poon, Martha. "From New Deal Institutions to Capital Markets: Commercial Consumer Risk Scores and the Making of Subprime Mortgage Finance." *Accounting, Organizations and Society* 34, no. 5 (2009): 654–74.

Porter, Katherine. "Bankruptcy and Financial Failure in American Families." In *Broke: How Debt Bankrupts the Middle Class,* edited by Katherine Porter, 1–24. Palo Alto, CA: Stanford University Press, 2012.

Povinelli, Elizabeth. *Economies of Abandonment: Social Belonging and Endurance in Late-Liberalism.* Durham, NC: Duke University Press, 2011.

Rebhun, L.A. *The Heart Is Unknown Country: Love in the Changing Economy of Northeast Brazil.* Palo Alto, CA: Stanford University Press, 1999.

Reid, Carolina. "Sought or Sold? Social Embeddedness and Consumer Decisions in the Mortgage Market." Working Paper 2010–09. San Francisco: Federal Reserve Bank of San Francisco, December 2010. www.frbsf.org /community-development/files/wp2010–09.pdf.

Riles, Annelise. *Documents: Artifacts of Modern Knowledge.* Ann Arbor: University of Michigan Press, 2006.

Rofel, Lisa. *Desiring China: Experiments in Neoliberalism, Sexuality, and Public Culture.* Durham, NC: Duke University Press, 2007.

Roitman, Janet. *Anti-Crisis.* Durham, NC: Duke University Press, 2013.

———. *Fiscal Disobedience: An Anthropology of Economic Regulation in Central Africa.* Princeton, NJ: Princeton University Press, 2005.

Ross, Andrew. *Creditocracy and the Case for Debt Refusal.* New York: OR Books, 2013.

Sangree, Hudson, and Phillip Reese. "Homeownership in Sacramento Plummets to Lowest Level in 40 Years." *Sacramento Bee,* May 12, 2014. www .sacbee.com/news/business/real-estate-news/article25985.

Sassen, Saskia. *Expulsions: Brutality and Complexity in the Global Economy.* Cambridge, MA: Belknap Press, 2014.

Schulz, Kathryn. "When Things Go Missing: Reflections on Two Seasons of Loss." *New Yorker,* February 13 and 20, 2017, 66–75.

Schuster, Caroline E. *Social Collateral: Women and Microfinance in Paraguay's Smuggling Economy.* Berkeley: University of California Press, 2015.

Sciacca, Annie. "In Costly Bay Area, Even Six-Figure Salaries Are Considered 'Low Income.'" *San Jose Mercury News,* April 22, 2017. www.mercurynews .com/2017/04/22/in-costly-bay-area-even-six-figure-salaries-are-considered-low-income/.

Scott, James. *The Moral Economy of the Peasant: Rebellion and Subsistence in Southeast Asia.* New Haven, CT: Yale University Press, 1977.

———. *Weapons of the Weak: Everyday Forms of Peasant Resistance,* New Haven, CT: Yale University Press, 1985.

Segal, David. "Debt Collectors Face a Hazard: Writer's Cramp." *New York Times,* October 31, 2010.

Seiler, Michael, Andrew Collins, and Nina Fefferman. *Strategic Default in the Context of a Social Network: An Epidemiological Approach.* Washington, DC: Research Institute for Housing America Special Report, October 2011. www.mba.org/assets/Documents/Research/RIHA/78456_10923_Research_ RIHA_Default_Report.pdf.

Seligman, Amanda. *Block by Block: Neighborhoods and Public Policy on Chicago's West Side*. Historical Studies of Urban America. Chicago: University of Chicago Press, 2005.

Sennett, Richard, and Jonathan Cobb. *The Hidden Injuries of Class*. New York: W. W. Norton, 1972.

Shimpach, Shawn. "Realty Reality: HGTV and the Subprime Crisis." *American Quarterly* 64, no. 3 (2012): 515–42.

Shipton, Parker. *Mortgaging the Ancestors: Ideologies of Attachment in Africa*. New Haven, CT: Yale University Press, 2009.

Silver-Greenberg, Jessica, and Michael Corkery. "Loan Complaints by Homeowners Rise Once More." *New York Times*, February 18, 2014.

Simmel, Georg. *The Philosophy of Money*. Trans. Tom Bottomore and David Frisby. New York: Routledge Classics, 1978.

Simoni, Alessandra, Guilherme Cardoso, Luisa Pessoa de Oliveira, and Rodrigo Bulamah. "Pigs and Mobile Phones: A Conversation with Marilyn Strathern." *Revista Proa* 2, no. 1 (2010): 1–12.

Sorkin, Andrew Ross. "Unlikely Fund-Raiser for Trump and Party." *New York Times*, May 10, 2016.

Squires, Catherine. "Coloring in the Bubble: Perspectives on Black-Oriented Media on the (Latest) Economic Disaster." *American Quarterly* 64, no. 3 (2012): 543–70.

Stack, Carol B. *All Our Kin: Strategies for Survival in a Black Community*. New York: Basic Books, 1975.

Stack, Steven, and Ira Wasserman. "Economic Strain and Suicide Risk: A Qualitative Analysis." *Suicide and Life-Threatening Behavior* 37, no. 1 (2007): 103–12.

Stein, Kevin, and Kristina Bedrossian. *Race to the Bottom: An Analysis of HAMP Loan Modification Outcomes by Race and Ethnicity*. San Francisco: California Reinvestment Coalition, July 2011.

Stein, Kevin, and Sarah Brett. *Chasm between Words and Deeds VIII: Lack of Bank Accountability Plagues Californians*. San Francisco: California Reinvestment Coalition, April 2012.

Story, Louise. "Home Equity Frenzy Was a Bank Ad Come True." *New York Times*, August 15, 2008. www.nytimes.com/2008/08/15/business/15sell.html.

Stout, Noelle. *After Love: Queer Intimacy and Erotic Economies in Post-Soviet Cuba*. Durham, NC: Duke University Press, 2014.

————. "#Indebted: Disciplining the Moral Valence of Mortgage Debt Online." *Cultural Anthropology* 31, no. 1 (2016): 81–105.

————. "Petitioning a Giant: Debt, Reciprocity, and Mortgage Modification in the Sacramento Valley." *American Ethnologist* 43, no. 1 (2016): 1–14.

Strathern, Marilyn. *The Gender of the Gift: Problems with Women and Problems with Society in Melanesia.* Berkeley: University of California Press, 1988.

Stuart, Guy. *Discriminating Risk: The U.S. Mortgage Lending Industry in the Twentieth Century.* Ithaca, NY: Cornell University Press, 2003.

Sullivan, Teresa A. Warren, and Jay Westbrook. *The Fragile Middle Class: Americans in Debt.* New Haven, CT: Yale University Press, 2000.

Thompson, E.P. "The Moral Economy of the English Crowd in the 18th Century." *Past and Present* 50 (1971): 76–136.

Tsing, Anna. "Sorting Out Commodities: How Capitalist Value Is Made through Gifts." *HAU: Journal of Ethnographic Theory* 3, no. 1 (2013): 21–43.

Walley, Christine. *Exit Zero.* Chicago: University of Chicago Press, 2013.

Warner, Michael. *Publics and Counterpublics.* New York: Zone Books, 2002.

Warren, Elizabeth, and Deborah Thorne. "A Vulnerable Middle Class: Bankruptcy and Class Status." In *Broke: How Debt Bankrupts the Middle Class,* edited by Katherine Porter, 25–39. Palo Alto, CA: Stanford University Press, 2012.

Wasserman, Jim. "Underwater Mortgages—To Pay or Walk Away?" *Sacramento Bee,* March 8, 2009.

Weiner, Annette. *Inalienable Possessions: The Paradox of Keeping-While-Giving.* Berkeley: University of California Press, 1992.

Weston, Kath. *Families We Choose: Lesbians, Gays, Kinship.* New York: Columbia University Press, 1997.

White, Brent. "The Morality of Strategic Default." UCLA Law Review Discourses; Arizona Legal Studies Discussion Paper No. 10–15. Tucson: University of Arizona, James E. Rogers College of Law, May 22, 2010. http://ssrn.com/abstract=1597835.

————. "Take This House and Shove It: The Emotional Drivers of Strategic Default." Arizona Legal Studies Discussion Paper No. 10–17. Tucson: University of Arizona, James E. Rogers College of Law, last revised May 15, 2010. https://papers.ssrn.com/sol3/papers.cfm?abstract_id=1603605.

Wiese, Andrew. *Places of Their Own: African American Suburbanization in the Twentieth Century.* Chicago: University of Chicago Press, 2004.

Williams, Brett. *Debt for Sale: A Social History of the Credit Trap.* Philadelphia: University of Pennsylvania Press, 2004.

Yanagisako, Sylvia. *Producing Culture and Capital: Family Firms in Italy.* Princeton, NJ: Princeton University Press, 2002.

Zaloom, Kaitlin. *Out of the Pits: Traders and Technology from Chicago to London.* Chicago: University of Chicago Press, 2006.

Zelizer, Viviana. *The Social Meaning of Money.* New York: Basic Books, 1994.

Index

abandonment: of development projects, 65 *fig*; of homes, 56, 63 *fig*, 64 *fig*, 66, 87, 122, 175, 177; social and economic, 5–7, 123–24. *See also* evictions; squatting, as form of resistance

Abu-Lughod, Lila, 29

ACCE (Alliance of Californians for Community Empowerment, formerly ACORN), 90, 91, 191–92, 233n25

"accumulation by dispossession" theory, 57

ACORN (Association for Community Organizations for Reform Now). *See* ACCE

activism. *See* protests

Adams, Vincanne, 10–11, 166

adjustable-rate mortgages (ARMs), 74, 88, 232n22

affective labor, 158–64

African American communities. *See* racial and ethnic inequality

agricultural industry, 42, 55, 125, 228n1

algorithmic models, 151–53, 169, 170, 206. *See also* automation

America Underwater, 181–82

Ameriquest Mortgage, 44, 45

anomic suicide, 187. *See also* suicide

Anthony, Jerry, 234n5

appraisal, 41

Asian American communities, 17, 42

automation, 123, 146. *See also* algorithmic models

bailout program, 8–11, 165–66, 206, 209. *See also* HAMP (Home Affordable Modification Program); TARP (Troubled Asset Relief Program)

Baker, Rhonda, 184

banking, history of criminality in, 59–61, 72. *See also* mortgaging

Bank of America: civil disobedience against, 193; complaints and litigation against, 204, 242n3; fraudulent and negligent practices of, 9, 10, 165, 235n16; mortgage modification program of, 144 *fig*, 167

bankruptcy: of entire cities, 4; of homeowners, 119, 136, 149–50, 175, 188, 234n5; of lending companies, 47

Bear, Laura, 20

Berlant, Lauren, 114

Besteman, Catherine, 14–15

CALIFORNIA SERIES IN PUBLIC ANTHROPOLOGY

The California Series in Public Anthropology emphasizes the anthropologist's role as an engaged intellectual. It continues anthropology's commitment to being an ethnographic witness, to describing, in human terms, how life is lived beyond the borders of many readers' experiences. But it also adds a commitment, through ethnography, to reframing the terms of public debate—transforming received, accepted understandings of social issues with new insights, new framings.

Series Editor: Robert Borofsky (Hawaii Pacific University)

Contributing Editors: Philippe Bourgois (UCLA), Paul Farmer (Partners In Health), Alex Hinton (Rutgers University), Carolyn Nordstrom (University of Notre Dame), and Nancy Scheper-Hughes (UC Berkeley)

University of California Press Editor: Naomi Schneider